RUTHLESS DEMOCRACY

RUTHLESS DEMOCRACY

A MULTICULTURAL INTERPRETATION
OF THE AMERICAN RENAISSANCE

Timothy B. Powell

PRINCETON UNIVERSITY PRESS

PRINCETON, NEW JERSEY

LIBRARY OF CONGRESS CATALOGING-IN-PUBLICATION DATA

POWELL, TIMOTHY B., 1959

RUTHLESS DEMOCRACY: A MULTICULTURAL INTERPRETATION OF THE
AMERICAN

RENAISSANCE / TIMOTHY B. POWELL.

P.   CM.

INCLUDES BIBLIOGRAPHICAL REFERENCES (P.) AND INDEX.

IBSN 0-691-00729-2 (ALK. PAPER)   ISBN 0-691-00730-6 (PBK.: ALK. PAPER)

1. AMERICAN LITERATURE—MINORITY AUTHORS—HISTORY AND CRITICISM.

2. LITERATURE AND SOCIETY—UNITED STATES—HISTORY—19TH CENTURY.

3. AMERICAN HISTORY—19TH CENTURY—HISTORY AND CRITICISM.   4. PLURALISM
(SOCIAL SCIENCES) IN LITERATURE.   5. ETHNIC GROUPS IN LITERATURE.

6. MINORITIES IN LITERATURE.   7. DEMOCRACY IN LITERATURE.

8. ETHNICITY IN LITERATURE.   I. TITLE

PS153.M56 P69 2000

810.9'920693—DC21   99-053218

CHAPTER 2: JOHN ROLLIN RIDGE APPEARED IN "BEYOND THE BINARY:
RECONSTRUCTING CULTURAL IDENTITY IN A MULTICULTURAL CONTEXT"
ED. TIMOTHY B. POWELL (NEW BRUNSWICK: RUTGERS UP, 1999).

THIS BOOK HAS BEEN COMPOSED IN GALLIARD TYPEFACE

THE PAPER USED IN THIS PUBLICATION MEETS THE MINIMUM REQUIREMENTS
OF ANSI/NISO Z39.48-1992 (R1997) *PERMANENCE OF PAPER*

WWW.PUP.PRINCETON.EDU

PRINTED IN THE UNITED STATES OF AMERICA

1   3   5   7   9   10   8   6   4   2

CONTENTS

CONTENTS

ACKNOWLEDGMENTS

I WOULD LIKE to begin by thanking my mother-in-law, Bobbye Troutt, who died very suddenly and tragically just before I completed work on *Ruthless Democracy*. It is a great sadness that she is not here to help celebrate the completion of a project which took almost ten years to bring to fruition. Over the last decade Bobbye provided me with the emotional support to keep fighting, the savvy to outduel political opponents, and the courage to articulate my own vision. I think of her every day and I hope that she is proud of what we accomplished together.

I would also like to thank the rest of my family. My wife, Eve Troutt Powell, whom I love more than life itself. My son, Jibreel, whose humor, questions, and boundless energy make me never want to stop learning. My mother and father, Dave and Lucia, who always welcomed me home from my far-flung adventures with open arms. I would also like to thank my cousins, Dave and Barb McDonald, whose invitation to Cairo almost twenty years ago set all of this in motion to a funky, unpredictable beat. My brother John and his family, my brother-in-law and sister-in-law David and Margot and their families, my many cousins, aunts, uncles, and in-laws all provided an endless stream of support and a keen sense of who I am.

In addition to my family there have been many friends both in and out of the academy to whom I am deeply indebted for their support. I would like to thank Houston Baker, whose spirit energized the book in its earliest stages and who gave me the strength to question and challenge the canon. I also want to thank Herman Beavers, Rosemarie Garland Thomson, Barbara McCaskill, David Schoenbrun, Miranda Pollard, John Inscoe, the Morrows, Florence Dore, George Kesel, the Denises, and the Jardims, all of whom are dear friends.

Finally, I would like to thank all of the people who read the manuscript in various phases of (un)readiness and (un)steadiness. Michael T. Gilmore, Wai-Chee Dimock, Sacvan Bercovitch, all played fundamentally important roles in shaping the work as a dissertation. Dana Nelson, John Lowe, Bill McFeely, Lucy Maddox, Eric Lott, Priscilla Wald, Don Pease, Ronald Takaki, and Diane Price-Herndl all provided encouragement, insight, and expertise to help make *Ruthless Democracy* a better book. I also want to thank the Mellon foundation for providing me with support while I was a graduate student at Brandeis University and the Center for the Humanities at the University of Georgia for a fellowship that allowed me to complete the manuscript.

RUTHLESS DEMOCRACY

HISTORICAL INTERLUDE

THE DEATH OF MOLUNTHA

In October 1786, in the transnational space where the sovereignty of the United States and the Shawnee Nation overlapped, a confrontation occurred between a Shawnee chief named Moluntha and Colonel Benjamin Logan over the question of the Shawnee's legal ownership of their ancestral homelands. Logan rode into the Shawnee camp with a company of U.S. cavalry soldiers, mounted and armed, led by a color guard proudly bearing the American flag. Moluntha walked out to greet Logan holding a copy of the Miami Treaty, signed earlier that same year, legally entitling him to the land on which he and his people stood. In his other hand Moluntha carried an American flag held high in the air as a symbol of welcome to the soldiers, a sign that the Shawnee came in peace. Colonel Logan was under orders that "if any person, under any description or any color, attempts to come to the army, all persons are forewarned to receive them in a friendly manner." And yet, as Moluntha sat down and entered into negotiations with the colonel, one of Logan's men came up behind him and buried the blade of an axe in Moluntha's skull.[1]

It is here, in this violent clash of the imagined communities of "America," that the central conflict of *Ruthless Democracy* comes sharply into focus. The moment just before Moluntha falls constitutes an instance of profound hope—when two men from vastly different cultures approach one another, each bearing the U.S. flag. For this flickering instant the promise of "America" as a symbol capable of embracing richly disparate peoples within the inclusive democratic rhetoric of the Declaration of Independence seems hauntingly possible. This hope is utterly shattered, however, by the soldier's ruthless act of nativist violence, as Moluntha falls to the earth, shrouded in the American flag, while the papers entitling him to the ground into which his blood seeps blow off into the vast continental expanse of the American frontier. Thus the unfulfilled promise of America's rhetorical commitment to the proposition that "All men are created equal" gives way to the white cultural backlash of fear and racism, turning the American Dream suddenly and irrevocably into the American Nightmare. It is a nightmare which has haunted this country since its inception—a peculiar kind of "American" psychosis, which takes possession of the cavalry soldier, compelling him to ignore the authority of his commanding officer as well as the treaty which has been ratified by the U. S. government and driving him to commit an act of violence so sudden and so extreme that Logan himself was left shocked and shaken by the deed.[2]

This cultural aporia—the seemingly unresolvable conflict between the multicultural history of the country and the violent will to monoculturalism that prevents the nation from coming to psychological terms with its own ethnic diversity—is the historical, literary, and psychological dilemma that will be studied at length in the course of this book. Embedded within the narrative fragment of Moluntha's massacre lie the questions that the coming chapters must engage and attempt to answer: Why has it been so difficult for the country to acknowledge and accept its historic multicultural character? What are the cultural origins of these destructive forces of psychological denial and nativist violence that seem to demand and effectively enforce a monocultural sense of national unity? And, finally, how would our critical conception of "America" be different if we were able to think beyond the forces of monoculturalism and to reimagine the nation's identity in terms of its multicultural history?

INTRODUCTION

THEORIZING RUTHLESS DEMOCRACY

IN THE SUMMER of 1851, while working on the final revisions of *Moby-Dick* on his farm in Pittsfield, Massachusetts, Herman Melville wrote to his good friend and neighbor Nathaniel Hawthorne to express his fears about how his new book would be received. In the letter Melville reveals his deeply conflicted feelings about his desire to "boldly declare . . . [the] Truth" and, on the other hand, his painful awareness that to do so is "ludicrous"—"Try to get a living by the Truth—and go to the Soup Societies."[1] Having already had the manuscript of *Typee* heavily edited to remove his attempts to represent the atrocities committed by white colonizers and missionaries in the name of "civilizing" the Marquesas Islands,[2] Melville was understandably wary of his upcoming journey to New York to see his editor, whom he refers to in the letter as "the malicious Devil [who] is forever grinning in upon me, holding the door ajar." Interestingly, Melville is also clearly anxious about what Hawthorne will think of the book and nervously wonders aloud whether "when you see or hear of my ruthless democracy on all sides, you may possibly feel a touch of a shrink."[3]

What draws me to the term "ruthless democracy" as a title for this multicultural project is the metaphorical quality of Melville's phrase. For the image encompasses both the nation's unrelenting drive toward cultural diversity as well as the brutal historical violence which was carried out in the name of extending, in the rhetoric of the nineteenth century, America's "empire for liberty."[4] Likewise, Melville's anxiety about Hawthorne's anticipated "touch of a shrink" metaphorically evokes the psychological flinch that the nation has historically exhibited in the face of its own inextricably multicultural character and the nativist contraction of citizenship which has typically been the response to any further diversification of the nation's cultural identity. Taken together, Melville's "ruthless democracy" and Hawthorne's anticipated "shrink" represent the object of my analysis.

. . . . .

The period known as the American Renaissance is, of course, one of the best-known and most fruitful periods in the history of American literature. In the exceedingly brief span between 1850 and 1855 such notable works as Melville's *Moby-Dick* (1851), Emerson's *Representative Men* (1850), Hawthorne's *Scarlet Letter* (1850) and *The House of the Seven Gables* (1851), Thoreau's *Walden* (1854), and Whitman's *Leaves of Grass* (1855) all appeared in print for the first time. What interests me, given the multicultural focus of this analysis, is that within this same five-year period women novelists rose to a position of commercial dominance for the first time and, significantly, William Wells Brown's *Clotel; or, The President's Daughter* (1853) (the first African American novel), and John Rollin Ridge's *The Life and Adventures of Joaquín Murieta, the Celebrated California Bandit* (1854) (the first Native American novel) were both published as well. By juxtaposing the canonical works of Nathaniel Hawthorne, Henry David Thoreau, and Herman Melville with the writings of Harriet Beecher Stowe, John Rollin Ridge, and William Wells Brown, I have sought to reconfigure the geographical and cultural margins of the American Renaissance and, in doing so, to present a more historically accurate understanding of the multicultural complexities of "American" identity.[5]

The term "American Renaissance" was originated by F. O. Matthiessen in 1941. Writing just before the United States entered World War II, Matthiessen redefined both the shape and the meaning of the canon of American literature. Prior to Matthiessen's *American Renaissance*, the canon had consisted of Whittier, Holmes, Longfellow, Lowell, Emerson, and Hawthorne. Matthiessen, privileging literature that was "dedicated to the possibilities of democracy,"[6] reconfigured the canon around the writings of Emerson, Whitman, Hawthorne, Thoreau, and Melville. A testimony to the critical force of Matthiessen's work is the fact that for the rest of the twentieth century this conception of the American Renaissance has served as a fixed point of reference, whether to esteem or to array against, for new evolutions of the canon.

Sacvan Bercovitch's *American Jeremiad* (1978), for example, sought to recover the canonical origins of "American" identity by demonstrating how "our classic American writers" (i.e., Emerson, Thoreau, Hawthorne, and Melville) utilized the tradition of the jeremiad first developed by Cotton Mather, Increase Mather, and John Winthrop.[7] In 1985, Jane Tompkins successfully argued in *Sensational Designs* for the inclusion of sentimental novels written by white women, or what she deemed "The Other American Renaissance," by demonstrating how Harriet Beecher Stowe, Susan Warner, and Maria Cummins outsold such canonical contemporaries as Hawthorne and Thoreau.[8] Four years later David S. Reynolds further expanded the topography of "American literature" with *Beneath the American Renaissance*, demonstrating how the works of "major" writers such as Melville and Whitman were deeply influenced by "a tremendous body of submerged writings that have been previously hidden from view."[9] And, most recently, Donald Pease has used Matthiessen's conception of the canon of "American literature" as an antithetical leverage point against which to define what he terms the "New Americanists"—a new generation of scholars who "return questions of class, race, and gender from the political unconscious of American Studies"[10]—in a series of collected volumes entitled *Cultures of United States Imperialism* (1993, coedited with Amy Kaplan), *Revisionary Interventions into the Americanist Canon* (1994), and *National Identities and Post-Americanist Narratives* (1994).

I conceive of *Ruthless Democracy* working within this tradition and, at the same time, as once again expanding the meanings of "American literature" by reimagining the American Renaissance in a multicultural context. By including Hawthorne, Thoreau, and Melville I have sought both to acknowledge and to challenge the work of Matthiessen and Bercovitch by demonstrating, first, that these writers continue to be of the utmost importance to an understanding of "American" identity but, second, that these critically familiar works come to be seen very differently when read side by side with women, black, and Native American writers. Likewise I have attempted to incorporate and expand upon the contributions of both Tompkins and Reynolds, who extended the canon in important new directions yet chose to leave intact fundamental distinctions between masculine and feminine literature (Tomkins) and high and low literature (Reynolds). Finally, I have set out to productively complicate Pease's conception of "post-Americanist narratives" by taking into consideration not only race, class, and gender but other forms of cultural difference, such as ethnic, religious, sexual, and regional identities.

I have chosen the American Renaissance as the focal point of this multicultural analysis because this is the period which has traditionally formed the basis of new conceptions of the canon of U.S. literature when contemporary forces converge in such a way to demand that the nation's identity be reimagined. With the political activism of the 1960s a distant memory, the dismantling of the welfare state now a political reality, and the end of affirmative action apparently looming on the horizon of the twenty-first century, the canon of American literature has begun to change once again—this time with increased emphasis on representing the multicultural nature of our national identity. The country's conflicted feelings toward its own historic multicultural identity can be seen reflected in the fact that this new curriculum is being instituted in secondary and higher education at the exact same moment that the affirmative action programs of the 1960s and 1970s are being dismantled.

There is good reason, therefore, to be skeptical of multiculturalism. What makes "multiculturalism" a vexed term is the fact that it has not been carefully formulated or, worse yet, that it has been more clearly defined by its opponents than its proponents. In the national bestseller *The Disunit-*

ing of America: Reflections on a Multicultural Society, Arthur M. Schlesinger writes that acceptance of the tenets of multiculturalism will invariably lead to the "disintegration of the national community, apartheid, Balkanization, [and] tribalization."[11] And yet the fact that Schlesinger uses the terms *"multiculturalism"* and *"Afrocentrism"* (my emphases) interchangeably throughout the book reveals both his own gross misunderstanding of these concepts and the failure of multiculturalists to adequately define the terms of the debate.

The other central problem that multicultural scholars must confront is the need to distinguish this new concept of multiculturalism from older, theoretically problematic forms of liberal pluralism. Pluralism maintains that the nation can acknowledge its ethnic differences and yet retain its central coherence through ideological consensus about what it means to be an "American." As William V. Flores and Rina Benmayor note in "Constructing Cultural Citizenship," the problem with this conception of national identity is that "by taking for granted that public space can be and is culturally neutral, pluralism endorses the dominant culture as normative. More serious is pluralism's silence on inequality and power relations in the country. While expression of difference is permitted, challenges to power relations are suppressed."[12] Multiculturalism, too often, has been co-opted by state and corporate narratives as a way to mask social inequalities with a rhetoric that celebrates cultural differences. Therefore, if the term "multiculturalism" is to be retained, it must be carefully redefined in opposition both to liberal pluralism and to Schlesinger's apocalyptic accusations of "the disuniting of America."

The so-called "Culture Wars" of the 1990s have produced an abundance of alternative theoretical paradigms: "critical multiculturalism," "insurgent multiculturalism," "transformative multiculturalism."[13] Amidst this proliferation of rhetoric, there are two works that I would like to single out as being particularly important in shaping *Ruthless Democracy.* Wahneema Lubiano's conception of "radical multiculturalism" offers a meaningful response to "empty, noncritical pluralism" by calling for a new analytical focus on "contestation" as the "driving force" for multicultural analysis.[14] Likewise, Ronald Takaki's *A Different Mirror* makes an important contribution to the developing field of multiculturalism by recovering the lost historical voices of Asian, African, Latino, and Native Americans and bringing all of these cultures together to construct a much richer and more diverse portrait of "America."[15]

Just as I have sought to both incorporate and revise critics of the American Renaissance, so too have I attempted to engage and extend the work of Lubiano and Takaki by inventing a new form of criticism, "historical multiculturalism." Whereas Lubiano's work takes aim at explicitly political issues, openly addressing university hiring practices and corporate culture, "historical multiculturalism" is more self-consciously grounded in what Homi Bhabha calls "lived perplexity."[16] While I agree with Lubiano's ideology, I would like to see multicultural theory advance from political rhetoric into carefully researched historical and literary analysis. As Christopher Newfield and Avery F. Gordon observe in "Multiculturalism's Unfinished Business," " 'Multiculturalism' in the 1990s came to denote not so much any particular position in an argument about race relations but the argument itself."[17] While holding onto the energy of Lubiano's "radical" critique and her focus on "contestation," I have tried to devise a more ideologically convoluted paradigm that emerges out of specific historical situations and that inextricably complicates such familiar binaries as left/right, oppressed/oppressor, and self/other.

This is not to say that *Ruthless Democracy* does not have an explicit ideology. This book aggressively challenges a Eurocentric conception of the canon and implicitly calls for every Americanist to more fully engage Native American, Mexican American, Asian American, black, and women's literature and history as absolutely central to "American" identity. Like Lora Romero—who observes that cultural critics "seem unable to entertain the possibility that . . . individual texts could be radical on some issues (market capitalism, for example) and reactionary on others (gender or race, for example)"—I am calling for a more theoretically nuanced and historically accurate model for understanding the ideological complexities of these literary texts.[18] It is simply not true that all of the canonical works are hegemonic and all of the noncanonical ones subversive. What we need is a theoretical paradigm that will allow us to study carefully both Hawthorne's systematic erasure of Native Americans and his profound critique of the dominant white culture. The writers of color, analogously, must be held to the same standard. Rather than seeing John Rollin Ridge simply as a Cherokee "other" to Hawthorne's white "self," Ridge's literary attack on the dominant white society must be balanced with the awareness that he was a Confederate loyalist and a staunch defender of U.S. imperialism.

Like Ronald Takaki's *A Different Mirror*, one of the primary goals of *Ruthless Democracy* is to recover lost cultural voices and to allow those voices to speak freely on the page. Whereas Takaki separates these cultures into distinct chapters, I have attempted to study the myriad of ways in which Native American, Mexican American, Asian American, and African American cultures interact and intersect. And whereas Takaki decided not to include a history of the dominant white culture, I have self-consciously chosen to engage canonical authors and to demonstrate, for example, how Thoreau's conception of "the only true America" can be interpreted in light of black, Indian, Irish, and women's cultures. Because of the increasing specialization of Cultural Studies, scholars tend to study these ethnic and racial groups as distinct and separate fields. One of the central tenets of "historical multiculturalism" is that cultures do not exist in isolation but are inextricably intertwined in infinitely complicated ways. To study African American or Asian American or Chicano literature in isolation risks unwittingly reifying an essentialist conception of cultural identity. While I do not claim to be an "expert" in each of these fields, I have worked hard to try to detail the ways in which these cultures collide, co-alesce, and continually come together and come apart.[19]

"Historical multiculturalism" is founded on three fundamental herme-neutic principles.[20] The first is that "America" has *always* been a multicul-tural nation. Whether one takes the moment of national origin to be the tension between Native American nations before white contact, the land-ing of Columbus, the settlement of Jamestown, or the signing of the Dec-laration of Independence, the country has always been defined by and deeply conflicted about its inherent cultural differences. The second her-meneutic principle is that the historical multicultural context inextricably shapes the literary text (often in ways that the author never intended).[21] Stowe's *Uncle Tom's Cabin* provides a telling example of this principle. After being harshly criticized for sending virtually every single surviving black character to Africa at the end of the novel, Stowe claimed that she had not *meant* to support the views of the American Colonization Society. Regardless of Stowe's intent, the conclusion to the most famous abolition-ist novel of the nineteenth century provides a meaningful insight into white America's deep-seated ambivalence about whether there was a place for free blacks in "America." To limit this study solely to the ways in which these authors *knowingly* engaged the multicultural perplexities of the time risks blinding ourselves to a deeper understanding of how the forces of monoculturalism could assume the guise of "logic," "aesthetics," or even "sanity." Although the writers were often unaware of the monocultural subtext in their work, these forces are still clearly discernable in the literary text.[22] Finally, the third principle is that a theoretically nuanced under-standing of this period requires taking into consideration a multiplicity of contesting cultural voices that are each allowed to articulate the imagined community of the nation on their own terms.[23] Unlike liberal pluralism's emphasis on unity, this study does not attempt to reduce "America" to a single ideological concept. Instead, what begins to come into focus when these sharply contrasting cultural constructions of the national imaginary are set in dialogic relation is an infinitely complicated aporia that cannot be resolved in the name of ideological consistency or logical clarity.

In philosophical terms an aporia is an "insoluble conflict between rheto-ric and thought . . . a lacuna between what a text means to say and what it is constrained to mean."[24] In *Margins of Philosophy*, Derrida defines an aporia as a philosophical space in which logical contradictions are allowed to coexist such that time both "is" and "is not."[25] In this case the contradictions that will be studied at length are the assertions that "America is a democratic nation and that it is not"; that "America is a racist nation and that it is not." In historical terms, this aporia can be formulated as a confrontation between the dominant white society's intractable will to monoculturalism and the explosion of cultural diversity between 1845 and 1855. The midpoint of the nineteenth century was a time of tremendous social flux, marked by the beginnings of the women's movement, the national debate about slavery, the "Indian problem," and the massive influx of Irish immigrants fleeing the potato famine. In literary terms, this aporia is perhaps best described by the image of the vortex at the end of *Moby-Dick*, when the "ruthless democracy" of the *Pequod*'s multicultural crew collides with the destructive whiteness of the whale: "concentric circles seized the lone boat itself and all its crew . . . and spinning, animate and inanimate, all round and round in one vortex, carried the . . . Pequod out of sight."[26]

. . . . .

One of the most intriguing questions about the American Renaissance is, What caused this sudden explosion of literary expression that produced not only the first acknowledged masterpieces of American literature but also an outpouring of novels by African Americans, Native Americans, and women? To understand this unprecedented proliferation of literature requires situating these expressive works in a richly nuanced historical context. Between 1850 and 1855 the question of just who was, or was not, an "American" remained painfully unclear. This uncertainty produced a unique social climate that encouraged writers from many different cultures to recreate the nation in their own image. Out of this swirling debate emerges the literature of the American Renaissance.

While the terms "multiculturalism" and "monoculturalism" are products of the late twentieth century, I want to demonstrate conclusively in the following historical overview that their use is not anachronistic. Rather, the crisis of national identity brought on by an ever-increasing diversity of cultures constitutes a definitive characteristic of the antebellum period. The nation's unconscious impulse to multiculturalism was driven by two powerful forces: the imperialistic drive across the continent in the name of Manifest Destiny and the capitalist demand for immigrant labor to fuel the burgeoning industrial revolution, which together brought hundreds of thousands of Mexicans, Indians, Chinese, and Irish into the country. This expansion, in turn, set off equally powerful forces of monoculturalism which sought to counter the increasing cultural diversity of the nation by legislatively constricting the boundaries of "American" citizenship. In the case of Indians and African Americans, these forces of cultural exclusion were so powerful that mere denial of civil rights was not enough; white anxiety demanded that "less civilized" races be physically removed from the country. This will to monoculturalism was not limited only to the dominant culture. Violent forces of racist exclusion created a counterimpulse to ethnic nationalism that proved to be equally separatist. This explosion of competing forms of nationalism complicated "American" identity geometrically, giving birth to a vast multiplicity of imagined communities within the internationally recognized geographic borders of the United States. These conflicting forces of inclusion and exclusion—which made the nation increasingly more culturally diverse in spite of its own innermost fears of multicultural disunity and racial inter-mixing—created the vortex out of which the literature of the American Renaissance emerged.

One of the most powerful historical impulses driving this vortex was the nation's conflicted will to empire. In less than a thousand days, from the annexation of Texas in 1845 to the conclusion of the Mexican-American War in 1848, the United States more than doubled in size, expanding its borders to continental proportions. With the diplomatic victory over Great Britain in Oregon, which extended the northern boundary of the country to the forty-ninth parallel in 1846, followed by the conquest of Mexico just two years later, the country became gripped by an imperial intoxication. Walt Whitman, writing in the Brooklyn *Daily Eagle*, proclaimed that "We pant to see our country and its rule far-reaching."[27] Manifest Destiny, while buttressing the dominant white society's narcissistic impression of itself as an empire operating under the auspices of divine Providence, nevertheless aggravated a deep-seated nativist anxiety about the ever-increasing multicultural complexity of the nation. Senator Lewis Cass gave these fears succinct expression when he stated in the midst of the Mexican-American War that "we do not want the people of Mexico. . . . All we want is a portion of territory . . . generally uninhabited."[28]

The problem was, of course, that these vast territories *were* inhabited. Historians estimate that seventy-five thousand Spanish-speaking people occupied the lands ceded to the United States by Mexico. According to the terms of the Treaty of Guadalupe Hidalgo, which ended the Mexican-American War in 1848, all Mexicans who remained in the ceded territories would "enjoy all of the rights of citizens of the United States . . . and [be] protected in the free enjoyment of their liberty and property."[29] By 1853, however, Anglo squatters had moved onto every rancho around San Francisco. In a bizarre cultural shift, Anglos effectively appropriated the title of "native" while deeming Mexican Americans to be "foreigners" on lands to which they held legal deeds.[30]

The acquisition of this "empire for liberty" exacerbated the already perplexing question of just who the "We" of the constitutional "We the People" was meant to include. This continental expanse, for example, contained not only thousands of indigenous Native Americans but seventy thousand members of those Eastern nations who had been relocated west of the Mississippi by the Indian Removal Act of 1830 so that they would be, in the words of the Senate Committee on Indian Affairs, "outside of us."[31] Unable to push the Indians any further west, Governor Peter Burnett of California vowed in his annual speech of 1851 to undertake a "war of extermination" against the Native American nations of California, a war which he promised would "continue to be waged between the two races until the Indian race becomes extinct."[32] When it became obvious that Native Americans could not simply be annihilated, they were removed. Authorized by a series of appropriation acts in the 1850s, the federal government relocated Native American nations onto reservations carefully situated so as to be legally within the jurisdiction of the U.S. government yet outside the constitutional parameters of citizenship.[33]

This collision between the forces of imperial expansion and the nativist contraction of "American" citizenship created a proliferation of competing nationalisms. During a debate at the end of the Mexican-American War about whether Indians and Mexicans living in the conquered territories should be given U.S. citizenship, John C. Calhoun announced on the floor of the United States Senate that "we have never dreamt of incorporating into our Union any but the Caucasian race. . . . Ours, sir, is the Government of a white race."[34] This impulse to cultural separatism was not, however, confined solely to the dominant white society. Convinced that African Americans were a "nation within a nation" and that "our country . . . despises us, and bids us begone, driving us from her embraces," Martin Delany called for blacks to leave the United States and attempted to buy land on the west coast of Africa in order to establish an independent nation.[35] In Texas, Juan "Cheno" Cortina organized twelve hundred Mexicanos to rebel against the newly formed "American" government with the intent of reasserting their Mexican identity rather than being assimilated both physically and culturally into the United States.[36] In Ohio, German immigrants formed "colonies" in order to continue to worship and educate their children in their own language.[37] And in California, Chinese immigrants lived and worked in tightly organized and closed communities, in response to racist accusations that they were "semibarbarians" and had no more right to be in California than "flocks of the blackbirds have in a wheatfield."[38]

The most divisive issue fragmenting the country into competing cultural nationalisms and complicating America's conflicted will to empire was, of course, the extension of slavery. As each new state formed out of the vast expanse of the continental empire applied for membership in the Union the question of slave versus free brought the nation closer to the brink of civil war. Gradually two distinct and antagonistic forms of nationalism took shape, each claiming to be the "true" ideological descendants of the founding fathers. Northerners like Henry Ward Beecher (Harriet Beecher Stowe's brother) fought for the right to imagine the nation on their own terms by arguing that "the South . . . is not worthy to bear rule . . . this continent is to be from this time forth governed by Northern men, with Northern ideas, and with a Northern gospel."[39] To which southerners responded by invoking their own interpretation of "America's" revolutionary origins, insisting that northern legislators were "just such a government as incited the Revolutionary patriots to throw off British allegiance. They [too] denied the right of a foreign people, of the same blood, language, religion and government, to legislate for them."[40]

The aporia of "American" identity—the ceaseless interplay of coming together and coming apart—can be clearly seen in the Compromise of 1850. Struggling to hold the Union together, Henry Clay and Daniel Webster devised a political scheme whereby California was admitted as a free state in return for the institution of the Fugitive Slave Law that gave southern slaveholders legal rights over runaway slaves in the North.[41] The Compromise of 1850, however, did as much to fragment national unity as it did to tenuously hold the Union together. More than any other single event, the enactment of the Fugitive Slave Law galvanized the immediate-abolition movement, setting off riots in the North to free recaptured slaves and compelling Harriet Beecher Stowe to write *Uncle Tom's Cabin*, which revealed the horrors of slavery to millions of readers. The Compromise, finally, merely papered over the deeply divisive contradiction that Frederick Douglass poignantly identified in an address of 1852 entitled "The Meaning of July Fourth for the Negro":"To drag a man in fetters into the grand illuminated temple of liberty and call upon him to join in joyous anthems [is] inhuman mockery and sacrilegious irony."[42]

With the growing strength of the immediate-abolition movement raising the "specter" that four million African Americans might imminently be set free, the impulse to cultural exclusion also gained proportionately in strength. The American Colonization Society (ACS), for example, advocated a policy of gradual emancipation, with the newly freed slaves being "returned" to their "native Africa" in order to preserve the narcissistically fragile illusion that the United States was, in the words of an ACS writer, "a white man's country."[43] Throughout the Midwest, states instituted what were known as the Black Codes, fearful that emancipated slaves in the South would migrate north into the "free" states. Article 13 of the revised Indiana constitution, for example, declared that no Negro or mulatto could settle in or enter the state, that all contracts with Negroes were void, and that persons hiring or encouraging Negroes to settle in Indiana were subject to a five-hundred-dollar fine.[44]

This psychological and social impulse to racial and cultural exclusion was, however, inextricably complicated by the industrial revolution's reliance upon immigrant and slave labor and the need for expanding economic markets. Although the industrial revolution began in this country in the 1830s, it did not gain full strength until just before the period which produced the American Renaissance. Spurred by the annexation of Texas, with its vast cotton fields, and the conquest of California, with its ports opening outward to important new markets in China and Japan, America rose for the first time to a position of commercial dominance on the world market. "We hold England by a cotton string," a foreign minister boasted to James Buchanan after the annexation of Texas.[45] The growth of the industrial revolution, however, demanded an army of cheap labor both to pick the cotton (thereby deepening both northern and southern whites' commitment to slavery) and to run the textile mills of the Northeast.

Mill owners initially experimented with using white farmers' daughters to staff their factories, attempting to tightly regulate the women by keeping them quartered in specially built boardinghouses, where their day was strictly regimented. In 1846, a minister from Lowell, Massachusetts praised these boardinghouses, where the "keeper" enforced rigid rules and submitted regular reports to factory supervisors, as being an effective "system of moral police."[46] The inclusion of women in the labor force of the factory system in turn raised perplexing questions about women's political exclusion from the enfranchised community of citizenship. Empowered by their new role in the industrial revolution and galvanized by oppressive working conditions such as the twelve-hour day, female mill-workers in Lynn, Massachusetts organized under the banner "American Ladies Will Not Be Slaves" and began a politicization of feminist issues that deeply destabilized American society.[47] This challenge was most clearly articulated in 1848 at the Seneca Falls Convention, when Elizabeth Cady Stanton issued the call for women's suffrage:"resolved, that it is the duty of women of this country to secure for themselves their sacred right to the elective franchise."[48] In response to this threat to the nation's patriarchal order, popular periodicals of the time began to advocate what might be deemed a form of internal exile also related to the cultural contraction of "American" citizenship. The *Ladies Literary Cabinet*, for example, wrote that "the welfare of the State" relied upon "the good government of families"—with "good government" being founded on the implicit notion that women should remain cloistered within the "domestic circle" and out of the workplace and the voting booth.[49]

It is telling of the complex interrelationship of historical forces of inclusion and exclusion that in 1848, the year of the Seneca Falls Convention, women began to be replaced in the factories by Irish immigrants willing to work for less and without room and board.[50] The promise of democratic equality and economic opportunity, combined with the potato famine in Ireland, led to a massive influx of Irish Catholics. At its peak, in the late 1840s, immigrants from Europe poured into New York harbor at the rate of more than ten thousand a day.[51] Driven by this surge of cheap labor the industrial revolution took off, particularly in the Northeast, with the railroad network expanding from forty-two hundred miles in 1843 to nearly twenty-five thousand miles in 1857.[52] As Thoreau wryly observed in *Walden*, "the rails are laid on [the Irish], they are covered with sand, and the cars run smoothly over them."[53]

While Irish labor drove the rapid expansion of the nation's internal economy, this massive influx of Catholics fueled fears of what Lyman Beecher (Stowe's father) called the threat of "Popish Tyranny."[54] In response to this perceived threat, the nativist movement quickly gained strength. Political nativism was an influential, if not well-remembered, force in the social vacuum created by the demise of the Whig party. Reaching the crest of its power in 1854, Nativists in Massachusetts took the governorship, every seat in the senate, and all but a few of the seats in the state house of representatives.[55] It is interesting that, unlike the American Colonization Society or the Indian Removal Act, the Nativist Party did not seek to deport the Irish. Because of their race and the integral part they played in the industrial revolution, the Irish were reluctantly acknowledged to be too valuable to exclude entirely.[56] Instead, nativists like Samuel F.B. Morse advocated that "the laws of the land be so changed, that NO FOREIGNER WHO COMES INTO THE COUNTRY AFTER THE LAW IS PASSED BE ENTITLED TO THE RIGHT OF SUFFRAGE."[57]

The growing reliance on immigrant labor to support the burgeoning capitalist economy quickly fractured the country along class lines. By 1855, foreign-born immigrants constituted half of New York City's population and 72 percent of the work force.[58] By 1860, more than half of the nation's wealth was owned by 5 percent of the population.[59] In turn, a new class of Americans came into being, what Boston city missionary Joseph Tuckerman called a separate "*caste*—cut off from those in more favored positions."[60] In 1850, for example, the New York police commissioner gave visibility to the nation's class divisions and the horrendous conditions under which the lower classes were condemned to live when he reported that the year before there had been 10,567 infant deaths in contrast to 6,411 adult deaths and acknowledged that there were currently almost three thousand vagrant children living in New York City alone.[61]

Once again, the dominant white society responded to this cultural diversification by seeking to reassert, through exclusion, a distinctly monocultural sense of "American" identity. Charles Loring Brace, for example, founder of the New York Children's Aid Society, implemented what he

called a "Placing Out System," designed to rid American cities of an "ignorant, debased, permanently poor class" by removing the city's impoverished children to new homes in the West. Between 1853 and 1895 Brace
removed ninety thousand boys, sometimes without parental permission,
to families in the West who had no contractual obligation to adopt or even
keep them and who often turned the boys loose after a few months.[62]
Brace's justification was that "dissipated and vicious parents[,] by habitu-
ally neglecting due care and provision for their offspring, shall thus forfeit
their natural claim to them . . . [and] be removed from them . . . till the
claim of the parent be reestablished by continued sobriety, industry, and
general good conduct."[63]

Thus, by the middle of the nineteenth century, "American" identity had
reached a point of profound crisis. The influx of Irish Catholic immigrants
effectively called into question unspoken assumptions about the nation
being an essentially Protestant nation. The advent of the immediate-abolition movement, in conjunction with the women's movement, began fundamentally important debates about the meaning(s) of "freedom" in a
democratic society. With the rapid development of the industrial revolution, the growing visibility of the impoverished inner city dispelled the
myth that "America" was a classless society. Atrocities like the Trail of
Tears likewise shattered the illusion that Indian Removal was being carried
out in benevolent consideration of what was best for Native Americans.
And, finally, the nativist backlash against Mexican American landowners
in California revealed the hidden cultural boundaries that inscribed the
privileges of citizenship.

·　·　·　·　·

It is in response to this historical crisis of national identity that the proliferation of literature known as the American Renaissance arises. As Benedict
Anderson observes in *Imagined Communities*, "the novel and the newspaper . . . provided the technical means for 're-producing' the kind of imagined community that is the nation."[64] Because it was radically unclear at
the midpoint of the nineteenth century whether "America" would suddenly change such that women, blacks, Mexican Americans, Native Americans, and Catholics would be admitted into the full rights of citizenship,
it was a period in which writers from virtually every segment of society
felt compelled to write novels in an attempt to expand the cultural boundaries of the imagined community of "America." And yet, Benedict Anderson's theory that literature plays a fundamentally important role in the
creation of national identity leaves unanswered a number of questions
which are of particular importance to a multicultural interpretation of the
American Renaissance. Who, for example, possesses the right to imagine

"America"? Does each writer have the freedom to imagine the nation equally on his or her own terms? And, finally, how does one theorize the nation in the face of a multiplicity of imagined communities which coincide imperfectly, if at all, and sometimes utterly contradict one another?

Because *Ruthless Democracy* is founded on contestation rather than consensus, canonical writers have been carefully situated in dialogic relation to African American, Native American, and women writers to foreground these contradictions. The theoretical basis for this model is Bakhtin's notion of "heteroglossia," a paradigm that engages "a multiplicity of social voices and a wide variety of their links and interrelationships (always more or less dialogized)." As Bakhtin observes, "at any given moment of its historical existence, language is heteroglot from top to bottom: it represents the co-existence of socio-ideological contradictions between . . . different socio-ideological groups . . . between tendencies, schools, circles and so forth, all given a bodily form." These languages, Bakhtin continues, "do not exclude each other, but rather intersect with each other in many different ways."[65] Following Bakhtin, I have sought to bring together the voices of middle-class New Englanders, Cherokee survivors of the Trial of Tears, Mexicano bandits in California, women abolitionists, fugitive slaves living in Europe, and South Sea islanders working on American whaling boats.

I want to emphasize that the works of Harriet Beecher Stowe, William Wells Brown, and John Rollin Ridge have not been chosen simply because standards of "political correctness" deem it necessary to mention a woman, a black, and a Native American in any contemporary sample of "American literature." These works constitute a fundamentally important dimension of this project precisely because they productively complicate any unified or monolithic conception of "American" identity. To be sure these works cannot be considered literary "masterpieces" that resonate with the cadences of Shakespeare or continue the Puritan tradition of the jeremiad. Ridge's *The Life and Adventures of Joaquín Murieta* is a dime novel full of heaving bosoms and narrow escapes, while much of William Wells Brown's *Clotel* is plagiarized from a short story by Lydia Maria Child. What makes these works worthy of inclusion in the hallowed realm of the "American Renaissance" is the fact that they force Americanists to rethink and remap the cultural and geographic boundaries of the nation. The authors and literary texts included here have been chosen because they each offer important insights into the nation's persistent denial and deep-seated fears of its own inextricably multicultural identity. To focus only on Hawthorne, Melville, Thoreau, and Emerson—almost literally a neighborhood in New England—critically inscribes an inherently limited view of "American" identity in the mid–nineteenth century. In contrast,

I hope to provide a more historically compelling portrait of the contentious years leading up to the Civil War, a period in which the ever-increasing cultural diversity of the nation's population strained the country's commitment to its discursive democratic origins to the point of national crisis.

Ruthless Democracy should not be read, therefore, as simply a literary revision of the American Renaissance. The reader expecting to find long, sustained chapters of literary analysis will be surprised (though I hope not disappointed) to discover that the book focuses as much on America's multicultural history as it does on its culturally diverse literature. I firmly believe that literature provides a unique (and underutilized) resource for exploring the psychological contradictions of the nation's troubled relationship to its own historic multicultural identity. Hawthorne's insight that white entitlement to the New World is founded on "so excellent a counterfeit of right," for example, exposes the innermost fears of the dominant white society, fears the rhetoric of Manifest Destiny was deeply invested in evading. To emphasize the interrelationship of history and literature, I have preceded each chapter with a "historical interlude" which introduces the central themes to be explored more fully in the chapter that follows. The real subject of *Ruthless Democracy* is, therefore, not simply a revision of the canon of American literature, but rather an argument for how engaging a multiplicity of cultural perspectives (both historical and literary) can lead to a greater understanding of the richly complicated, infinitely conflicted nature of "American" identity.

What makes this study itself a "ruthless democracy" is the fact that each of the six authors considered here is given equal theoretical weight. No critical hierarchy implicitly privileges Hawthorne and Melville as "major" writers while tacitly diminishing the importance of Ridge or Brown by deeming them to be representative of "minority" cultures. As Bakhtin notes in "Discourse in the Novel," "the novel . . . denies the absolutism of a single and unitary language—that is, [it] refuses to acknowledge its own language as the sole verbal and semantic center of the ideological world . . . [but is] conscious of the vast plenitude of national and . . . social languages—all of which are equally capable of being 'languages of truth.' "[66] In giving each author a democratically equal voice, however, it is important not to lose sight of the political, social, and economic inequalities that work to shape the margins of these literary constructions of the imagined community of the nation. The fact, for example, that William Wells Brown wrote the first African American novel while living in exile because of the Fugitive Slave Law must not be underestimated. Rather, his fractured family life needs to be theorized in relation to the fragmented narrative of the novel. And yet, in a ruthless literary democracy, these stylistic problems do not diminish the critical importance of Brown's literary construction of "America" in relation to, for example, Melville's *Moby-Dick*.

.   .   .   .   .

Ruthless Democracy explores two distinct yet interrelated aspects of America's multicultural identity. The first section of the book, entitled "Beyond New England," is dedicated to expanding Matthiessen's conception of the American Renaissance beyond the Northeast and to exploring the multicultural complexities within the geographic boundaries of the United States. The second half, entitled "Toward a Transnational Understanding of 'American' Identity," extends this historical multicultural study beyond the geographical borders of the United States by mapping neglected aspects of what I am calling "the American Diaspora."

The opening chapter, "History Imagined 'Fantastically Awry,' " commences in the heart of New England and interrogates how canonical American literature perpetuates the illusion of monoculturalism by obscuring the multicultural origins of "America." Hawthorne begins *The House of the Seven Gables*, for example, by asserting that Matthew Maule (a white New Englander) was "the original occupant of the soil"—effectively erasing the Naumkeag Indians who lived on the land and gave the town its name before it became "Salem." Hawthorne's novel, however, also excavates the dark recesses that lie buried beneath discursive layers of white disavowal by exploring the Pyncheon family's persistent desire for the "lost Indian deed" and the crisis of indigenity that haunted the dominant white society in the wake of a series of Supreme Court rulings giving legal title to Native Americans. This exceedingly complicated dialectic of disavowal and desire provides the theoretical foundation for understanding the nation's deeply conflicted relationship to its own multicultural history. The second chapter, on John Rollin Ridge's *The Life and Adventures of Joaquín Murieta*, expands the margins of the American Renaissance from New England, to the deep South, to Indian Territory, to Alta California. Ridge's novel offers an important dialogical response to Hawthorne, articulating the racial rage of Cherokee Indians who had been removed on the Trail of Tears and Mexican Americans who had been dispossessed of their lands in California. Having extended the cultural and geographical borders of the American Renaissance across the continent, I return in the third chapter to New England, to read Henry David Thoreau's *Walden* in terms of this new historical multicultural context. Here again the forces of disavowal and desire collide; Thoreau's literary masterpiece provides a vivid illustration of both the nativist impulse to cultural exclusion and the persistent influence of African American, Native American, Irish, and women's culture on canonical literature.

Whereas the first half of *Ruthless Democracy* complicates the tendency of Americanists to privilege the literature of New England as being representative of "America," the second half sets out to "think beyond the nation," by exploring "America's" transnational borders.[67] The conclusion of Harriet Beecher Stowe's *Uncle Tom's Cabin*, for example, in which virtually every surviving African American character is sent off to Liberia, raises important historical questions about the relationship of the "colony" of Liberia to the United States and the conflicted nature of American imperialism in the nineteenth century. Stowe's novel reveals not only the ambivalence of the white leaders of the American Colonization Society, who founded Liberia to "rid" the United States of its black population, but also the contradictory feelings of those black Americans who chose to repatriate to this "little black America" on Africa's shores. William Wells Brown's *Clotel* further extends the transnational borders of the nation, forcing the reader to consider the plight of runaway slaves who had to flee the country because of the Fugitive Slave Law. Brown's novel effectively maps the American Diaspora by clearly demonstrating that these fugitive slaves, although living outside the geographic borders of the country, adamantly believed the United States to be their "native land." Herman Melville's *Moby-Dick* likewise extends the cultural and geographic borders of the imagined community of "America" by tracing the erratic course of the *Pequod* around the Cape of Good Hope through the China Sea into the South Pacific and detailing the cultural conflict on board. Just as Ridge's novel reveals the multicultural complexity within the nation, Melville's "ruthless democracy" uncovers nineteenth-century America's transnational economic markets and the international diversity of the American labor force.

This all-too-brief list of six authors—Hawthorne, Ridge, Thoreau, Stowe, Brown, and Melville—does not establish a new, definitive conception of the canon analogous to Matthiessen's *American Renaissance*. The theoretical construct of "ruthless democracy" refuses analytic closure, opting instead for an open-ended and inherently fluid dialogue that engages an intentionally disparate grouping of cultural voices. As Bakhtin notes, a dialogic approach like the one employed in this study is "not a logical, systematic, purely semantic fullness with every point represented; no, it is a historical and concrete plenitude of actual social-historical languages that in a given era have entered into interaction, and belong to a single evolving contradictory unity."[68]

I want to be clear, therefore, that William Wells Brown's voice is not meant to be the "authentic" voice of the African American community. One of the problems with trying to inscribe a "representative" portrait of the cultural diversity of antebellum America is the danger of assigning too much critical weight to the first African American and Native American novels. The historical multicultural matrix of this particular "ruthless democracy" should be seen as extending beyond the margins of this analysis. Brown's perspective, in other words, needs to be theoretically situated in dialogic relation not only to Harriet Beecher Stowe but to black women writers such as Harriet Wilson and Harriet Jacobs, as well as to black nationalists like Martin Delany and Henry Highland Garnett, who vehemently disagreed with Brown's assimilationist tendencies. Likewise, John Rollin Ridge should not be misconstrued as being representative of all Native American tribes or even all members of the Cherokee Nation. I sincerely hope that other scholars will continue to expand and complicate this historical multicultural model of the American Renaissance by situating Ridge's voice in relation to Sioux, Navaho, Creek, and Iroquois perspectives from the nineteenth century. The six writers and literary texts discussed here should be thought of as a synecdoche, a suggestive evocation of a much larger and much more culturally complicated array of voices that taken together constitute the "single evolving contradictory unity" of "American" identity.

The problem, of course, with engaging the indeterminacy of a multicultural transnational conception of the national imaginary is the question of what "American" identity means in this new context. Can we even speak of "American" identity in any singular sense of the term? As Bakhtin points out, with the "deepening of dialogical essence . . . fewer and fewer hard elements ('rock bottom truths') remain that are not drawn into dialogue."[69] The point of this historically and theoretically complex analysis is not simply to deconstruct any and all conceptions of national identity, as Arthur Schlesinger fearfully depicts multiculturalism as doing in *The Disuniting of America*. As Ernesto LaClau and Chantal Mouffe have written in describing their theory of "radical democracy," an initial phase of "dispersion, detotalization, or decentering of certain positions with regard to others" constitutes a necessary first step toward reintroducing "a certain notion of totality." The difference between a monolithic and a radically deconstructed sense of national identity, LaClau and Mouffe argue, is that a decentered understanding of national identity would "no longer involve an underlying principle that would unify 'society,' but [would engage] an ensemble of totalizing effects in an open relational complex."[70] In other words, the project of *Ruthless Democracy* is not to reduce "America" to a single unifying ideological construct—like Matthiessen's "possibilities of democracy" or Bercovitch's "consent"—but rather to allow these different voices to coexist in a fluid, infinitely complicated, never-ending dialogue.

What the book sets out to uncover, then, is not a "rock bottom truth" but the aporia or unresolvable conflict between the nation's historic multicultural identity and its insistent will to monocultural unity. What I will attempt to make critically visible is the complicated form of cultural exchange which occurs in spite of the nation's deep-seated psychological fears of racial intermixing and the legislative and imaginative attempts to keep the myriad of cultures distinctly separate from one another. This multicultural hybridity—a fractal mosaic that cannot be fixed but can nevertheless be identified in the midst of the ceaseless interplay of the nation's coming together and coming apart—constitutes the new conception of "American" identity created by *Ruthless Democracy*'s transnational reconfiguration of the American Renaissance.[71]

PART I

BEYOND NEW ENGLAND

HISTORICAL INTERLUDE

THE CIVIL POLITY DERANGED

In February 1824, Governor G. M. Troup of Georgia wrote to the secretary of war, John C. Calhoun, to call upon newly elected President Andrew Jackson to enact the legislation of Indian Removal. The stated purpose of Troup's letter was to convince Calhoun that Georgia possessed legal right to "occupy the country which is their own, and which is unjustly withheld from them."[1] The problem was that "the country" which Troup identified as his "own" made up the heart of the Cherokee Nation, occupied by more than seventeen thousand Native Americans who had called the land their "own" since time immemorial. In straining to make his point, Troup's letter provides a revealing insight into the crisis of indigenity within the dominant white society and the logic of monoculturalism used to justify white entitlement to Indian lands.

Troup begins his appeal to Calhoun by imploring him to remind President Jackson that Georgia's compact with the United States called for Indian title to the land to be extinguished "as early as the same can be peaceably obtained, on reasonable terms."[2] In compensation for "having endured so long and so patiently," Troup insists that Georgians be granted "the land which was their birthright."[3] Troup's appeal, however, unravels in the face of historical fact: not only did the Cherokee continue to occupy their ancestral homelands but the United States government had negotiated any number of treaties with the Cherokee which provided de facto recognition that the land legally belonged to the Cherokee to sell or trade. It is a problem of jurisprudence of which Troup is acutely aware, for he turns in his next sentence to attacking the idea that "primitive aboriginal rights are such now, as they were before the discovery of the land" as being an "insult and mockery." Obviously aware that the charge of "insult" cannot legally establish Georgia's claim to Cherokee land, Troup concludes by admitting, "I am sorry I cannot support [my views] by matter-of-fact information of official character. To me this is impossible."[4]

And yet this surprisingly honest acknowledgement does not compel Troup to withdraw his request that the president implement a "proposition for removal" of the Cherokee, but instead only makes his tone more strident. Unable to provide "matter-of-fact information of official character," Troup turns to the logic of monoculturalism and the idea that the cultural borders of "America" should be drawn strictly along racial lines—a view Troup was well aware that Calhoun shared. Troup thus concludes with the argument that "Of all the old States, Georgia is the only one whose political organization is incomplete; her civil polity is deranged; her military force cannot be reduced to systematic order and subordination: and all because Georgia is not in the possession of her vacant territory."[5]

In these closing lines of Troup's appeal the aporia that underlies "American" identity becomes visible for a flickering moment, revealing the profoundly conflicted attitudes of white America in the face of the nation's historical diversity. On the one hand, Troup readily admits that the State of Georgia remains somehow "incomplete" without the Cherokees' land—a conception of "wholeness" that is inherently multicultural. And yet, at the same time, a culturally diverse conception of the nation remains unimaginable to Troup. Confined by the logic of monoculturalism, Troup worries aloud that military "order and subordination" cannot be maintained in the face of Cherokee presence. Troup even goes so far as to argue that the "civil polity is deranged" while the Cherokee retain control over their ancestral homelands. "Order" and even sanity are thus predicated, for Troup, upon a condition of monocultural coherence that leads him to covet the Cherokee's primordial relationship to the land and to demand Cherokee removal.

A deep-seated desire for "completeness" thus comes directly into conflict with a sense of "order" deeply rooted in what I am calling the logic of monoculturalism. In an earlier letter Calhoun had inquired as to the possibility of "part of [Georgia's] territory" being set aside "for the settlement of the Indians" or that the Cherokee "incorporate into and amalgamate with [white] society." To which Troup responds that it is an "absolute certainty" that "Georgia will never give her assent" to having Cherokee Indians within her borders either freely mixing as citizens or isolated on reservations.[6] Confronted with the possibility of this unimaginable community, Troup attempts to restore "order" and sanity to his world by boldly writing the Cherokee out of historical existence (i.e., ending his letter with the summation, "all because Georgia is not in the possession of her *vacant* territory"). With a turn of the phrase seventeen thousand Cherokee have disappeared—a form of discursive removal that ominously foreshadows Jackson's Indian Removal Act six years later and the Trail of Tears eight years after that.

Troup's phrase, "the civil polity is deranged," provides an unintended though highly meaningful insight into the dominant white society. For Troup inadvertently captures the fundamental psychological conflict that results from being a historically multicultural country with an insistently monocultural sense of national identity. The aporia inscribed in Troup's closing argument provides a fitting historical juxtaposition to a multicultural analysis of *The House of the Seven Gables*. All of these same themes underlie Hawthorne's literary construction of the national imaginary: the unresolved tension between desire for Indian lands and the unwillingness of whites to recognize Native Americans as part of the imagined community of "America"; the related impulse to try to resolve this dilemma by discursively erasing the nation's multicultural origins; and, finally, the cursed awareness within the dominant white society that they had "no matter-of-fact information of official character" to justify their tenuous legal claim to the land.

CHAPTER ONE

NATHANIEL HAWTHORNE: HISTORY IMAGINED

"FANTASTICALLY AWRY"

The House of the Seven Gables, antique as it now looks,
was not the first habitation erected by civilized man on
precisely the same spot of ground. Pyncheon Street formerly
bore the humbler appellation of Maule's Lane, from the
name of the original occupant of the soil.
(Nathaniel Hawthorne, *The House of the Seven Gables*)

SOMETHING IS WRONG. How could Matthew Maule, a white New Englander, possibly be construed as "the *original* occupant of the soil" here in the opening pages of Hawthorne's *The House of the Seven Gables* (1851)? In *The Indian Population of New England in the 17th Century*, S. F. Cook notes that the specific area of what is now Salem, Massachusetts, where Hawthorne sets his novel, was home to the Naumkeag Indians, whose numbers just before white contact Cook estimates at one thousand. The Naumkeag were part of the Pennacook Confederation, whose population at the time of arrival was, according to historians' best estimates, approximately twelve thousand.[1] We do not, unfortunately, have primary documents detailing how the Naumkeag felt about the arrival of whites or their perception of the English longing for Indian land or those strange but powerful things the Englishmen called "deeds." What we do know for certain, however, is that the Naumkeag *were there*.

It is not difficult, of course, to understand how Hawthorne erases the Naumkeag from his literary construction of the historical origins of the nation. "History" begins, according to the monocultural logic which narrowly confines Hawthorne's perspective of America's past, with the appearance of "civilized man"—and "civilized" here clearly means "white." The more difficult question is *why* does Hawthorne leave Native Americans out of this literary archeology in search of the "name of the original occupant of the soil"?[2] Given the central and enduring place of Hawthorne in every construction of the canon, from the Young American series in the mid–nineteenth century to Matthiessen's *American Renaissance* in the mid–twentieth, this elision constitutes an important point of entry for understanding the role of the canon in erasing the multicultural history of the nation from the white page of "American literature."[3]

The first step in undertaking a multicultural interpretation of Hawthorne's romance is to try to restore Native Americans' repressed historical existence.[4] And yet to bring Indians back into the picture by juxtaposing Hawthorne's literary construction of early American "history" with population figures of the *true* "original occupant[s] of the soil" directly violates Hawthorne's warning in the well-known preface to *Seven Gables*. Because *Seven Gables* is a romance, Hawthorne cautions against the "exceedingly dangerous form of criticism" which brings his "fancy pictures . . . into positive contact with the realities of the moment" (16). As Susan Mizruchi writes in *The Power of Historical Knowledge*, "history's representation in *The House of the Seven Gables* is a phenomenon continually evaded: history is most vividly evident as an absent cause."[5] In order to better understand the psychological, cultural, and social forces that create this blindness to the multicultural origins of "America" requires critically reconstructing the "absent cause" that leads Hawthorne to imagine history "fantastically awry" by depicting a white man as the "original" inhabitant of "the soil."

In the spirit of Melville's "ruthless democracy," I will ignore Hawthorne's "touch of a shrink" in the preface to *Seven Gables* and pursue this "dangerous species" of historical multicultural criticism, in order to better understand the intricate contradictions of Hawthorne's representations of Native Americans in his literary construction of the imagined community of "America." On the surface, it appears that Hawthorne has discursively removed Indians from "history" in much the same way that Andrew Jackson physically removed Indians from the land twenty years earlier. And yet, despite Hawthorne's opening disavowal of Native Americans' historical existence, throughout the course of the narrative the Pyncheon family longs for a "lost Indian deed" that, it turns out, is hidden at the spiritual center of the House of the Seven Gables, behind a portrait of the Pyncheon patriarch. This dialectical interplay of the Pyncheons' desire and Hawthorne's disavowal will provide the theoretical basis for an analysis that extends beyond *The House of the Seven Gables* to an interrogation of the nation's infinitely conflicted relationship to its inextricably multicultural origins.

These contradictory representations of Native Americans in *The House of the Seven Gables* can be explained in part by situating Hawthorne's romance in a detailed historical context. Hawthorne's literary career coincides exactly with the age of Indian removal, in which the Creek, Choctaw, Chickasaw, Seminole, and Cherokee nations were moved west of the Mississippi. In 1830, for example, the year that Andrew Jackson signed the Indian Removal Act, Hawthorne published his first short story, "The Hollow of Three Hills," in the *Salem Gazette*. Two years later, Indian removal reached a point of national crisis when the Cherokee took their case all the way to the United States Supreme Court, where Chief Justice John Marshall ruled that Indians were "the undisputed possessors of the soil."[6] That same year, 1832, Hawthorne published his first critically important tales, including "My Kinsman, Major Mollineux" and "Roger Malvin's Burial"—a tale about what Hawthorne deemed "one of the few incidents of Indian warfare naturally susceptible of the moonlight of romance."[7] In 1837, the year that Hawthorne published *Twice Told Tales*, the Trail of Tears began, which eventually led to the death of more than four thousand Cherokee Indians. And finally, in 1851, one year before the federal government began moving Native Americans onto reservations, Hawthorne published his second novel, *The House of the Seven Gables*, which declares Matthew Maule to be "the original occupant of the soil."

The goal of this analysis is not, however, to determine Hawthorne's political views on Indian removal or Jacksonian ideology.[8] I am not interested in fathoming the question of whether Hawthorne *meant* to explore white anxiety about dispossessing Indians of their land. To the contrary, what interests me is Hawthorne's "epistemology of unknowing";[9] that is to say the psychological machinations which allowed Hawthorne (and/or his readers) to believe that Matthew Maule really was "the original occupant of the soil." By juxtaposing Hawthorne's romantic representation of "history" with such "realities of the moment" as Jackson's Indian removal policies, Marshall's Supreme Court decisions, and the Trail of Tears, I will demonstrate how "the lost Indian deed" can be read as a metaphor for the centrally important, though deeply conflicted, place of Native Americans in the national imaginary. In doing so, I will also illustrate how a multicultural analysis of the American Renaissance radically reinterprets F. O. Matthiessen's assertion that canonical American literature is dedicated to "the possibilities of democracy."[10]

The "Absurd Delusion" of the Indian Deed

The Indian deed—situated at the heart of the House of the Seven Gables and yet alternately described as "lost," "impalpable," and "worthless"— constitutes the focal point of this literary analysis of white America's ambivalent relationship to the ineluctable historical fact that the nation is built on Indian land. Originally procured by the family patriarch, Colonel Pyncheon, back in the seventeenth century, the Indian deed granted the Pyncheons title to a "tract of Eastern lands . . . in the state of Maine" and was "signed with the hieroglyphics of several Indian sagamores" (285). The document was "lost" when Colonel Pyncheon traded it to Matthew Maule as part of a deal to obtain a portion of the land on which the House

of the Seven Gables was subsequently built (182). Ironically, the deed was
not lost at all but rather was hidden "in a recess in the wall" (285) of
the Pyncheon family mansion by Maule's son, one of the carpenters who
constructed the House of the Seven Gables, so that Colonel Pyncheon
could not reclaim it after he succeeded in having Maule put to death for
the crime of witchcraft.

The Indian deed plays an exceedingly complicated role in both Hawthorne's romantic construction of the nation and the Pyncheon family's
sense of entitlement to the land. On the one hand, the importance of the
"lost Indian deed" is systematically disavowed throughout the course of
the narrative. In the opening pages of the tale Hawthorne seems to dismiss
the Indian deed, describing it as nothing more than an "impalpable claim"
and "an absurd delusion of family importance" (31). What makes the Pyncheons' dream "absurd" is a muted awareness that, as Hawthorne writes,
"in the course of time, the territory [granted by the deed] was partly
regranted to more favored individuals, and partly cleared and occupied by
actual settlers. These last, if they ever heard of the Pyncheon title, would
have laughed at the idea of any man asserting a right on the strength of
moldy parchment" (31). At the end of the novel, therefore, when the
hiding place of the "lost Indian deed" is revealed and the document itself
finally recovered by the Pyncheons, Holgrave summarily dismisses it as
having "long been worthless" (285).

And yet while the "moldy parchment" may be legally "worthless" to
the Pyncheons, the "lost Indian deed" has a very real psychological value
that cannot be so easily dismissed. Throughout the novel the Pyncheons
continue to look longingly toward the "ancient map of the Pyncheon territory eastward" (87), which supposedly depicts what was granted in the
Indian deed and which encompasses lands "more extensive than many a
dukedom or even a reigning prince's territory, on European soil" (30).
Given the social instability of the relatively new capitalist economy—"in
this republican country," Hawthorne writes, "amid the fluctuating waves
of our social life, somebody is always at the drowning point" (48)—the
hope of a "dukedom," even if it is a "delusion," clearly plays an important
role in the Pyncheons' narcissistic sense of self-worth by making the
"poorest member of the [Pyncheon] race to feel as if he had inherited a
kind of nobility" (31).

This aporia—defined by the endless interplay of desire and disavowal—
comprises the hermeneutical foundation of my historical multicultural
analysis. Theoretically, this critical paradigm is indebted to Eric Lott's
conception of "the dialectical flickering of racial insult and racial envy" in
Love and Theft, his study of blackfaced minstrelsy in nineteenth-century
America. As Lott notes, the commercial success of minstrelsy's "blacking

up" during the antebellum age led to a corresponding "blackening" of American popular culture on a level that escaped most of minstrelsy's performers and its patrons. Lott's insightful analysis thus goes beyond simply asking whether minstrelsy was racist to an understanding of both the deep-seated racial *fear* within the white working-class audience that paid to see the obsequious, racist stereotypes of Zip Coon, Jim Crow, and Uncle Tom, as well as the racial *fascination* for what whites perceived to be black culture's alluring sense of "cool, virility . . . [and] abandon." This deeply conflicted relationship, Lott notes, constitutes "a peculiarly American structure of racial feeling."[11]

Hawthorne's contradictory representations of Indians as both historically absent and integral to the Pyncheon family myth mirrors the paradoxical feelings of the dominant white society toward "the original occupant[s] of the soil." On the one hand, whites insisted that Native Americans were unfit for citizenship and had to be removed beyond the geographic borders of the nation for their own preservation. On the other hand, Indians played a culturally important (if not openly acknowledged) role in helping whites to fashion an identity for themselves as "native Americans." If we take the architecture of the House of the Seven Gables to be an example of what Lauren Berlant calls "the National Symbolic," the central (though forgotten) place of the "lost Indian deed" can be read as a metaphor for the multicultural hybridity that lies hidden behind the canonical exterior of "American" identity.[12]

The question, of course, which every undergraduate wants to know is whether Hawthorne *meant* the Indian deed to represent cultural hybridity? As Robert J. C. Young writes in *Colonial Desire: Hybridity in Theory, Culture, and Race*, multicultural hybridity often takes place at an "unintentional [or] unconscious level."[13] To focus on the question of authorial intent risks losing sight of the unresolved contradictions between white America's narcissistic image of itself as a country founded on democratic freedom and its repressed awareness of the horrific violence committed in wresting (or buying) the land away from the indigenous inhabitants of the New World. As Frederic Jameson observes in *The Political Unconscious*, it is a critical mistake to reduce literary analysis to simply a matter of authorial intent. Within the literary text, Jameson notes, "the social contradiction . . . must, however reconstructed, remain an absent cause, which cannot be directly or immediately conceptualized by the text . . . [but] takes the form of the *aporia* . . . the unthinkable and the conceptually paradoxical, that which cannot be unknotted by the operation of pure thought." Following Jameson, it can be said that the "lost Indian deed," hidden away in the dusty inner recesses of the House of the Seven Gables, embodies the multicultural unconscious of Hawthorne's literary text.[14]

Disavowal: Discursive Indian Removal

It is, admittedly, a critically difficult task to excavate the "lost Indian deed" and to interpret what the "hieroglyphics of several Indian sagamores" (285) mean to Hawthorne's literary construction of the imagined community of the nation. To recover the significance of this "yellow parchment," buried below "a century's dust," it is first necessary to dig beneath several layers of denial that Indians even existed. In this description of the map of the territory to which the Pyncheons are entitled by the "lost Indian deed," for example, Hawthorne's romance works to discursively remove Native Americans from "history" altogether: "[The map was] the handiwork of some skillful old draftsman, and grotesquely illuminated with pictures of Indians and wild beasts, among which was seen a lion; the natural history of the region being as little known as its geography, which was put down most fantastically awry" (44). Blurring the line between "fancy" and "reality" which he strives to protect in the preface, Hawthorne's text couples the image of "Indians" with the image of a "lion" to suggest that the historical accuracy of the map is "fantastically awry." Indians become the product of the "old draftsman['s]" imagination; their presence in the picture, along with the lion, is used as proof of how "little known" the "natural history of the region" truly was. And thus the substitution of what Eric Hobsbawm calls an "invented tradition"[15] is neatly in place. Indians have become fiction, a product of the white imagination gone "fantastically awry." And fiction, the assertion that Indians (like lions) were never indigenous to the region, has become "history."

The psychological contradiction inherent in the fact that Hawthorne attempts to imagine Native Americans out of historical existence in his description of the map of those very lands titled to the Pyncheons by the "lost Indian deed" provides a telling example of the anxiety within the white community surrounding the "Indian question." This anxiety manifests itself in the form of an aporia whereby Indians both do and do not exist in Hawthorne's romantic reconstruction of "history." It is theoretically important not to collapse this contradiction for the sake of ideological clarity, for the conflicted impulse to at once possess Indian title and deny Native Americans' historical existence makes up a constitutive, if puzzling, part of the crisis of indigenity within the dominant white community.[16] These contradictions can be explained in part by setting Hawthorne's literary romance in dialogic relation to the legal debate about white entitlement which erupted during Hawthorne's lifetime.

The legal right of whites to the North American continent was called into question during the nineteenth century by a series of Supreme Court decisions known as the Marshall trilogy. The first of these cases, *Johnson v. McIntosh* (1823), involved the question of the validity of purchases of land from the Indians prior to the Revolutionary War and has been called the "singlemost important textual interpretation of the law governing the rights of indigenous tribal peoples."[17] Marshall ruled against the legality of Indian deeds, reaffirming white entitlement to the New World on the basis of the Doctrine of Discovery, which held that "the rights of the original inhabitants . . . to complete sovereignty . . . was denied by the original fundamental principle, that discovery gave exclusive title to those who made it." European conquest, Marshall decided, gave whites "an exclusive right to extinguish the Indian title of occupancy."[18]

The problem was, as Robert Williams points out in *The American Indian in Western Legal Thought*, that by making white Americans' legal claim to the land dependent on the British conquest of the New World, Marshall called into question the "principal liberating thematics of the Revolutionary era, which envisioned America as a land freed of the Norman Yoke."[19] Marshall's ruling that "conquest gives a title which the Courts of the conqueror cannot deny" and his open acknowledgment that white entitlement was "maintained and established by the sword" thus shattered white Americans' view of themselves as a formerly *colonized* nation that came into being through a revolutionary assertion of independence.[20] By grounding white entitlement to the New World in the Doctrine of Discovery, Marshall's decision forced whites to openly acknowledge that their claim to the land was based on the fact that genealogically they were the *colonizers*.

The next two cases in the Marshall trilogy involved the Cherokees' attempts to fight the State of Georgia in the U.S. court system. In the first case, *Cherokee Nation v. Georgia* (1831), the Cherokee claim was dismissed by Marshall on the grounds that the Cherokee were a "domestic dependent nation" and therefore could not file suit as an internationally recognized nation.[21] One year later the Cherokee were back in court. This time, in *Worcester v. Georgia* (1832), Marshall reversed his earlier ruling by calling into question the Doctrine of Discovery: "Did these adventurers, by sailing along the coast and occasionally landing on it, acquire for the several governments to whom they belonged, or by whom they were commissioned, a rightful property in the soil from the Atlantic to the Pacific, or rightful dominion over the numerous people who occupied it?" Such a notion, Marshall wrote, was "absurd." While the Doctrine of Discovery "regulated the right given by discovery among the European discoverers," Marshall ruled that it "could not affect the rights of those already in possession." Marshall thus concluded that "The Indian nations had always been considered as distinct, independent political communities, retaining their original natural rights, as the undisputed possessors of the soil, from time immemorial." Georgia's attempt to extend its laws over the Cherokee was thus found to be "unconstitutional, void, and of no effect."[22]

This crisis of white entitlement came close to toppling the entire democratic structure of the United States government. Andrew Jackson, determined to remove the Cherokee from Georgia, refused to enforce the Supreme Court's decree. "John Marshall has made his decision," Jackson wrote, "let him enforce it if he can." As Jackson stood idly by, white speculators in Georgia burned, looted, and raffled off the Cherokees' ancestral homelands. John Ross, the leader of the Cherokee nationalist party, returned home from Washington, D.C. to find whites occupying his house and was brazenly ordered to turn over the horse on which he was sitting.[23] Supreme Court Justice Joseph Story wrote in the midst of the crisis, "I yield slowly and reluctantly to the conviction that the Constitution cannot last."[24]

The situation only grew worse when, six years later, the federal government forced the Cherokee to remove to Indian Territory. Removal of the Cherokee began on March 3, 1837. One missionary wrote, "it is mournful to see how reluctantly these people go away . . . even the stoutest hearts melt into tears when they turn their faces towards the sun—& I am sure that this land will be bedewed by a Nation's tears—if not with their blood." A year later forced removal began with the Cherokee being rounded up into detention camps, where dysentery, and cholera raged. On the march, which averaged 116 days (though the government had provided provisions for only 80 days), epidemics of measles, whooping cough, pleurisy, and bilious fever broke out. A traveler from Maine who encountered the Cherokee in the southern part of Kentucky wrote that "on the road where the Indians passed . . . they buried fourteen or fifteen at every stopping place, and they make a journey of ten miles per day on average."[25] In all, historians estimate that more than four thousand Cherokee died.[26]

The Trail of Tears provoked a sense of horror in many members of the white community. The American Peace Society, for example, called the "oppressed Cherokees" an "American Poland," hopelessly seeking "a refuge from the perfidy of a nation, which, to the cruelty of the Russian despotism, adds the hypocrisy of a claim to republicanism."[27] Ralph Waldo Emerson wrote to President Martin Van Buren in April 1838 protesting the federal government's treatment of the Cherokee: "a crime is projected that confounds our understandings by its magnitude,—a crime that really deprives us as well as the Cherokee of a country . . . for how could we call the conspiracy that should crush these poor Indians our government, or *the land that was cursed by their parting and dying imprecations* our country, any more?" (my emphasis). The "crime[s]" inflicted upon the Cherokee threatened the very "name of this nation" and America's perception of itself as being an "omen of religion and liberty."[28] Emerson's fear that the land itself was "cursed by their parting and dying imprecations" clearly resonates with Hawthorne's literary representation of the "curse" that emanates from the Pyncheons' repressed awareness that the land on which the House of the Seven Gables was built had been obtained as a result of unspoken atrocities committed against "the original occupant of the soil."

The Trail of Tears can be said to represent the final stage of the crisis of white indigenity in the first half of the nineteenth century. The brutality of Cherokee removal proved to be a grim fulfillment of Marshall's observation in *Johnson v. McIntosh* that white entitlement to the land was "maintained and established by the sword." The tragedies that occurred on the long walk from Georgia to Indian Territory in what is now the state of Oklahoma were well documented in newspapers throughout the country. These atrocities provided a chilling insight for many white Americans into the dark realities that underlay the beneficent rhetoric used to officially describe Indian removal. President Martin Van Buren, for example, in his annual address in December 1838 briefly referred to Cherokee removal as "the difficulties which have arisen from the peculiar and impracticable nature of the Indian character," noting that the situation had reached a "happy and certain consummation" due to the "wise, humane, and undeviating policy of the Government."[29] The historical realities that underlay this "happy" rhetoric were, however, too painful for many whites to acknowledge. "The steps of this crime follow each other so fast," Emerson wrote, "that the millions of virtuous citizens . . . *must shut their eyes* until the last howl and wailing of these tormented villages and tribes shall afflict the ear of the world" (my emphasis).[30]

The political turmoil surrounding Indian Removal makes it easier to understand why Hawthorne deems it "dangerous" to bring his romantic construction of Matthew Maule as "the original occupant of the soil" into direct contact with the "realities of the moment." Just as horrific physical violence was used to remove the Cherokee, so too does Hawthorne's erasure of the Naumkeag constitute a form of epistemic violence. Rather than resorting to the overly simplistic explanation that "Hawthorne was a racist," we can achieve a deeper insight by studying what Philip Fisher calls the "cultural work" of the literary text.[31] Struggling to resolve the crisis of white entitlement that very nearly toppled the American democratic system in 1832, Hawthorne works to disavow Marshall's ruling that the Cherokee were the "undisputed possessors of the soil from time immemorial" by discursively removing Indians from his literary construction of early American "history."

The inner workings of Hawthorne's discursive act of removal can be more clearly seen in an earlier short story, "Roger Malvin's Burial" (1832). In the opening paragraph of the tale, which recounts a skirmish with the Pequawket Indians known as "Lovewell's Fight," Hawthorne writes that "imagination, by casting certain circumstances judicially into the shade, may see much to admire in the heroism of a little band who gave battle to twice their number in the heart of the enemy's country."[32] One "circumstance" which Hawthorne self-consciously pushes outside the margin of the white page is the fact that Lovewell and his men were not "defending the frontier" but were, in reality, on a scalping raid (they collected ten pounds sterling in bounty for each Indian scalp).[33] Just as Hawthorne casts the "realities" of American imperialism "judicially into the shade" in this earlier historical tale, so too does his later romance carefully omit the multicultural complexities of colonial history.

What makes *Seven Gables* of greater critical interest than "Roger Malvin's Burial" is that, although it elides Native Americans' historical presence, it openly acknowledges and explores the dominant white society's most closely guarded secrets regarding their tenuous claim to entitlement. Hawthorne's description of the elaborate edifice of the House of the Seven Gables, for example, reveals the anxiety that underlies the arrogance of white America's rhetoric of conquest: "There is something so massive, stable, and almost irresistibly imposing in the exterior presentment of established rank and great possessions that their very existence seems to give them a right to exist; at least, so excellent a counterfeit of right, that few poor and humble men have moral force enough to question it, even in their secret minds" (36). Hawthorne here strips away the "almost irresistibly imposing" facade of America's "massive" and seemingly "stable" claim to the New World, exposing the fears that lurked in the "secret minds" of those brave enough to question whites of "established rank and great possessions." In a remarkable, if fleeting, moment Hawthorne's canonical text reveals the repressed awareness that white America's discourse of ownership—from John Winthrop's claim that the land was "*vacuum domicilium*" (i.e., legally vacant) in the seventeenth century to Marshall's argument for the Doctrine of Discovery in the early nineteenth—was nothing more than "so excellent a counterfeit of right."[34]

What this historical multicultural analysis uncovers is a much more ideologically complex understanding of Matthiessen's famous assertion that the writers of the American Renaissance were dedicated to "the possibilities of democracy." Matthiessen celebrates the writings of Hawthorne, Melville, Emerson, Thoreau, and Whitman as giving "fulfillment to the potentialities freed by the Revolution, to provide a culture commensurate' with America's political opportunity."[35] I would argue, however, that whereas Matthiessen acknowledges the class conflict in *Seven Gables*, there is a racial dimension to Hawthorne's critique which implicates him more fully in the Pyncheons' "crimes" than Matthiessen's nationalistic paradigm is willing to allow.[36] On the one hand, Hawthorne sharply criticizes the social inequalities of colonial America. His description of Colonel Pyncheon's role in Matthew Maule's execution, for example, exposes the horror that lies hidden beneath the discourse of nationalism used to justify white imperialism in the name of founding a New Jerusalem: "It was a death that blasted with strange horror the humble name of the dweller in the cottage, and made it seem almost a religious act to drive the plow over the little area of his habitation, and obliterate his place and memory from among men" (21). On the other hand, Hawthorne himself actively participates in "obliterat[ing]" Native Americans' "place and memory from among men" by removing them from his literary construction of early "American" history. I agree with Mathiessen that Hawthorne's romance reveals the "possibilities of democracy"; in my view, however, these "possibilities" include not only a longing for justice and equality but also an implicit desire for a monocultural utopia.

Desire: The Lost Connecting Link

As Lucy Maddox observes in *Removals: Nineteenth-Century American Literature and the Politics of Indian Affairs*, "the place of Indians in national culture" was fundamentally important to "the process of constructing a new-nation ideology."[37] In the preface to *Edgar Huntly* (1799), for example, Charles Brockden Brown self-consciously discussed his use of Indian subject matter to derive a uniquely "American" cultural identity. Brown wrote that "the field of investigation, opened to us by our own country, should differ essentially from those which existed in Europe." Rather than "Gothic castles and chimeras," Brown insisted that American writers needed to concentrate on "the incidents of Indian hostility, and the perils of the Western wilderness." "For a native of America to overlook these," Brown concluded, "would admit of no apology."[38] Similarly, when William Gilmore Simms set out to write "an *American* romance" that would be distinguished from the romances of Sir Walter Scott by the fact that his "material could be furnished by no other country,"[39] he chose as his subject white settlers' engagement with the Yemassee Indians in South Carolina. Native American subject matter thus helped the first generation of "American" novelists to distinguish themselves from their British predecessors and, interestingly, to distance themselves from their own genealogical whiteness by allowing them to fictively refashion themselves as "native[s] of America."

This thematic of white desire for and appropriation of Native American subjectivity plays out again and again in the first few decades of the nineteenth century. At the end of Lydia Maria Child's *Hobomok* (1824), for example, Hobomok voluntarily takes himself "far off among some of the red men in the west," leaving behind a son who assimilates into the dominant white society—"His father was seldom spoken of; and by degrees his Indian appellation was silently omitted"—thereby resolving the crisis of white indiginity through the sentimental trope of marriage.[40] At the end of *The Pioneers* (1823), James Fenimore Cooper likewise imagines the seamless transition from Indian to white possession of the title "Native American" by constructing a scene in which Chingachgook—"the last of his people who continued to inhabit this country"—dies with a medal of George Washington around his neck. Tellingly, Cooper tells us at the same time that Leatherstocking "got the Indian habits."[41] As Brian Dippie has observed, between 1824 and 1834 more than forty novels were published which imagined the disappearance of Native Americans from the land.[42] A careful analysis of "desire" for Native American subjectivity in Hawthorne, however, needs to go beyond the important and groundbreaking work of Dippie's *Vanishing Americans* and Maddox's *Removals*. A fully realized multicultural exegesis needs to explain not only how Indians are effaced from the text of white writers but how Native Americans continue to exert a profound cultural influence on "American" identity even after they supposedly "disappeared."

To come at this problem through Hawthorne's romance is a difficult critical endeavor, given that Indians have been doubly removed, as it were, from Hawthorne's literary construction of the imagined community of "America." If, as Jacques Derrida has theorized, a linguistic "glyph" signifies the presence of the absence of the thing-in-itself,[43] then Indians have been twice removed from Hawthorne's romance. Native Americans do not appear directly in the text but instead are present only in the form of "the hiero*glyph*ics of several Indian sagamores" on a "*lost* Indian deed" or, in deconstructive terms, as an absent presence of an absence. Unlike the novels of Brown, Simms, Child, and Cooper, there are no Indian characters represented directly in Hawthorne's romantic reconstruction of American "history." "Native Americans" have, in fact, become white: Hawthorne describes Matthew Maule as "the *original* occupant of the soil" (20), Phoebe Pyncheon as "a *native* of a rural part of New England" (75), and Holgrave as "the representative of many compeers in his *native* land" (170, my emphases). In this sense, Hawthorne's romance works to undo the crisis of the Marshall ruling by effacing the indigenous inhabitants of the soil from history and transferring the legal rights of indigenity to whites.

The absence of any Indian characters in *Seven Gables* can be explained in part by the historical context within which Hawthorne was writing. By the time *The House of the Seven Gables* was published, the work of Indian removal had been completed. By as early as 1842, the War Department informed President Tyler that "there is no more land east of the Mississippi, remaining unceded, to be desired by us."[44] This physical removal of

Indians from the land was followed by a second wave of discursive removal which attempted to scientifically justify Jackson's policies by arguing that the extinction of Native Americans was imminent and inevitable. In 1854, for example, Josiah C. Nott and George R. Gliddon wrote in one of the foundational works of American anthropology, *Types of Mankind*, that "Nations and races, like individuals, have each an especial destiny: some are born to rule, and others to be ruled. . . . Some races, moreover, appear destined to live and prosper for a time, until the destroying race comes, which is to exterminate and supplant them." Nott and Gliddon's theories are founded on a logic of monoculturalism that disavows the possibility that a multicultural society could even exist, leading them to conclude that, "It is clear as the sun at noon-day, that in a few generations more the last of these Red men will be numbered with the dead."[45] As Patricia Nelson Limerick argues in *The Legacy of Conquest*, however, scholars of Native American and white American culture must not allow themselves to become inadvertently caught up in this nineteenth-century worldview that Indians were fated to "disappear" by 1850 but must struggle instead to critically recover the persistent and enduring place of Indians in American history.[46]

As Hawthorne's romance clearly demonstrates, just because there may not have been any more Indian territory to be "desired" by the dominant white culture after 1842 does not mean that white longing for Native Americans' sense of oneness with the land had necessarily abated or that Indians did not continue to play a meaningful role in the cultural construction of "American" identity. White America's persistent desire for Native American subjectivity can be clearly seen in the Pyncheons' undiminished hope to recover the "lost Indian deed." When young Phoebe Pyncheon comes from the countryside to live with Clifford and Hepzibah in the House of the Seven Gables, for example, one of the first things that her cousin does is to "[bid] Phoebe to step into one of the tall chairs, and inspect the ancient map" (87), almost as if this experience of unfulfilled longing for the "lost Indian deed" were part of her initiation into the family. Hepzibah explains that "there existed a silver mine, the locality of which was precisely pointed out in some memoranda of Colonel Pyncheon himself" (30). But after Colonel Pyncheon's death "some connecting link had slipped out of the evidence" proving the Pyncheons' claim to the land. "The bare justice or legality of the claim," Hawthorne writes, "was not so apparent after the Colonel's decease, as it had been pronounced in his lifetime," when he had the "force of character to achieve it" (30). This lack of "evidence" to the contrary, Hepzibah explains to Phoebe that "it was for the interest of all New England that the Pyncheons should have justice done to them" (87).

The Pyncheons' deep-seated anxiety that "some connecting link" to the land itself had been lost can be read, on one level, as a literary reflection of Marshall's ruling in *Worcester v. Georgia* (1832) that the "Cherokee nation [was] a sovereign nation, authorized to govern themselves"[47] and that whites therefore had no real basis for their claim of legal entitlement. On a deeper historical level, the Pyncheons' desire for the "lost Indian deed" can be understood as a longing for a legal talisman that would ward off the dominant white society's cursed awareness that their possession of the land was based on a series of atrocities, ranging from the Pequot massacre in 1637, when Captain John Underhill attempted to cut off "all Remembrance of them from the Earth,"[48] to the Trail of Tears in 1838.

It is meaningful, in this regard, that the "curse" which haunts the Pyncheon family down through the ages is intertwined in Hawthorne's narrative with the Pyncheons' loss of the Indian deed. The curse, in fact, comes upon the family at almost the precise moment that the Indian deed is "lost" and departs when it is recovered. The curse commences, for example, when Matthew Maule is executed for the crime of witchcraft and excoriates the Pyncheon family from the gallows, back in the seventeenth century. At almost this precise same moment, "the old wizard, hanged though he was" (182) obtains the Indian deed from Colonel Pyncheon who, "bartered [his] Eastern territory for Maule's garden ground" (285). Interestingly, the curse ends some two hundred years later on the same day that Holgrave, a distant ancestor of Matthew Maule, weds Phoebe Pyncheon and reveals to his bride the "recess in the wall" where the ancient deed was hidden by one of Maule's sons. Hawthorne even gestures toward making this link between the curse and the "lost Indian deed" explicit, when he notes that "popular belief pointed to some mysterious connection and dependence, existing between the family of the Maules and these vast unrealized possessions of the Pyncheons" encompassed by the Indian deed (182). The fact that Hawthorne here attributes the "connection" to "popular belief" does not necessarily mean that he is dismissing the idea as insubstantial, for earlier in the narrative, he observes that "tradition . . . sometimes brings down truth that history has let slip" (29).

This "mysterious connection and dependence" between the "lost Indian deed" and the curse that haunts the Pyncheon family needs to be understood in psychological rather than strictly legal terms. Like the dominant white society's deep-seated ambivalence about whether Indians could be considered "Americans," Hawthorne's representation of Native Americans in *Seven Gables* is characterized by a "flickering dialectic" of disavowal and desire. Because of this social uncertainty, Hawthorne appraises the "Indian deed" as being simultaneously "valuable" and "worthless." At the end of the novel, for example, when Holgrave reveals the location of the "folded sheet of parchment . . . signed with the hieroglyphics of several Indian sagamores, and conveying to Colonel Pyncheon and his heirs, forever, a vast extent of territory at the eastward" (285) he immediately announces that the Indian deed "is what the Pyncheons sought in vain, while it is *valuable*; and now that they find the treasure, it has long been *worthless*" (285, my emphases).

In legal terms the deed is indeed "worthless," given that Marshall ruled in *Johnson v. McIntosh* (1823) that all Indian deeds predating the Revolutionary War were legally "extinguished."[49] What makes the deed "valuable" to the Pyncheons is not, however, the "treasure" of the silvermine rumored to exist on this eastern tract of land. The "value" of the "lost Indian deed" lies in its ability to help assuage the Pyncheons' "perpetual remorse of conscience" (173) that comes from the repressed awareness that their entitlement to the land is grounded on nothing more than "so excellent a counterfeit of right" (36). Native American subjectivity, as embodied in the "lost Indian deed," thus plays a profoundly important role in helping the Pyncheons feel at one with the land, in much the same way that Charles Brockden Brown's Indian subject matter helps him to create a fictional identity as "a native of America."

Even if the sense of entitlement granted by the Indian deed is nothing more than "an absurd delusion of family importance," it proves to be a psychologically important "delusion." Working to "resolve" the Pyncheons' crisis of indigenity, the deed makes them feel that they possess a legal document "conveying to Colonel Pyncheon and his heirs, *forever*, a vast extent of territory" (285). It does not matter, on this delusional level, that the "territory" which the deed entitles the Pyncheons to is not the cursed ground on which the House of the Seven Gables sits. It is enough that the Pyncheons have in their possession a legal document that essentially entitles them to forget the atrocities they committed in taking possession of the land.

Analogously, Indian deeds historically alleviated whites' repressed awareness that the land itself was "cursed by [Indians'] parting and dying imprecations." As Thomas Jefferson wrote in *Notes on the State of Virginia*, "That the lands of this country were taken from [Indians] by conquest, is not so general a truth as is supposed. I find in our historians and records, repeated proofs of purchase."[50] Likewise John Quincy Adams wrote that whites "entered into negotiations with [Native Americans], purchased and paid for their rights and claims . . . and procured deeds. . . . In short, I see not how the Indians could have been treated with more equity or humanity than they have been in general in North America."[51] In both instances the historical existence of Indian deeds is (mis)construed to arrive at a distorted version of the "truth" which actively forgets white "conquest" of the New World and perpetuates the "delusion" that "Indians could [not] have been treated with more equity."

Hybridity: The Curse of "American" Identity

In the closing pages of Hawthorne's romance the character of Holgrave, a direct descendant of Matthew Maule, reveals the hiding place of the "lost Indian deed" which has eluded the Pyncheons for some two hundred years. Placing his finger on the "secret spring" behind the portrait of Colonel Pyncheon, Holgrave releases the latch, bringing to light "a folded sheet of parchment" covered with "a century's dust" (285). As he does so, Clifford Pyncheon cries out, "Ah, I remember now! I did discover it, one summer afternoon, when I was idling and dreaming about the house, long, long ago. But the mystery escapes me" (284). Because the "machinery had been eaten through with rust," the "portrait, frame and all, tumbled suddenly from its position, and lay face downward on the floor" (285). At the precise moment that Holgrave reveals the long desired "lost Indian deed," he turns to Phoebe and asks her "how will it please you to assume the name of Maule? As for the secret, it is the only inheritance that has come down to me from my ancestors" (285).

It is a signal moment in *The House of the Seven Gables*, for Hawthorne here reveals the multicultural hybridity that lies deep within his literary representation of the National Symbolic. Hawthorne's description of the "lost Indian deed," hidden behind a portrait of the Pyncheon patriarch— a "Puritanic-looking personage in a skull cap, with a laced band and a grizzly beard" (44)—is a striking metaphor both for the central place of Indians in the national imaginary and the way in which Native American subjectivity is covered over by the iconography of Puritan patriarchy. The portrait of Colonel Pyncheon, "holding a Bible in one hand, and in the other an iron sword hilt," lying face down on the floor embodies the collapse of the national myth in the wake of Marshall's invalidation of the Doctrine of Discovery (which held that European entitlement to the New World was "established and maintained by the sword"). It is a powerful critique of the foundational fictions of "American" identity, for Hawthorne had earlier described the portrait as being "so intimately connected to the fate of the house, and so magically built into its walls, that, if once it should be removed, that very instant the whole edifice would come thundering down in a heap of dusty ruin" (184).

The insight that Hawthorne provides into the cultural hybridity of "American" identity proves, however, to be evanescent. The conclusion of *Seven Gables* is a confusing nexus of revealing/concealing and remembering/forgetting in which illuminated moments of insight are quickly transformed into darkened ones of willed blindness. Clifford's hopeful ejaculation—"Ah, I remember now!"—is rendered harmless by his immediate rejoinder that "the mystery escapes me" (284). Likewise, Holgrave no sooner reveals his identity as a descendant of Matthew Maule and his knowledge of the Indian deed's whereabouts than he is suddenly changed into a "conservative," who advocates the "calm of forgetfulness" (282).

Holgrave's sudden change appears especially disingenuous and has been criticized by generations of disenchanted Americanists. From a multicultural perspective, Holgrave's bourgeois posturing and his failure to articulate the rage of the dispossessed collapses the dialogic complexity of the marriage between the Maules and the Pyncheons. Holgrave's silence disappoints because earlier in the narrative Hawthorne had positioned him to be the one character in the novel who could see through the dominant society's "counterfeit of right": "Now and then, perchance, comes in a seer, before whose sadly gifted eye the whole structure melts into thin air, leaving only the hidden nook, the bolted closet, with the cobwebs festooned over its forgotten door, or the deadly hole under the pavement, and the decaying corpse within" (211). It is tempting, certainly, to imagine Hawthorne as the "seer" with a "sadly gifted eye," able to pierce through the "big, heavy, solid unrealities" of white America's rhetoric of entitlement (210). And yet, having momentarily brushed aside "the cobwebs festooned over [the] forgotten door" leading to the psychological source of the curse, Hawthorne securely bolts the door shut again at the end of the novel by having Holgrave renounce his hereditary gift of insight.

Invoking the power of sentimentalism, Hawthorne writes of Holgrave's marriage to Phoebe Pyncheon: "The bliss which makes all things true, beautiful, and holy shone around this youth and maiden. They were conscious of nothing sad or old. They transfigured the earth and made it Eden again" (277). Like Lydia Maria Child's *Hobomok*, Hawthorne attempts to resolve the crisis of white indigenity through the sentimental trope of marriage. And yet, whereas Child confronted white America's deepest fears of miscegenation by imagining the marriage of a white woman to a Native American, Hawthorne attempts to circumvent the prejudice of his age by having Phoebe Pyncheon marry a direct descendant of "the original occupant of the soil" who, according to Hawthorne's romantic reconstruction of "history," is white. What Hawthorne "transfigure[s]" at the end of the novel, therefore, is not "the earth" but the nation's inextricably multicultural history.

Hawthorne's romance concludes by supporting the illusion that "America" was a monocultural utopia. Rather than being the one character in the novel who can see beyond the artifice of American innocence, Holgrave turns out to be an agent of forgetfulness. "In this age," Hawthorne writes of Holgrave's beliefs, "the moss-grown and rotten Past is to be torn down, and . . . [the] dead corpses buried, and everything to begin anew" (168). As Ernest Renan writes in "What is a Nation?"

"Forgetting, I would even go so far as to say historical error, is a crucial factor in the creation of a nation."[52] Writing in the service of nation building, Hawthorne's romance preserves the myth of monocultural unity by perpetuating the "historical error" that "the original occupant of the soil" was white.

It is telling that at this moment in the narrative, having renounced his lineage and embraced Phoebe Pyncheon's newly inherited estate, Holgrave announces that the "curse" which has haunted the Pyncheons for more than two hundred years has been lifted. Hawthorne's Edenic vision of the nation, embodied in Holgrave's dizzying rise through the class system and his middle-class amnesia that leaves him "conscious of nothing sad or old," is founded on an act of unknowing in which the Pyncheons' painful awareness of their family's past crimes simply vanishes at the end of the novel. The curse of "American" identity cannot, however, simply be forgotten. If what causes the Pyncheons' psychological trauma in the first place is the repressed memory of the unjustifiable acts committed in taking possession of the New World, then this willed forgetfulness at the end of the novel does not dispel the curse but only signals the beginning of yet another cycle of disavowal.

Analogously, the curse of being a multicultural country with a monocultural sense of national identity did not disappear in Hawthorne's lifetime but continued to haunt the nation in the form of the "Indian question." Because it was no longer possible to simply continue pushing Native Americans ever westward after the conclusion of the Mexican-American War in 1848, the question of what to do with "the original occupant[s] of the soil" reached the point of crisis at the midpoint of the nineteenth century. In an effort to resolve this dilemma, a report was commissioned by the House of Representatives in 1848 investigating the possibility of the "confederate tribes" in Indian Territory being allowed to "elect . . . a delegate to Congress, who shall have the same powers, privileges, and compensation as the delegates of the respective territories."[53]

The text of the "Indian Territory" report by the Committee on Indian Affairs recounted the long history of the federal government's numerous promises to various Indian nations to eventually accept them into the Union. In 1778, for example, the government negotiated a treaty with the "Delaware nation" which stated that they could "form a State . . . and have a representative in Congress: *Provided*, nothing contained in this article is to be considered as conclusive until it meets with the approbation of Congress." Similarly, in 1785, the federal government signed a treaty with the Cherokee stipulating "that the Indians may have full confidence in the justice of the United States, respecting their interests, [that] they shall have the right to send a deputy of their choice, whenever they think fit, to Congress." The report concluded with the recommendation that

"By giving them a representative in Congress, they would feel that they were no longer considered inferiors, strangers . . . but part and parcel of ourselves, possessing the rights and enjoying the privileges of citizens."[54] The recommendation was, however, ignored. Like Hawthorne's representation of the paradoxical place of "the lost Indian deed" in his literary construction of the national imaginary, Native Americans found themselves at almost the exact center of the country (in what is now the state of Oklahoma) and yet excluded from the imagined community of American citizenship.

To conclude that the forces of disavowal triumph in the end would, however, be historically inaccurate. The rejection of the Indian Territory Report, like the institution of an all-white "Eden" in the closing pages of *The House of the Seven Gables*, does not mean that the forces of white disavowal effectively crushed the multicultural hybridity of "America" out of existence. The conflicted, though enduring, place of Native Americans in the national imaginary can be seen in the federal government's search for a new iconographic representation of the national identity during the age of the American Renaissance. In 1854, just six years after denying Native Americans admission into the Union, the United States mint placed on the three-dollar gold coin the figure of "an Indian princess . . . [her] head crowned with a circle of feathers, the band of which is inscribed LIBERTY." In 1859, James B. Longacre modified the design for the "Indian Head cent," which, as Cornelius Vermeule remarks in *Numismatic Art in America*, went on to become "perhaps the most beloved and *typically American* of any piece great or small in the American series."[55]

Just as Hawthorne appropriates Native Americans' historical subject position by pronouncing Matthew Maule to be "the original occupant of the soil," the "Indian Head cent" was not actually a representation of a Native American figure but simply a depiction of the white, female icon of Liberty adorned with an Indian headdress.[56] The "Indian Head cent" thus constitutes a haunting image of how, even after Jackson's Indian removal policies had been fully enacted, Indian subjectivity continued to be absolutely central to whites' sense of themselves as "native Americans." It is revealing, furthermore, of the nation's hesitancy to fully acknowledge its own historic multicultural identity that it would recognize the cultural importance of Native Americans only after they had been placed on reservations and the 1848 Indian Territory initiative rejected. Even though Native Americans were tragically displaced and systematically denied access to the rights of citizenship, their fundamentally important contribution to the multicultural hybridity of "American" identity could never be completely disavowed.

HISTORICAL INTERLUDE

THE SHIFTING BORDERS OF CITIZENSHIP

On September 1, 1849, delegates from all over California convened in Monterey to draw up the state constitution and to define the cultural boundaries of "WE, the people of California." The convention took place almost exactly one year after the discovery of gold at Sutter's Mill was announced in the newspapers of New York. Enticed by accounts of streets paved with gold, tens of thousands arrived from New England, Mexico, Europe, Australia, Hawaii, China, and South America—making California one of the most culturally diverse places in America even before it had been accepted into the Union as a state. The debates surrounding the racial qualifications for citizenship thus provide a unique insight into the clash between the historical forces of monoculturalism and multiculturalism as the nation struggled to reconcile its rapidly diversifying population with its all-inclusive democratic rhetoric.

The concept of "freedom" in California was sharply constrained by invisible cultural parameters. On the one hand, the "Declaration of Rights" in the state constitution opened with the proposition that "All men are by nature free and independent, and have certain inalienable rights, among which are those of enjoying and defending life and liberty."[1] On the other hand, many of the white delegates were extremely wary of incorporating California's culturally diverse population into the imagined community of constitutional citizenship. As Henry Tefft, a lawyer from Wisconsin who had only resided in California for four months prior to the convention, explained: "When the State proclaims all men free and equal . . . the declaration means nothing more nor less than this: they [non-whites] are free to remain at home; but they are not free to come here and degrade white labor—free to disturb the social and political harmony of the state."[2]

The logic of monoculturalism that so severely limited the democratic promise of the phrase "All men are by nature free" came into sharper focus when the delegates arrived at section 1 of article 2, "Right of Suffrage." The statement drafted by the constitutional committee limited the legal right to vote to "Every white male citizen of the United States." Mr. Gilbert, a "native" of Alta California, requested clarification. Gilbert explained that "the meaning of the word 'white,' in the report of the committee, was not generally understood in his country [Mexico], though well understood in the United States."[3] The "meaning of the word 'white' " in California was complicated by the fact that the Treaty of Guadalupe Hidalgo, which ended the Mexican-American War the year before, guaranteed that "Mexicans now established in territories previously belonging to Mexico . . . who shall prefer to remain in said territories, may either retain the title and rights of Mexican citizens, or acquire those of citizens of the United States."[4]

The debate over who would be included in the cultural construct of "citizenship" finally came down to conflicting interpretations of "whiteness"—a hermeneutic struggle that brought the Anglo and Californio contingents, both of whom were well represented at the constitutional convention, into open antagonism.[5] Speaking on behalf of the "Californians," Mr. Noriego explained what he called "the true signification of the word 'white.' " Noriego argued that "Many citizens of California have received from nature a very dark skin; nevertheless, there are among them men who have heretofore been allowed to vote, and not only that, but to fill the highest public offices [before the U.S. invasion]. It would be very unjust to deprive them of the privilege of citizens merely because nature had not made them white." He then concluded his statement by saying, "But if, by the word 'white,' it was intended to exclude the African race, then it was correct and satisfactory." Speaking on behalf of the Anglo contingent, Mr. Botts replied that he "had no objection to color, except so far as it indicated the inferior races of mankind. He would be perfectly willing to use any words which would exclude the African and Indian races. . . . His only object was to exclude those objectionable races—not objectionable for their color, but for what their color indicates."[6]

The Californio contingent thus negotiated a fragile compromise on "the meaning of the word 'white,' " and the wording of section 1 of article 2 was changed to include "Every white male citizen of the United States, and every white male citizen of Mexico." This tenuous inclusion of Mexican Americans into the imagined community of "California," based on the mutually agreed-upon exclusion of "the African and Indian races," did not last long. In 1857 the cultural borders of "whiteness" and "citizenship" contracted once again: Manuel Dominguez, who signed the California constitution in October 1849, was prohibited from testifying in court because of his Indian blood.[7]

As Priscilla Wald notes in *Constituting Americans*, "the story of the nation" is composed of both "national narratives" and "untold stories." "National narratives of identity," Wald writes, "seek to harness the anxiety surrounding the question of personhood, but what they leave out resurfaces" in the form of "untold stories" that disrupt the "official story."[8] If the California constitution inscribes the institutional account of California citizenship, then John Rollin Ridge's *The Life and Adventures of*

Joaquín Murieta, the Celebrated California Bandit (1854), written by a Cherokee survivor of the Trail of Tears about a dispossessed Mexican American, provides a critically important counternarrative, revealing the multicultural history of the state that has carefully been edited out of the "official story."

CHAPTER TWO

JOHN ROLLIN RIDGE: EXTENDING
THE BORDERS OF "AMERICA" FROM
NEW ENGLAND TO ALTA CALIFORNIA

I intend to kill the Americans by 'wholesale,' burn their
ranchos, and run off their property at one single
swoop. . . . When I do this, I shall wind up my career. My
brothers, we will then be revenged for our wrongs, and
some little, too, for the wrongs of our poor bleeding country.
(John Rollin Ridge, *The Life and Adventures
of Joaquín Murieta*)

T O MOVE from Nathaniel Hawthorne's *The House of the Seven Gables* (1851), with its canonically stylized prose and carefully crafted symbolic architecture, to the multicultural complexities of John Rollin Ridge's *The Life and Adventures of Joaquín Murieta, the Celebrated California Bandit* (1854), a dime novel in which virtually every page is saturated with unrelenting racial rage, is admittedly a critically jarring transition. This juxtaposition not only shifts this analysis of the American Renaissance from the Puritan-influenced traditions of New England to the frontier violence of California, from the canonical to the noncanonical, but moves it across racial and class lines as well. Such a sudden and dramatic shift radically dislodges the discursive foundations of received notions of the American Renaissance. My intent in doing so is to call into question the extent to which Hawthorne, Melville, Thoreau, and Emerson (who literally were neighbors in a corner of New England) can be seen as representative of "American" identity.

Although *The Life and Adventures of Joaquín Murieta* can be categorized as "popular fiction," the first Native American novel nevertheless makes an important contribution to this historical multicultural analysis in that it remaps the geographic and cultural boundaries of Matthiessen's "America." Ridge's life and writing reveal the dark underside of the American Dream and the crueler "possibilities of democracy." Born at the height of the Cherokee renaissance, Ridge's father and grandfather were among the most important chiefs of the Eastern Cherokee. The Ridge family and the Cherokee Nation made every attempt to assimilate into the dominant white society. "*Our* wish has been *their* law," argued William Wirt before the Supreme Court, "They . . . pursued our course of education, adopted our form of government, [and] embraced our religion."[1] Nevertheless, in 1838, the Cherokee were dispossessed of their lands in one of the most horrific incidents of Indian removal, the Trail of Tears.[2] After moving to Indian Territory the Cherokee Nation was torn apart by internal strife, and Ridge subsequently fled to California with his brother Aeneas and their black slave Wacooli in search of a new life. Following a short and unsuccessful stint as a gold miner, Ridge wrote *The Life and Adventures of Joaquín Murieta* in 1854 about a mythical/historical Mexicano who, having been driven off his land by white nativists, devoted his life to "reveng[ing] . . . the wrongs of our poor bleeding country."[3]

To open Ridge's novel is to enter an entirely different "America" from the one imagined in Hawthorne's romance.[4] Whereas Hawthorne's text consists of a vast expanse of unbroken and unspoken whiteness, Ridge's pages are filled with "a number of Cherokees," a "Digger Indian," "poor, miserable, cowardly Tejon" Indians, "industrious Chinamen," and a "Mexican . . . wrapped in his *serape*." And whereas Hawthorne depicts all of his characters as "native" to New England, Ridge deconstructs the myth of white indigenity by fracturing the white community along ethnic lines, peopling his pages with "peddling Jews," "two or three Frenchmen," "three or four Germans," and "a Dutchman." Ridge's novel, in this sense, sheds light on the nation's historic multicultural heritage that Hawthorne "casts judicially into the shade."[5]

By focusing on California in the volatile period following the Mexican-American War and the gold rush, Ridge's novel provides a rare literary insight into what was undoubtedly one of the most multicultural and deeply conflicted regions of the country in the years leading up to the Civil War. The conquest of Texas, New Mexico, and California in 1848 raised perplexing questions about America's image of itself as a country born of revolutionary resistance to colonization. In California legal questions surrounding America's imperial conquest of Mexico were complicated by the fact that, unlike white colonization of Indian lands in the East, Californio *hacendados* were well educated and possessed legal deeds to their extensive ranchos. The dominant white society's anxiety about the state's cultural diversity was exacerbated even further when gold was discovered in 1848. Within six months more than fifty thousand prospectors arrived from all over the world, leading Hinton Helper to describe California as "a complete human menagerie" in *The Land of Gold* (1855).[6] California's petition to enter the Union one year later upset the fragile balance between slave and free states and precipitated a national crisis, tenuously resolved by the Compromise of 1850. California's origins and its multicultural population thus raised perplexing questions that called into doubt some of the nation's most revered myths—that "America" was a republican country devoted to fighting imperialism in the New World and dedicated to the democratic ideal that "all men are created equal."

Ridge's personal experience with the horrors of Indian removal and his literary account of a Mexican American's rage lay bare the conflict between democratic inclusion and racist exclusion at the heart of "American" identity. Admittedly, Ridge's novel will not remind Americanists of Thoreau's introspective aphorisms or Melville's soaring theological flights. What makes John Rollin Ridge's *Life and Adventures of Joaquín Murieta* an important consideration to add to the evolving critical conception of the American Renaissance is that it provides a meaningful dialogical response to Hawthorne's monocultural conception of "America" and the constructs of national identity that have been built upon Hawthorne's texts. By confronting the rage of Ridge's novel, born of the cruelty of Cherokee dispossession, Americanists are forced to rethink F. O. Matthiessen's celebration of "democracy."[7] Likewise, Ridge's account of the atrocities inflicted upon Mexican Americans in the early years of California statehood productively complicates and queries Sacvan Bercovitch's notion that "America" is a symbol of "consent."[8] What Ridge's *Life* reveals is the inextricably complicated and deeply contentious multicultural hybridity which was utterly characteristic of America in the mid–nineteenth century but which has been overlooked by scholars of the American Renaissance because of their narrow, monocultural focus on New England.

Indian Removal and the Failure of Democracy

The final pages of Hawthorne's *The House of the Seven Gables* read like a capitalist fantasy of American democracy—a classless society in which "all men" are able to participate equally in the economy and to rise freely through the social structure. With the death of Judge Pyncheon at the end of the romance, "Clifford became rich; so did Hepzibah; so did our little village maiden, and through her that sworn foe of wealth and all manner of conservatism, the wild reformer—Holgrave!" Even Uncle Venner, whom Hawthorne describes as a "man at the very lowest point of the social scale," is suddenly transported in the closing moments of the novel into the ubiquitous middle class of Hawthorne's "America."[9] Such moments provide the basis for F. O. Matthiessen's claim that the literature of the American Renaissance is "devoted to the possibilities of democracy."[10] To contrast this romantic, monocultural utopia, however, with the brutal realities of Indian removal as experienced by the family of John Rollin Ridge exposes the dark underside of America's discourse of democratic equality. Ridge's life—which spans years of Supreme Court decisions involving the Cherokee, the Trail of Tears, and the violent nativism of the California gold rush—utterly belies this myth of equal opportunity and democratic freedom.

The Ridge family, one of the wealthiest and most powerful in the Cherokee Nation, were devoted to the possibility that they could adapt and survive alongside the dominant white society. John Rollin's grandfather, the Ridge, fought with Andrew Jackson in the Creek War of 1811 and attained the rank of major. Leading more than five hundred Cherokee at the battle of Horseshoe Bend, Major Ridge and his troops helped to defeat the Creek Nation and to bring glory to Andrew Jackson as an "Indian fighter." General Jackson later praised the Cherokee for their support: "You have shown yourselves worthy of the friendship of your Father, the President." President Madison, in turn, bestowed medals on a dozen Cherokee leaders for their bravery in combat and their support of the United States. This political and military alliance proved, however, to be short-lived. When Major Ridge returned home from the Creek War, he discovered that white volunteers had stolen horses, killed hogs and cattle, and taken the crops and clothing of the Cherokee with whom they had fought side by side in battle.[11]

Major Ridge, nevertheless, continued to work diligently to help the Cherokee try to assimilate into the dominant white culture. He welcomed missionaries into the nation and encouraged his people to convert to Christianity and to learn English. In 1818 he sent his son, John Ridge (John Rollin's father), north to study at the American Board of Commissioners for Foreign Missions (ABCFM) school in Cornwall, Connecticut, along with his cousin Elias Boudinot (who would later publish the *Cherokee Phoenix*, the first Native American newspaper). While in Connecticut, both Ridge and Boudinot fell in love with and married white women from the town. Having provoked the white community's fear of miscegenation, Ridge and Boudinot were denounced by area newspapers, castigated by local preachers, and burned in effigy.[12] It is revealing of the conflicted nature of the multicultural hybridity of "American" identity that the people of Cornwall supported the education of Indians so long as they remained "Foreign." The threat of intermarriage, however, unveiled the racism hidden behind the ABCFM's rhetoric of reform.

John Rollin Ridge was born in 1827 in the heart of the Cherokee Nation (now northern Georgia), on a farm of 419 acres tended by eighteen African American slaves.[13] Two years after Ridge's birth, Cherokee country was flooded by white prospectors searching for gold. In response to pressure from whites in Georgia, Jackson signed the Indian Removal Act in 1830, calling for all Native Americans to be relocated west of the Mississippi. The Ridges and their fellow Cherokee initially struggled against white occupation. Major Ridge, wearing a horned buffalo headdress, led a force of thirty warriors against white settlements at Beaver Dam and Cedar Creek in an unsuccessful war to reclaim lost lands. John Ridge traveled to Washington, where he met with Secretary of War John Henry Eaton and President Jackson, reminding them of his father's loyal service in the Creek War and pleading with the government to honor past treaties. Frustrated with the federal government's intransigence, the Cherokee finally launched two suits against the state of Georgia. After Andrew Jackson refused to uphold the Supreme Court decision that the Cherokee possessed legal entitlement to their lands, John and Major Ridge grew increasingly doubtful that the Cherokee could hold out against white encroachment. Worried that the Cherokee would lose all of their lands and gain nothing in return, in December 1935 they helped to negotiate the Treaty of New Echota, which provided that the Cherokee would exchange their lands in the East for 13,800,000 acres in the West, plus a payment of $4,500,000 and an annuity to support a school fund in the nation. Upon adding his mark to the other signatures, Major Ridge reportedly announced, "I have signed my death warrant."[14]

In 1838 sixteen thousand Cherokee set off on what would become known as the Trail of Tears. Because the Ridge family had cooperated with the government, they were allowed to travel separately to Indian Territory. The family would, however, be haunted by the ghosts of the more than four thousand Cherokee who died along the way. A year later Ridge's father and grandfather were assassinated by Cherokee nationalists in revenge for signing the Treaty of New Echota. John Ridge was killed before the eyes of his young son. Many years later John Rollin would describe the scene:

> Two men held him by the arms and others by the body, while another stabbed him with a dirk twenty-nine times. . . . He raised himself on his elbow and tried to speak, but the blood flowed into his mouth and prevented him. . . . Then succeeded a scene of agony the sight of which might make one regret that the human race had ever been created. It has darkened my mind with an eternal shadow.[15]

Despite the fact that Major Ridge had fought side by side with Andrew Jackson in the Creek War, John Ridge had attended white schools, and John Rollin himself was half-white, the Ridge family and the Cherokee Nation were brutally and systematically excluded from the imagined community of "America." It is telling, however, of the power of America's democratic ideals that, despite the Trail of Tears and its bloody aftermath, Ridge would continue to cling tenaciously to the hope that the Cherokee could be accepted into the Union. Ridge's hope, however, was inextricably

complicated by the federal government's refusal to honor its many promises to democratically include the Cherokee into the Union as a state.

A careful analysis of Andrew Jackson's annual address of 1830—the year
that the Indian Removal Act was signed into law—exemplifies the dupli-
citous role that democratic rhetoric played in convincing the Cherokee to
remove to Indian Territory. Jackson cannily invoked the rhetoric of the
Declaration of Independence to make it seem as if Indian removal were
being carried out in accordance with the nation's democratic principles.
Seeking to justify his controversial mandate, Jackson asserted that removal
"will separate the Indians from immediate contact with settlements of
whites, *free* them from the power of the States; enable them to *pursue
happiness* in their own way." "What good man," Jackson concluded,
"would prefer a country covered with forests and ranged by a few thousand savages to our extensive *Republic* . . . filled with all the *blessings of
liberty, civilization, and religion?*" (my emphases).[16] Thus, according to
the strictures of Jackson's ruthless democracy, the "blessings of liberty"
granted whites the right to be free of the Cherokee but not the right of
the Cherokee to live freely on their own land.

As a teenager John Rollin Ridge became caught up in the bloody civil
war that divided the Cherokee Nation in the years immediately following
the Trail of Tears. In an attempt to save her son from the traditional
Cherokee obligation to avenge one's father's death, Ridge's mother sent
John Rollin to be educated at the Great Barrington Academy in her native
New England. Obsessed with his filial duty, Ridge returned to Indian Territory two years later and killed a Cherokee nationalist who he believed
had been involved in the assassination. Fearing that he would not receive
a fair trial or that he would be killed in retribution, Ridge was forced to
flee the Cherokee Nation. In the spring of 1850, filled with dreams of
fabulous wealth and boundless opportunity, Ridge left for the goldfields
of California.[17]

Ridge's American Dream did not survive long in the Golden State. Horrified by the putrid working conditions and vicious nativism in the mines,
he abandoned the quest for gold soon after arriving in California. While
working for local newspapers such as the *Golden Era*, Ridge became interested in the stories swirling around the Mexican *bandito* Joaquín Murieta.
In the spring of 1853, goaded by the horrific accounts of murder and
robbery in the press, the California state legislature offered a five-thou-
sand-dollar reward for Joaquín, dead or alive. Captain Harry Love and his
rangers chased Murieta and his band for three months and finally succeeded in killing Joaquín and his lieutenant, Three-Finger Jack. Murieta's
head was cut off, preserved in a pickle jar, and displayed throughout the
state. Ridge published his historical romance, *The Life and Adventures*

of Joaquín Murieta, the following year. Although he never received any royalties ("my publishers, after selling 7000 copies put the money in their pockets [and] fled," he wrote to his cousin), Ridge's novel was widely read in pirated copies.[18] M. G. Vallejo, an important member of the Californio community, recalls in his *testimonio* of 1872 how Joaquín Murieta mobilized the Mexican American community: "the majority of the young men that had so unjustly been dispossessed, thirsty for vengeance, took off to join the band of Joaquín Murieta and under the command of this fearsome bandit they were able to avenge some of the wrongs inflicted upon them by the North American race." In her excellent study of the Californio *testimonios*, *Telling Identities*, Rosaura Sánchez attributes Vallejo's description of Murieta to Ridge's romance.[19]

Ridge's use of the character of Joaquín Murieta is exceedingly complicated and provides a meaningful glimpse into the multicultural complexities of nineteenth-century America. On the one hand, Murieta gives voice to the rage which many Native Americans and Mexican Americans felt at a time when lynch mobs were more powerful than the state government in the California mining camps. On the other hand, the only Cherokee characters in the book fight on the side of Captain Love and willingly help the white rangers by lynching suspected members of Murieta's gang (138). One must be careful, therefore, of a simplistic binary analysis of Ridge's novel that immediately assumes an ideological alliance between the romance's Cherokee author and its Mexicano protagonist. By having the Cherokee abet the white rangers at the end of the novel, Ridge reenacts his grandfather's decision to fight on the side of Andrew Jackson in an apparent last-ditch attempt to convince his white readers of Cherokee loyalty.[20]

This ideological complexity can also be seen in Ridge's newspaper writings. In an article entitled "The Cherokees. Their History—Present Condition and Future Prospects" published in the Clarksville (Texas) *Northern Standard* just before he left for California, Ridge condemned "the policy of the United States government" which "removed [the Cherokee] . . . producing confusion and bloodshed, whose effects are yet fearfully apparent." And yet in the same article Ridge also writes that "I would advocate a measure . . . which looks to the events of making the Cherokee nation an integral part of the United States, having Senators and Representatives in Congress, and possessing all the attributes, first of a territorial government, and then of a sovereign State."[21] Like his father and grandfather, Ridge maintained this hope throughout his lifetime. John Rollin Ridge's American Dream was, however, based on a very different ideological conception of "America." During the Civil War the Ridge family sided with the South, hoping that a confederate victory would allow the Cherokee to become part of the new southern nation. Ridge vehemently attacked the federal government in his editorials and joined the Knights of the Golden Circle, a secret society dedicated to deposing Lincoln. His cousin Stand Waite was the last Confederate general to surrender his sword.[22]

Ridge's life and work thus reveal the hope as well as the despair of America's ruthless democracy. The Cherokee, more than any other Indian nation, tried endlessly to overcome the forces of racial exclusion in order to become "an integral part of the United States." Their faith in the promise of democratic inclusion, the violent assassination of Ridge's father and grandfather, Andrew Jackson's wanton disregard of the Supreme Court's constitutional authority, and Ridge's support of the Confederacy all suggest "possibilities of democracy" that F. O. Matthiessen never considers, much less incorporates, into his critical construction of "American" identity.

The problematic monocultural focus of Mathiessen's theoretical formulation of the American Renaissance stems from the fact that it is founded on what Frederic Jameson calls a "strategy of containment." Jameson defines this technique as a rhetorical device "which allows what can be thought to seem internally coherent in its own terms, while repressing the unthinkable . . . which lies beyond its boundaries." This "strategy of containment," Jameson continues, enables writers to "project the illusion that their readings are somehow complete and self-sufficient."[23] In other words, what allows Mathiessen to see Hawthorne as a writer "dedicated to the possibilities of democracy" and to overlook the discursive removal of Native Americans from his literary account of early American history is the fact that Mathiessen's "America" represses the cultural diversity that Ridge's life and work embody. Because Matthiessen "contains" his analysis by only taking into consideration white, male, middle-class writers from New England, he is able to argue convincingly that each of these authors works to strengthen democratic principles. To bring John Rollin Ridge's voice into the dialogue, however, shatters Matthiessen's "strategy of containment" and compels (I hope) Americanists to reconsider the previously "unthinkable" multicultural complexities of the American Renaissance.

The Limits of Consent

The Life and Adventures of Joaquín Murieta opens with a familiar invocation of the American Dream. Ridge notes that Joaquín "was a Mexican, born in the province of Sonora of respectable parents and . . . remarkable for a very mild and peaceful nature" (8). Tired of "the uncertain state of affairs in his own country, the usurpations and revolutions which were of such common occurrence," Murieta "resolved to try his fortunes among the American people, of whom he had formed the most favorable opinion" (8). In the spring of 1850, intoxicated with stories of enormous gold nuggets and instant fortune, Joaquín begins "in the honest occupation of a miner in the Stanislaus placers" and soon gains "the confidence and respect of the whole community around him," while "fast amassing a fortune from his rich mining claim" (8). Within a few months he is able to build a "comfortable mining residence in which he domiciled his heart's treasure—a beautiful Sonorian girl" named Rosita (9).

This archetypal image of the American Dream is, however, shattered by the forces of white nativism. A band of "lawless men, having the brute power to do as they please" invade Murieta's fragile utopia and insist that "they would allow no Mexicans to work in that region" (10). When Joaquín resists, he is "struck . . . violently over the face," and his mistress is "ravished . . . before his eyes" (10). Determined to overcome white America's "prejudice of color" and "unmanly cruelty and oppression," Murieta moves further north into the hills where "he might hope for peace." As Ridge notes, "his dream was not destined to last" (10). Once again a nativist band of "unprincipled Americans" force him from "his little home surrounded by its fertile tract of land . . . with no other excuse than that he was 'an infernal Mexican intruder'!" (10).

Ridge's novel documents, with harrowing detail, the transformation of the American Dream into the American Nightmare. Murieta, in spite of the atrocities he has endured, strives "to labor on with unflinching brow and with that true *moral* bravery, which throws its redeeming light forward upon his subsequently dark and criminal career" (11). Having been chased from the mines, Joaquín struggles to make a living by dealing monte. And yet, once again, the forces of racism intervene. While riding through a mining camp on a horse that his brother lent him, a white Californian accuses Murieta of horse theft, ties him to a tree, and brutally whips him. The white mob then "proceeded to the house of his half-brother and hung him without judge or jury" (12). It is at this point, Ridge writes, that "wanton cruelty and the tyranny of prejudice reached their climax" (12). Transfigured by rage, Murieta's "soul swelled beyond its former boundaries, and the barriers of honor," leading Joaquín to vow that "he would live henceforth for revenge and that his path should be marked with blood" (13). Thus in a few short months Murieta's hope and optimism for "America" is crushed by the forces of racial exclusion and white America's will to monoculturalism. Having left Mexico "fired with enthusiastic admiration of the American character," Murieta "contracted a hatred to the whole American race, and was determined to shed their blood whenever and wherever an opportunity occurred" (14).

Ridge's novel thus openly contests Sacvan Bercovitch's critical assertion that "America" is a symbol of "consent." In *The American Jeremiad* and *The Rites of Assent*, Bercovitch argues that the nation has historically been able to transform dissenting voices into "a mode of cultural cohesion and continuity." "America is a symbolic field," Bercovitch writes, whose opposing voices only serve to "reaffirm the ideals" of the nation. Using the literature of the American Renaissance as a basis of proof, Bercovitch conceives the nation as a "*concordia discors*" which he defines as "a thousand aggressively independent individuals and sects all saying the same thing." This inherently monological conception collapses the multicultural complexities of American history, leading Bercovitch to conclude in *The Rites of Assent* that "the rhetoric of consensus molded what was to all appearances the most heterogeneous 'people' in the world into the most monolithic of modern cultures."[24] As Ridge's account of California after the American conquest demonstrates, however, the racial boundaries of this "monolithic" society were policed by forces of white nativism that violently excluded Mexican Americans, whether they consented to the ideals of "America" or not.

An example of just how limited Bercovitch's definition of "America" is can be seen in *The Rites of Assent*. Bercovitch writes that "The American was not (like the Frenchman or the Latin American) a member of 'the people' . . . he could denounce servitude and oppression while concerning himself least, if at all, with the most enslaved and inadequately represented groups in the land. Those groups were part of 'the people,' perhaps, but not the *chosen* people; they were in America but not of it."[25] Like Matthiessen, Bercovitch utilizes a "strategy of containment" to project the discursive illusion that his conception of "America" is "somehow complete and self-sufficient."[26] Bercovitch's theory of "consensus" works perfectly well for what he calls, in *The American Jeremiad*, "our classic American writers" (Melville, Thoreau, Hawthorne, and Emerson). His depiction of Holgrave, for example, as "the hero, who joins the consensus, marries a daughter of the Puritans, and transforms class-conscious radicalism into suburban self-improvement" is both accurate and insightful.[27] Problems occur, however, when the cultural boundaries of Bercovitch's "America" are extended beyond "the *chosen* people" to include Native Americans like John Rollin Ridge, whose family was shattered by the Trail of Tears, or Mexican Americans like Joaquín Murieta, whose rage was forged by the terrible atrocities committed against Mexicanos in the early years of California statehood.[28]

A careful reading of Ridge's novel reveals that Joaquín Murieta's "consent" has little to do with his acceptance into the imagined community of "America." Murieta comes to the United States seeking democratic freedom and economic prosperity only to discover virulent racism and limited opportunities. Ridge observes of white Americans that "a feeling was prevalent among this class of contempt for any and all Mexicans, whom they looked upon as no better than conquered subjects of the United States, having no rights which could stand before a haughtier and superior race" (9). It is interesting that even after he is attacked by nativist mobs, Joaquín struggles to hold on to the ideals of "America." Ridge writes that Murieta considers the "lawless and desperate men" who attacked him to be "Americans [who] failed to support the honor and dignity of that title" (9). And yet after his lover is raped "before his eyes," his brother-in-law hanged "without judge or jury," and he himself "publicly disgraced with the lash," Joaquín "suddenly and irrevocably changed." Thus, in the final analysis, the "wanton cruelty and the tyranny of prejudice" that reigned in California following the Mexican-American War effectively destroys Murieta's American Dream, rendering meaningless the fact that he initially "consents" to the "symbol of 'America.' "

This is not to say, however, that Joaquín Murieta is not an "American." What we need is a new critical understanding of "America" which, to stand Bercovitch on his head, is founded not solely on those people who were *of* "America" (the "*chosen* people") but is instead constructed on the basis of who was *in* America. By not limiting national identity to the racial boundaries that defined and confined "citizenship" but instead theorizing the full dialogic complexity of the many different voices all struggling to imagine the nation on their own terms and in their own image, a very different conception of "America" begins to come into focus. The "America" that Ridge depicts consists of a never ending conflict between hope and despair, between democracy and racism. What Ridge's text documents is the constant coming together and coming apart of the country as these many different imagined communities collide, creating a charged atmosphere of nativism, racial rage, and competing nationalisms.

Ruthless Democracy as a Critical Paradigm

As José David Saldívar argues in *Border Matters: Remapping American Cultural Studies*, there is a pressing need at this time for "a new [paradigm] of U.S. cultural studies." Saldívar calls for a new critical methodology that "challenges the homogeneity of U.S. nationalism and popular culture" and "re-imagine[s] the nation as a site with many 'cognitive maps' in which the nation-state is not congruent with national identity."[29] By including John Rollin Ridge's *The Life and Adventures of Joaquín Murieta* in this new multicultural conception of the American Renaissance it becomes clear that older conceptions of "American" identity like Matthiessen's or Bercovitch's are not theoretically complicated enough to account for the contradictions and cultural conflicts that Ridge's novel inscribes. By extending the "cognitive map" from New England to the deep South, to Indian Territory, and finally to California and Mexico, Ridge's text explodes Bercovitch's notion that "America" is a "monolithic" society made up of a thousand voices "all saying the same thing." Having thrown open the cultural borders of the nation, the question now becomes how to formulate "American" identity anew.

In response to this need for a new critical paradigm for U.S. cultural studies I would like to suggest the historical multicultural model of "ruthless democracy." The metaphorical complexity of Melville's phrase is compelling in that it describes both the brutal racial exclusion carried out under the rhetorical guise of "freedom for all" and the unrelenting forces of cultural expansion that continued to diversify the population of the country in spite of white America's deep-seated fears of racial disunity and miscegenation. Too often, I think, academic discussions of multiculturalism become caught up in the binary view that "America" is either a democratic melting pot or a balkanized, disunified collection of nations within a nation.[30] The theoretical premise of "ruthless democracy," on the other hand, is that the country's will to monoculturalism and the historical forces of cultural diversity are almost equally powerful, that "American" identity needs to be reconceptualized not as a static, abstract ideology but as a ceaselessly fluid contestation, grounded in a historically detailed cultural context. California, in the chaotic years of the gold rush, provides a telling case study of America's "ruthless democracy," showing how the exceedingly complex multicultural nexus is created by the conflict between democratic/capitalist inclusion and racist/nativist exclusion.

In 1849, the New York *Herald* reported that men "are rushing head over heels towards . . . that wonderful California, which sets the public mind almost on the highway to insanity."[31] To Anglos, California was advertised as a place where "when the tide was out, the entire beach is covered with bright and yellow gold."[32] To Mexicans and South Americans, the discovery of gold in California was the fulfillment of the myth of El Dorado. In China, those who left the mainland in search of their fortune in the Occident were called *gam saan haak*, "travelers to Gold Mountain."[33] By the end of 1849, there were 80,000 Yankees, 8,000 Mexicans, and 5,000 South Americans in the mining districts.[34] The Chinese began arriving two years later and by 1852 historians estimate that there were more than 25,000 Chinese in the state. All told, the population of California increased 2500 percent from 1848 to 1852. The multicultural character of the state (and its attendant racism) can be clearly seen in the names of the mining camps and towns: German Bar, Irish Creek, Chinese Camp, Georgia Slide, Italian Bar, Dutch Flat, French Corral, Kanakia Bar, and Nigger Hill.[35]

This vertiginous expansion of cultural diversity brought on by the economic opportunity of the gold rush in turn set off a powerful backlash, as the forces of white nativism tried to contract the racial borders of the imagined community of "California" to ensure that political power remained in the hands of whites. Although the Treaty of Guadalupe Hidalgo had guaranteed that all Mexicans who remained in the conquered territories would automatically become U.S. citizens, the California state legislature enacted the Foreign Miners' Tax in 1850, which was aimed primarily at Mexican miners. The tax, twenty dollars a month, effectively banned them from the mines and hence from the kind of economic opportunity that forms the historical basis of the American Dream.[36] One year later, in 1851, the California Land Act stipulated that every claim in the state had to be reviewed and approved by U.S. courts. Individual cases dragged on indefinitely—the average time for settlement of a claim in California was seventeen years—and Californio *hacendados* were often driven to sell off large portions of their lands to pay the exorbitant legal fees of their Anglo attorneys. M. G. Vallejo, for example, who signed the California Constitution of 1849—with its declaration that "All men" possess the "inalienable right" of "acquiring, possessing, and protecting property"—was effectively dispossessed of his lands in Socol, California.[37] As Vallejo recalls in his *testimonio*, most of the Californios "lowered their heads before the California tribunals and allowed the squatters to take possession of their properties." One of the wealthiest individuals in the region before 1846, Vallejo lost his entire rancho to squatters by 1862, after years of costly litigation.[38]

Although the courts upheld the constitutionality of the Foreign Miners' Tax in *People v. Naglee* (1850), the nativist intent of the tax was never realized. As Rodolfo Acuña points out in *Occupied America: A History of the Chicanos*, rather than paying the exorbitant fee, 50–75 percent of the Mexicans abandoned their diggings and left the southern mines.[39] The tax was repealed in 1851, when it became clear that cheap labor was needed in the quartz mines, and when Anglo merchants complained to Sacramento that the exodus of Mexicans was destroying the state's economy.[40] As part of the protest to repeal the oppressive tax, the editor of the *Daily Pacific News* wrote, "the Mexican is, so far as the development of the resources of the country is concerned, the most useful inhabitant of California." A year later legislators reinstated the tax, although it was reduced from twenty dollars a month to only three.[41] After 1854, however, the tax was collected mainly from the Chinese, who came to occupy the unenviable position of California's most despised minority.[42]

The first Chinese immigrants came to California in 1849, arriving by the thousands in search of gold and economic opportunity.[43] When the state census revealed the surge in Chinese immigration, the forces of nativist exclusion were turned from the Mexicans toward the Chinese. In 1854, in *People v. Hall*, the California Supreme Court overturned a case in which a white man had been convicted of murder on the basis of the testimony of a Chinese witness. Redefining the fourteenth section of the constitution, which prohibited blacks and Indians from testifying against whites, the court imposed a strict binary view of race and "California" identity, ruling that "We are of the opinion that the words 'White,' 'Negro,' 'Mulatto,' 'Indian,' and 'Black person,' wherever they occur in our Constitution and laws, must be taken in their generic sense, and that . . . [this] necessarily excludes all races other than the Caucasian." In support of their decision, the justices wrote of the Chinese that "The anomalous spectacle of a distinct people, living in our community . . . whose mendacity is proverbial; a race of people whom nature has marked as inferior, and who are incapable of progress or intellectual development beyond a certain point . . . [demonstrates that] nature has placed an impassable difference [between the races]." The California Supreme Court thus concluded that Chinese immigrants should be banned from "not only the right to swear away the life of a citizen, but the further privilege of participating with us in administering the affairs of our government."[44]

Like Mexican Americans, the Chinese were too valuable to the state's economy to be entirely excluded. Chinese labor was fundamentally important to the construction of the transcontinental railroad and the enormous undertaking of attempting to link California ports to eastern industry. From 1866 to 1869, the railroad employed ten thousand Chinese workers to tunnel through the Sierra Mountains. After the completion of the railroad in 1869, eastern goods flooded the California market, forcing local manufacturers to cut back on labor costs by employing more Chinese. In *The Indispensable Enemy*, Alexander Saxton writes that by 1870 there were just under fifty thousand Chinese in the state comprising more than 20 percent of the California work force.[45] In the case of both Mexican and Chinese Americans, then, the capitalist need for cheap labor and new markets offset the racist backlash of the dominant white society, creating an unresolved tension at the heart of "California" identity.

The place of African Americans in the imagined community of "California" proved to be equally conflicted, although the terms of the debate centered around "freedom" rather than economics. A significant majority of the constitutional delegates agreed that slavery should be banned in the state of California. Their reasons, however, were not grounded in the political ideology of abolition but in a deep-seated racism. "If the people of this Territory are to be free against the curse of slavery," one delegate declared, "let them also be free from the herds of slaves who are to be set at liberty within its borders." Time and again the Anglo delegates tried to add an amendment to the constitution decreeing that "The Legislature shall, at its first session, pass such laws as will effectually prohibit free persons of color from immigrating to and settling in this State." White fear of black "freedom" and the haunting specter of miscegenation were cast in apocalyptic imagery: "Have they forgotten the burning of Pennsylvania Hall in Philadelphia? Where the freest and most unlimited freedom was extended to the dusky gentleman? Where the . . . scheme of engrafting the snow white rose upon the dark ebony . . . [caused] the sky [to be] lit up by the fiery elements?" Mr. Semple, from Kentucky, even went so far as to suggest that if "these herds of free negroes" were not kept out of California, he would prefer "being kept out of the Union to all eternity." "I am as anxious to become one of the bright stars of the glorious Union as any gentleman," Semple argued, "but [if] we are to come in with a curse upon us, from which we can never be redeemed. . . . I would take my rifle and defend the right [of racial purity] as freely as I did the flag of the United States when we achieved the right to this Territory."[46] The "curse" of being a multicultural country with a monocultural sense of national identity could not, however, simply be legislated out of existence.

The proposed Black Codes of California went unratified because of a lingering fear that the constitution of California would not be accepted by the United States Congress if it included a measure for the exclusion of African Americans. As the constitutional delegate Edward Gilbert argued, "If you insert in your Constitution such a provision or any thing like it, you will be guilty of great injustice—you will do a great wrong, sir—a wrong to the principles of liberal and enlightened freedom . . . before the great public of the United States and before all the nations of the world. Does any gentleman here believe, sir, that there is a man who has ever contended upon the floor of Congress . . . for the universal liberty of mankind who will sanction a Constitution that bears upon its face this darkest stigma?"[47] Gilbert's speech swayed the convention and the proposition, which had been accepted on the first vote, was overturned.[48] When confronted with the choice between excluding African Americans or being excluded from the Union, white nativists were forced to accept the foundational fiction of the nation's fundamental commitment to democracy and to shroud their racism in silence.

In the case of California's indigenous Indian nations, however, the vehemence and violence of white nativism was too powerful to silence. Governor Peter Burnett's threat of a "war of extermination" effectively gave white nativists free reign to massacre Native Americans.[49] Josiah Royce, an early historian of California, recounts attacks against "defenseless Digger Indians, whose villages certain among our miners used on occasion to regard as targets for rifle practice, or to destroy wholesale with fire, outrage, and murder."[50] Finally the federal government intervened in 1851 and U.S. Commissioners were able to negotiate that the various Indian nations residing within the state would be relocated onto some eight and one-half million acres of land set aside as reservations.[51] In the case of Native Americans, therefore, the rhetoric of democracy failed to embrace the indigenous peoples of California, leaving Indians legally relegated to being a nation within the nation. And yet, their legal status as "domestic dependent nations" did little to protect most Native Americans. In 1853, for example, the Kelsey family hired eighty Pomo Indians to work in their mine. When the mine failed, the Indians were left to fend for themselves in hostile territory. In retaliation, the Pomos killed a member of the Kelsey family. The United States army responded by massacring 250 Pomo Indians—an outcome which Captain N. Lyon of the Second Infantry described in his report as "a most gratifying result."[52]

Whereas the dominant white society was quite comfortable with defining "California" citizenship along strictly enforced racial lines, the issue of whether white women should be fully vested with civil rights proved to be a more ambiguous question. Charles T. Botts, originally from Virginia, argued that married women should not be given the right to own property, because "in the marriage contract, the woman, in the language of your protestant ceremony, takes her husband for better or worse; that is the position in which she voluntarily places herself, and it is not for you to withdraw her from it." Denouncing women's rights as "the doctrine of those mental hermaphrodites," Botts pleaded with the other delegates "not to lay the rude hand of legislation upon the beautiful and poetical position in which the common law places this contract"—effectively arguing that the subjugation of women was aesthetically "beautiful." In response J. M. Jones, representing San Joaquín, argued: "Are we to adopt laws which make man a despot of woman, and give woman no right because she has no representation?"[53] In the end the Californio conception of civil law that had been in place before the conquest, with its more liberal recognition of the property rights (though not the voting rights) of married women, prevailed. This victory can be attributed not to a desire for a multicultural conception of Californian identity or to an ideological commitment to women's rights but, more likely, to the fact that the population of California was 92 percent male in 1849, and it was thought that the civil law's protection of women's property rights might attract more white women to the state.[54]

Analogously, race played a significant role in allowing the Irish to gain entrance to the imagined community of "California" almost immediately. In contrast to the East Coast, where the huge influx of Irish Catholics fleeing the potato famine was fissuring "white" society along the lines of class, religion, and ethnicity, "whiteness" proved to be much more all-inclusive in California. In 1850, for example, a nativist critic in Lowell, Massachusetts wrote of the Irish who worked in the mills, "when we see

whole streets deserted by their former inhabitants and filled with
a low class of foreigners . . . we wonder that . . . [the state] should counte-
nance the policy [of unrestricted immigration] of which our American
citizens so justly complain."[55] One year earlier, on the other hand, the
newspaper *Alta California* had commented that "If there be a people
whose condition is worthy of a world-wide commiseration and sympathy,
it is that of tyrannized and famished Ireland." The inclusive power of
whiteness was such that by 1857 California had elected its first Irish U.S.
Senator.[56] As David R. Roediger has observed in his important study of
Irish assimilation, the Irish were able to play knowingly upon America's
obsession with race to cash in on what Roediger (after DuBois) calls "the
wages of whiteness."[57]

Hybridity Forged in the Midst of Racial Rage

By redrawing the boundaries of national identity to include not just the
"chosen people" but the full multicultural spectrum of the country, a very
different transnational conception of "American" identity begins to come
into focus, one that extends throughout the Americas to Mexico, Chile,
and Venezuela; across the Pacific to China and the South Sea Islands; and
across the Atlantic to Ireland, England, and Spain. The theoretical premise of a historical multicultural interpretation of America's "ruthless democracy" is not to collapse this infinitely complicated dialogic array of
voices speaking in different tongues to a single, static, ideological definition of national "identity." Instead, the critical challenge is to accurately
describe how this vast array of cultures come together—sometimes in
ideological unison, sometimes in violent conflict—to create an inherently
unstable yet endlessly fascinating aporia that, although it can never be
resolved, can still be called "America."

What makes John Rollin Ridge's *Joaquín Murieta* such an important
resource for understanding America's "ruthless democracy" is that this
first Native American novel articulates the nation's endlessly conflicted
relationship to its historical multicultural identity much more clearly and
insightfully than many canonical novels. Whereas Hawthorne's *House of
the Seven Gables*, for example, carefully represses the dialogic complexity
of the nation's origins, Ridge's novel explores the racial rage that has historically characterized America's cultural diversity. What Ridge's novel depicts with remarkable clarity is the power of racial rage to both deconstruct
and reconstruct national identities. The destructive quality of racial rage
can clearly be seen both in the mob's brutal attacks upon Murieta and in
his ruthless personal war of revenge. "Report after report," Ridge writes,
"came into the villages that Americans had been found dead on the high-

ways, having either been shot or stabbed and it was invariably discovered
. . . that the murdered men belonged to the mob who publicly whipped
Joaquín" (13). Murieta cannily uses the shared outrage within the Mexican American community to bring together a society that had been shattered by the Anglo invasion. "Appealing to the prejudice against the 'Yankees,' which the disastrous results of the Mexican War had not tended to
lessen in their minds," Murieta "soon assembled around him a powerful
band of his countrymen, who daily increased, as he ran his career of almost
magical success" (16). This dynamic nationalism, built on a communal
anger, transcends both cultural and class divisions. The Mexican American
rebels "induced the Indians to aid them in this *laudable* purpose" (26)
and established a network among "many large rancheros who were secretly
connected with the banditti, and stood ready to harbor them in times of
danger and to furnish them with the best animals that fed on their extensive pastures" (19).

The alliance between Indians and Mexicanos, however, begins unravel-
ing almost immediately. Ridge notes that "the ignorant Indians suffered
for many a deed which had been perpetrated by civilized [i.e., Mexican]
hands" (27). The tensions between the two groups is vividly represented
in the conflict between Murieta and Sapatarra, chief of the Tejon Nation.
Having captured Murieta and his men, Sapatarra "sent word to the 'The
Great Captain,' the county judge of Los Angeles." The judge, "supposing
the capture was the result of a little feud between some 'greaser' and the
Tejons" (39), advises Sapatarra to set the Mexicans free. The Tejon chief
has Murieta and his men "stripped entirely naked and . . . whipped." Declaring "the ends of justice satisfied," Sapatarra then turns the banditos
loose "as naked as on the day that they were born and stricken with a
blanker poverty than the veriest beggar upon the streets of London, or
New York" (40).

Despite Ridge's depiction of Murieta's rage as being the desire to "revenge . . . the wrongs of our poor bleeding country," one of the most
important theoretical contributions of the novel is the way it demonstrates
the inherent (and often overlooked) complexities of racial rage. Murieta
does not attack solely the men who whipped him, nor does he limit his
vengeance only to Anglos. The most frequent victims of his attacks are
the Chinese. As Remi Nadeau points out in *The Real Joaquín Murieta*,
nineteen of Murieta's twenty-four known victims were Chinese.[58] As
Ridge writes, "the miserable Chinamen were mostly the sufferers, and they
lay along the highways like so many sheep with their throats cut by the
wolves" (97). Ridge goes on to describe the decision of one of Murieta's
men "to kill Chinamen in preference to Americans" as being "a *politic*
stroke," since "no one cared for so alien a class, and they were left to shift
for themselves" (97, my emphasis). *The Life and Adventures of Joaquín*

Murieta thus provides a historically accurate, though ideologically convoluted, commentary on the multicultural "politics" of antebellum America.

The open conflict between white nativism and racial rage in the novel
creates a destructive vortex that eventually leads to the violent death of
Joaquín Murieta. Murieta is chased down by Captain Love, who "dis-
charged several balls into his body" (153). Love then shoots Joaquín's
first lieutenant, Three-Finger Jack, "through the head" in the final gun
battle. Because "it was important to prove, to the satisfaction of the public,
that the famous and bloody bandit was actually killed," Love "caused the
head of the renowned Murieta to be cut off" and placed in a jar full of
alcohol "for exhibition over a large portion of the State . . . to give the
public the actual sight of an object which had flung a strange, haunting
dread over the mind" (156). Like the closing image of Melville's "Benito
Cereno"—of Babo's "head, that hive of subtlety, fixed on a pole in the
Plaza, [that] met, unabashedly, the gaze of whites"[59]—Joaquín Murieta's
embalmed head symbolizes both the horror of white imperialism and the
persistence of racial rage. The "strange, haunting dread" that Murieta's
blank gaze invokes in the dominant white society can be read, in this
context, as the uncanny return of the multicultural perplexities that were
repressed from Hawthorne's canonical construction of "America" as a
monocultural utopia.

Despite the triumph of the forces of white nativism at the end of the
narrative, Ridge's novel describes in exquisite detail the multicultural hybridity of "American" identity. By "hybridity" I do not mean to suggest,
however, a return to the myth of America as a melting pot, where a multitude of different cultures are blended together into a single, ideologically
coherent national identity. Nor do I mean to invoke the idea of pluralism,
which conceives of the nation as an array of ethnicities within which cultural differences are respected and even celebrated without acknowledging
the racism and violence that lie just beneath the country's discourse of
democratic inclusion. "Hybridity," to the contrary, is a theoretical term
able to encompass Murieta's initial belief in the American Dream, the
tenuous alliance between Indians and Mexicanos forged of a shared racial
rage, as well as the horrific violence that leaves the Chinese and Murieta
himself slaughtered in the dust of California's hills.[60]

The form(s) of Ridge's novel embody this "hybridity." A literary archeology reveals, for example, that the narrative development of *Joaquín Murieta* is drawn from Mexican American *corridos*. In *"With His Pistol in His
Hand": A Border Ballad and Its Hero*, Americo Paredes writes that the
corrido has its origins in the Spanish romances sung by the conquistadors.
The modern form of the corrido, Paredes notes, crystallized following the
Mexican-American War in 1848. For Paredes, the corrido is defined as
much by its poetic structure of octosyllabic quatrains as by its content, the

clash of Mexican and Anglo cultures in the borderlands. The hero of the *corrido* "is always the peaceful man, finally goaded into violence by the *rinches* and rising in his wrath to kill great numbers of his enemy. His defeat is assured; at the best he can escape across the border, and often is killed or captured. But whatever his fate, he has stood up for his right."[61] Like the hero of the *corrido*, Murieta is described by Ridge as being distinguished by the "native honesty of his soul," (11) whose character "changed suddenly" when confronted by the racist violence of the Anglo conquerors. And, most importantly for Paredes's definition of the *corrido's* hero, Murieta dies finally "with his pistol in his hand," fighting to the very end "for his right."

Whereas the narrative development of *Joaquín Murieta* derives from the Mexican American *corrido*, the historical romance form of the novel which Ridge adopts can be traced back to Anglo-American culture. Originally conceived by British writers such as Sir Walter Scott, the historical romance form was popular in the United States and was adopted by many authors, including James Fenimore Cooper, William Gilmore Simms, and Nathaniel Hawthorne. Ironically, Ridge adopts a literary form commonly used by white writers to justify Andrew Jackson's Indian removal policies. William Gilmore Simms's *The Yemassee* (1835), for example, was published five years after the Indian Removal Act and three years before the Trail of Tears. In this historical romance Simms recounts the Yemassee Indians' extinction in the mid–eighteenth century in order to historically justify the "disappearance" of Native American nations from the South during the Jacksonian era. Simms writes, for example, that "it is utterly impossible that the whites and Indians would ever live together. . . . The nature of things is against it, and the very difference between the two, that of color . . . must always constitute them an inferior caste in our minds."[62] The "obvious superiority" of whites, Simms continues, dooms Native Americans to "sink into slavery and destitution."

Well aware of the power of the historical romance to define the cultural boundaries of the imagined community of the nation, Ridge ironically reverses Simms's discursive erasure of Native Americans from early American "history." In the preface to *Joaquín Murieta*, Ridge states his intention to "contribute my mite to those materials out of which the early history of California shall one day be composed" (7). The "mite" that Ridge contributes to the "history" of California statehood is not only an awareness of the multicultural complexities of Mexican American, Native American, and Chinese cultures within the state. In a larger context, Ridge's novel constitutes an important contribution to "American literature" because he reverses Simms's racist view that Indians were of "an inferior caste." After Murieta is captured by Sapatarra, for example, Ridge writes that "The poor, miserable, cowardly Tejons had achieved a greater triumph

over them than all the Americans put together!" (38). The inherent complexity of the multicultural hybridity of Ridge's romance is clearly illustrated here. On the one hand, Ridge's description of the Tejons' triumph
can be read as a antiracist statement, contesting the white stereotype of
Indians as ignorant. On the other hand, this passage also reveals Ridge's
own regional prejudice and his tendency throughout the narrative to depict California Indians as being culturally inferior (e.g., "poor, miserable,
and cowardly") to the "Five Civilized Tribes" of the Southeast.[63]

The multicultural complexity of the form(s) of *Joaquín Murieta* is further complicated by Ridge's thematic use of Cherokee myth. His most
explicit borrowing of Cherokee folklore comes in a passage where he writes
that Murieta's "extraordinary success . . . would almost lead us to adopt
the old Cherokee superstition that there were some men who bear
charmed lives and whom nothing can kill but a silver bullet" (139). A
more subtle, though prevalent, trace of Cherokee myth can be found in
Ridge's use of the trickster image. A number of passages throughout the
novel suggest that Ridge may have modeled Murieta in part on the character of Ûñtsaiyĭ' from Cherokee mythology. In what is perhaps a subtle link
to the gambler Ûñtsaiyĭ', Ridge notes in the novel that Murieta works for
a time dealing monte. Like Ûñtsaiyĭ', who is described in the myths as
knowing "how to take on different shapes, so that he always got away,"[64]
Murieta also has an uncanny ability to change shapes and assume disguises.

In the course of the narrative Murieta disguises himself as a Mexican
señorita to escape white Rangers (35); he "passes" as a white merchant
named Samuel Harrington to rescue members of his gang who have been
captured (95); and he disappears into the crowd as a Mexican beggar
wrapped in a *serape* (51). Playing upon the inability of white law enforcement agents to distinguish one Mexican from another, Ridge notes wryly
that Murieta "was actually disguised the most when he showed his real
features" and that he "frequently stood very unconcernedly in a crowd
. . . and laughed in his sleeve at the many conjectures which were made as
to his whereabouts and intentions" (31). Just as Ûñtsaiyĭ' is caught at the
end of the myth, so too is Murieta finally captured at the end of Ridge's
narrative. Despite his capture, however, Murieta can be read as a trickster
figure in the sense that he fools, and makes fools of, the whites who pursue
him and thus effectively subverts the power relations which Simms, for
example, attempted to inscribe in *The Yemassee*.[65]

In the final analysis, what John Rollin Ridge's *Life and Adventures of
Joaquín Murieta* reveals is a much more theoretically nuanced and historically accurate conception of Benedict Anderson's formulation that "the
novel . . . provided the technical means for 're-producing' the kind of
imagined community that is the nation."[66] For Ridge's novel demonstrates
that there is not one singular "imagined community" but a vast multiplic-

ity of communities, all imagining the nation on very different terms. In this novel the nativist mobs construct of "America," excluding "all Mexicans, whom they looked upon as no better than conquered subjects of the United States, having no rights which could stand before a haughtier and superior race" (9). There is the nation of Tejon Indians, who live within the geographic boundaries of the United States yet clearly reside outside of this nativist construct of "America." And, of course, there is Joaquín Murieta's imagined community, made up of "an organization of two thousand men" whose purpose is "to kill the Americans by 'wholesale' " (75), a nation within, and at war with, the larger nation that encompasses it. Ridge's literary text thus demonstrates that these multiple imagined communities do not remain separate but interact and come together, albeit often in a violent way, to mutually influence one another. The cultural hybridity of Ridge's novel provides a model for the historical form of the nation itself—a geographically defined entity containing multiple and embattled imagined communities, which, taken together in all of their contradictory and conflicted complexity, represent a new, radically deconstructed conception of the ruthless democracy of "American" identity.

HISTORICAL INTERLUDE

DEFINING "NATIVE AMERICAN"

In April 1844, one year before Henry David Thoreau began his "experiment" beside Walden Pond, riots ravaged the Kensington section of Philadelphia in a public struggle between white Protestants and Irish Catholics to define the cultural borders of "Native American" identity. On the first day of rioting a nativist mob marched through the Irish neighborhood of Kensington. The mob quickly dispersed, however, when confronted with a show of force from the Irish militia, who had been arming themselves for months in preparation for an attack. The nativists immediately reassembled at the George Fox Temperance Hall to pass a series of resolutions calling for "citizens" of Philadelphia to "visit with their indignation and reproach, this outbreak of a vindictive, anti-Republican spirit, manifested by . . . the alien population of Kensington." The next day nativist newspapers issued a call to all "Native Americans" to resist "the assaults of aliens and foreigners" by assembling once again in the heart of Kensington. Several thousand people answered the call. Just before they entered the meetinghouse, several shots were fired from the Hibernia Hose house, an Irish fire company, killing one of the marchers, a young man named George Shiffler.[1]

The next day nativist mobs stormed the Hibernia Hose house, burning it to the ground. By midnight more than thirty homes belonging to Irish Catholics had been burned and looted before the late arrival of military forces finally brought the rioting to a close. The next day the mayhem continued as whole rows of houses were set on fire. Protestants living in Kensington sought to protect themselves by hanging large banners from their homes adorned with the words "Native American," the sight of which brought cheers from the crowd. Moving through the streets of Kensington the mob eventually made their way to Saint Michael's Catholic Church. As the state militia watched, nativists burned the church and the seminary adjoining it. Finally the mayor of the city arrived on the scene to plead with the masses. Rioters, however, pushed past him and his military escort to set fire to Saint Augustine's Church, in the heart of the Irish neighborhood. Thousands of Irish families fled the city in the wake of the carnage and even the *Native American* was compelled to condemn the "wanton and uncalled for desecration of the Christian altar."[2]

In 1854, the same year that Thoreau published *Walden*, nativist mobs rained terror on Irish communities throughout New England. Posters appeared in the streets of Boston, signed by "A TRUE AMERICAN," reviling "all Catholics" as "liars, villains, and cutthroats."[3] Led by a preacher calling himself the "Angel Gabriel," nativists attacked the Irish settlement at Chelsea, Massachusetts and the Bellingham Catholic Church in May 1854. In June, the Catholic church at Coburg, Massachusetts was burned; on July 3, an armed mob attacked the Irish quarter in Manchester, New Hampshire and expelled Irish members of the community. And, finally, on the Fourth of July in 1854, nativists blew up and sacked the Catholic church in Dorchester, Massachusetts (less than thirty miles from Concord).[4]

To consider Thoreau's beloved masterpiece of American literature in relation to this nativist violence is, admittedly, disconcerting. Situating Thoreau's all-too-familiar canonical work within this unfamiliar historical context, however, calls attention to the nativist dimensions of *Walden*. Walking along the railroad causeway, for example, Thoreau "wonder[s] at the halo of light around my shadow" and "fanc[ies himself] one of the elect," in contrast to the "Irishmen," who "had no halo about them." Thoreau's conclusion—"it was only natives that were so distinguished"— reveals a nativist subtext that most literary critics have (consciously or unconsciously) overlooked for more than fifty years. In the chapter that follows I will work to excavate this troubling subtext. By uncovering the forces of cultural exclusion that lie hidden beneath the transcendental surface of Thoreau's text, I want to call into question not only how *Walden* mirrors the nativist violence of the age but how this logic of exclusion has been unwittingly adopted by scholars of the American Renaissance.

CHAPTER THREE

HENRY DAVID THOREAU:

"THE ONLY TRUE AMERICA"

John Field, an Irishman, . . . was discontented . . . yet he had
rated it as a gain in coming to America, that here you could
get tea, and coffee, and meat everyday. But *the only true
America* is that country where you are at liberty to pursue
such a mode of life as may enable you to do without these,
and where the state does not endeavor to compel
you to sustain . . . slavery and war.
(Henry David Thoreau, *Walden*)

It is clear that . . . the Declaration of Independence did not
mean . . . by equality that the [Catholic] minority should
be superior or equal to the majority. These points are clear,
and they at once settle the question as to the right of foreigners
who come to our shores and demand to be admitted
into the community on equal terms. . . . Independence
includes . . . the right to expel from the State of community,
any and all whom it may think uncongenial to its system.
(An American [Samuel F.B. Morse], "Imminent Dangers to
the Free Institutions of the United States
through Foreign Immigration")

LITERARY CRITICS and high school students alike know well the
above passage from Henry David Thoreau's *Walden* (1854) extol-
ling the virtues of "America" as a place where one is "at liberty"
to resist the federal government in the name of transcendental freedom.
Less widely acknowledged is the fact that Thoreau inscribes his famous
depiction of the transcendental ideal in contradistinction to the aspira-
tions of the Irishman John Field, whom, it would seem, Thoreau does
not consider to be part of "the only true America." Given his esteemed
reputation as a writer "obsessed with freedom" (in Stanley Cavell's
words),[1] Thoreau would not ordinarily be read in juxtaposition with the
nativist writings of Samuel F.B. Morse. And yet there is a certain resonance
between the nativist pamphlet and the literary "masterpiece" that needs
to be explored more fully. Like Morse, who defines "independence" in

terms of the "right to expel" undesirable ethnicities from the "State of community," Thoreau (in the passage just quoted and in others) appears to exclude the Irish from his literary construction of the imagined community of the nation.[2]

It is not only the Irish, however, who are excluded from this canonical conception of the "true America." Throughout the text, Thoreau depicts Native Americans as "extinct" or vanishing, even though in the first chapter he recounts having "seen Penobscot Indians, in this town, living in tents of thin cotton cloth."[3] Thoreau likewise represents African Americans as being a "race departed" (299), even though the census of 1850 indicates that there were more than two thousand blacks living in Boston at the time.[4] And, finally, any and all traces of the women who helped to support Thoreau while he was camped at Walden Pond (his mother, his sister, his aunt, and Lidian Emerson) are carefully edited out of his manuscript. To read Thoreau's canonical text in a multicultural context thus raises a number of important and perplexing critical questions: Is there a meaningful relationship between the epistemic violence of Thoreau's discursive erasures and the historical violence of political nativism that was on the rise during the years in which Thoreau was writing *Walden*? Why is it that Thoreau, a committed abolitionist and a dedicated scholar of Native American culture, would exclude blacks and Indians from his literary construction of the national imaginary? How does this multicultural study of *Walden* affect our understanding of Thoreau's central place in the canon of American literature?

My contention is not that Thoreau was a racist or that he knowingly erased Native Americans, African Americans, women, and the Irish from the pages of *Walden*. To the contrary, I believe the explanation for these erasures has more to do with Thoreau's philosophical beliefs than with his political ones.[5] To understand the relationship between Thoreau's transcendentalism and his discursive removal of Irish, blacks, women, and Indians we must read Thoreau's text in cultural as well as philosophical terms. In particular, I will focus my attention on Thoreau's strategy of transcendental reduction. In the opening pages of *Walden*, for example, Thoreau writes: "When one man has reduced a fact of the imagination to be a fact to his understanding, I foresee that all men will at length establish their lives on that basis" (113).[6] This transcendental reduction constitutes a fundamental part of Thoreau's philosophical project to "live a primitive and frontier life," in order to come to terms with "the essential laws of man's existence" (113).[7] And yet this transcendental assumption that "one" white, male, Protestant New Englander could represent "all men" proves troublesome when set in dialogic relation to the federal government's Indian Removal policy, the American Colonization Society's insistence that "the only remedy afforded us is to colonize their mother country [with repatriated African Americans],"[8] the patriarchal attitudes that conspired to keep women confined to the domestic sphere, and the mayor of Boston's proclamation that the Irish were "a race that will never be infused into our own"[9]—all of which share the logical assumption that the dominant white society was the "truest" representative of "America."

To be fair, it must be acknowledged that Thoreau almost certainly never *meant* to represent himself as the "one man" who would provide the philosophical model for "all men" or to connect himself explicitly with Indian Removal, African colonization, or nativism. "I would not have any one adopt *my* mode of living on any account," Thoreau writes in the opening chapter, "but I would have each one be very careful to pursue *his own* way" (158, original emphases).[10] Transcendentalism strives, by definition, to rise above the ceaseless flux of history and the antagonisms brought on by racial differentiation. "To walk even with the Builder of the universe," Thoreau notes in the conclusion, it is necessary "not to live in this restless, nervous, bustling, trivial Nineteenth Century, but [to] stand or sit thoughtfully while it goes by" (348). I am not interested, however, solely in exploring what Thoreau meant; rather, my goal is to historicize this self-consciously ahistorical philosophy, in order to demonstrate how Thoreau's transcendental reduction provides an important insight into the "nervous . . . Nineteenth Century." The fact that Thoreau remains unconscious of his underlying nativist subtext is precisely what makes these forces of exclusion so powerful and so persistent.[11] Scholars of the American Renaissance have, in turn, perpetuated this nativism by using the logic of transcendental reduction to elevate Thoreau to the status of the "one" representative man who embodies the values of the American canon. In *The Senses of Walden*, Stanley Cavell describes Thoreau's "experiment" beside Walden Pond as being "the national event re-enacted."[12] Lawrence Buell, in *Literary Transcendentalism*, takes Cavell's claim one step farther by arguing that "Thoreau's works . . . become, in effect, an account of the whole universe."[13] Americanists from Matthiessen to Bercovitch have adopted the logic of Thoreau's transcendental reduction—"what is true for one is truer still for a thousand" (158)—to provide the philosophical basis for the critical contention that writers from *one* region of the country, from *one* race, or of *one* gender could accurately represent *all* of "America."

Calling into question the logic of monoculturalism that underlies Matthiessen's conception of the canon constitutes only the first step in the larger project of *Ruthless Democracy*. In the first two chapters, I extended the cultural and geographic boundaries of the American Renaissance across the continent and beyond the great racial divide. I will conclude the first half of the book by returning to the heart of Matthiessen's New England, to demonstrate how even the seemingly most monological of canonical works draws upon the nation's repressed multicultural heritage.

My intent in this chapter is thus twofold. On the one hand, positioning Thoreau between John Rollin Ridge and Harriet Beecher Stowe calls attention to the absence of Native Americans and women in Thoreau's text and brings to light the nativist subtext underlying Thoreau's seemingly all-inclusive transcendental rhetoric. This deconstructive phase is not, however, the theoretical endpoint of this historical multicultural analysis. Rather, I want to instigate an important analytical turn here at the midpoint of the book—a turn toward *reconstructing* the multiplicity of cultural influences that lie buried more deeply still beneath Thoreau's nativist subtext. Thus I hope to demonstrate not only how Thoreau effaces Indians, blacks, women, and the Irish but also how each of these repressed cultures deeply informs Thoreau's literary construction of the "only true America."[14]

The White Man Comes, Pale as the Dawn

To begin, I want to return to Stanley Cavell's observation that Thoreau's "experiment" can be interpreted as "the national event re-enacted." With regard to the representation of Indians in *Walden*, Cavell's insight proves strikingly accurate (albeit in ways that Cavell never intended). Like the New World, where the earliest European settlers had to remove the indigenous occupants of the soil before they could lay claim to both the land and the title of "Native American," Thoreau's literary text constitutes a discursive site wherein European and Indian cultures simultaneously conflict and interact. This contestation plays out in terms of a complex dialectic of discursive erasure and cultural appropriation, whereby Indians gradually disappear as Thoreau slowly takes on both Native American customs and their closeness to "Nature." This act of discursive Indian Removal can be read as a kind of transcendental imperialism that, over the course of the narrative, eventually allows Thoreau to occupy the Native Americans' cultural subject position.

There can be no doubt of Thoreau's interest in and scholarly attention to Indian culture. Between 1845 and 1860 he filled eleven manuscript volumes with notes and observations on Native American culture. Four volumes of these Indian Notebooks were written between 1851 and 1854, when Thoreau was hard at work revising the manuscript of *Walden*.[15] Indeed, the text of *Walden* is replete with references to Native American crafts, myths, and folklore. In "Economy," Thoreau exalts the construction and efficiency of Indian wigwams. He does not eat salt, because "I do not learn that the Indians ever troubled themselves to go after it" (153). And in the chapter entitled "The Ponds," Thoreau laments the "poverty of [white] nomenclature" (250), which imposes the name

"Flint's Pond," and works to correct the misnomer by retelling the Indian myth which recounts the derivation of the pond's original name. Underlying this admiration of and desire for Native American culture, however, is a deep-seated ambivalence that leads Thoreau at certain key moments in the narrative to disavow and distance himself from Indians.

The complexity of Thoreau's ambivalent relationship to Native American culture can be seen in his parable of "the strolling Indian" in the opening chapter of *Walden*. As Leonard Neufeldt has pointed out, the description of the Indian's failure to sell his baskets can be read as a metaphorical account of Thoreau's own failure to successfully market his first book, *A Week on the Concord and Merrimack Rivers*—seven hundred copies of which, unbound and unsold, he eventually had to carry home from his publisher's warehouse in a wheelbarrow.[16] Thoreau does not, however, openly empathize with the Indian's struggle against the unforgiving capitalist marketplace. Instead, he cannily uses the Native American's exclusion from the economic sphere to solidify his own liminal position within and without the new, burgeoning capitalist economy that was quickly coming to define "America" in the mid–nineteenth century. "I too had woven a kind of basket of a delicate texture," Thoreau writes, but "instead of studying how to make it worth men's while to buy my baskets, I studied rather how to avoid the necessity of selling them" (119). Like the "strolling Indian," Thoreau feels marginalized by the nation's recent commitment to industrial capitalism. And yet Thoreau clearly distinguishes himself from Native Americans, whom he perceives to be outside the imagined community of economic citizenship. Thoreau implicitly justifies this exclusion by explaining that the Indian "had not discovered that it was necessary for him . . . to make something else which it would be worth [the white man's] while to buy" (119). He then carefully distances himself from the Indian by noting that "I have always endeavored to acquire strict business habits; they are indispensable to every man" (119), thus leaving the failure of *A Week* safely behind him and positioning himself within the economic sphere, without being beholden to it.

Thoreau studiously avoids basing the exclusion of Indians on the grounds of race. He deftly evades any suggestion of "prejudice" by insinuating, two paragraphs later, that the economic community of "America" is democratically open—"such problems of profit and loss, of interest . . . demand a universal knowledge" (120). Thoreau's use of the term "universal" is, however, both complicated and deceptive. Thoreau does not mean that *any* man or woman can reach this level of transcendental awareness but rather that the one exceptional individual who comprehends the "problems of profit and loss" can reach it. Thoreau's transcendental rhetoric here effectively masks the nativist subtext that runs throughout *Walden*. Beneath the seemingly all-inclusive language of "universal knowledge" lurks yet another version of the narrative of the Vanishing American. Indians never assimilated, Thoreau suggests, because in the end they failed "to make something which it would be worth [the white man's] while to buy" (119).

In this sense Thoreau's rhetoric closely mirrors the cultural logic that had been used to justify Indian Removal twenty years earlier. Senator Albert Gallatin asserted in 1836, for example, that "The Indian disappears before the white man, simply because he will not work. There was nothing to prevent the Indian from reaching the same state of agriculture and population [as the white man] but his own indolence."[17] Thoreau himself advocates a similar position in his journals. Writing in the wake of the Trail of Tears, Thoreau observes that "what detained the Cherokees so long was the 2923 plows which that people possessed; if they had grasped the handles more firmly, they would never have been driven beyond the Mississippi." Like the political rhetoric of the day, Thoreau predicates Indian Removal not on white greed but on the failure of the Cherokee to attain the "universal knowledge" of "profit and loss." Thus Thoreau concludes, "The African will survive, for he is docile, and is patiently learning his trade and dancing at his labor; but the Indian does not often dance, unless is the war dance."[18]

Given Thoreau's self-conscious effort to be democratic and inclusive in *Walden*, he never goes so far as to condemn Native Americans for "indolence," as Gallatin does in his political rhetoric. Nevertheless, the ambivalence that underlies Thoreau's philosophical discourse manifests itself in the fact that after this fictional account of "the strolling Indian" in the first chapter, Native Americans never again appear in bodily form. Instead, Thoreau depicts Indians either in abstract philosophical terms ("In the savage state every family owns a shelter as good as the best" [127]) or else in terms of Nature. Using naturalist imagery, Thoreau retells the history of the white conquest of the North American continent. "All the Indian huckleberry hills are stripped . . . [and] raked into the city" to make way for the "iron horse . . . breathing fire and smoke," Thoreau writes, adding somewhat ruefully that "it seems as if the earth had got a race now worthy to inhabit it" (191). The "once wild Indian pheasant" ("more indigenous even than the natives") is celebrated for its ability to "put nations on alert," even as Thoreau sadly notes that the bird is conspicuous now only for its absence (199–200). Finally, in "House Warming," having come across the "ground-nut (Apios tuberosa)" while digging "fish-worms," Thoreau eulogizes this "totem" of a "quite forgotten" and "almost exterminated" Indian nation (282).

To understand more fully how Thoreau uses Nature to explain the "disappearance" of Native Americans, it is necessary to go back to his journals, for it is there that he worked out the problem of how to translate cultural conflict into naturalistic detail. This entry from 1850, for example, provides an important insight into Thoreau's methodology: "A lone Indian woman without children, accompanied by a dog, wearing the shroud of her race, performing the last offices of her departed race. Not yet absorbed into the elements again; a daughter of the soil; one of the nobility of the land. The white man is an imported weed,—burdock and mullein, which displace the ground-nut."[19] Thoreau here strives to capture the exact moment when Native Americans vanished. The "lone Indian woman" is a barren figure, "without children," already wrapped in her burial "shroud." Thoreau thus transforms the cultural annihilation of Native Americans along the eastern seaboard into a natural process: the white man, "an imported weed," simply comes to "displace the ground-nut."

Thoreau's transcendental aesthetic—the beauty, simplicity, and common sense of Nature—must therefore be rigorously interrogated. To bring the nativist implications of this passage more sharply into focus, it is instructive to contrast Thoreau's naturalistic description with historical accounts documenting the disappearance of the "original occupant[s] of the soil." In 1676 an angry mob rioted and expelled the last remaining five hundred "praying Indians" from the town of Concord. After being removed to Deer Island in Boston Harbor, smallpox and dysentery then ravaged and killed most of Concord's surviving Indians.[20] According to Thoreau's transcendental rewriting of history, however, the indigenous occupants of the soil were "absorbed into the elements again," as if their "extermination" were an act of Nature rather than white nativism. Like Thoreau's haunting phrase from *A Week on the Concord and Merrimack Rivers*—"the white man comes, pale as the dawn"—the conquest of a continent is transfigured into a deceptively serene, even beautiful, naturalistic image.[21] Thus Thoreau's transcendental aesthetic, the beauty and majestic power of Nature, comes to be implicated in the literary removal of Indians from this canonical "masterpiece."[22]

Here again Thoreau's naturalistic rhetoric echoes the official discourse used to justify Andrew Jackson's Indian Removal policies. As Secretary of State Lewis Cass proclaimed at the height of Indian Removal, "the extinction of the Indians has taken place by the unavoidable operation of *natural causes,* and as the *natural consequence* of the vicinity of white settlements" [emphasis added].[23] It is a puzzling dialogic connection, given Thoreau's call for "civil disobedience," for active resistance of the federal government's efforts to extend the boundaries of the nation in the name of Manifest Destiny. Thoreau's transcendental reenactment of Indian Removal needs to be understood, however, not as a justification of government policy but rather in terms of the psychological fragility that underlies his philosophical authority.

As Homi Bhabha notes in *Nation and Narration*, "the claim to be representative [of the nation] provokes a crisis in the process of signification."[24] In *Walden* this "crisis" occurs as a result of Thoreau's attempt to collapse the multicultural complexity of the nation into a transcendental Oneness. Given that Thoreau grounds transcendental authority in a sense of oneness with Nature (e.g., "If we would indeed restore mankind . . . let us first be as simple and well as Nature ourselves") (164), Native Americans' historical and cultural primacy presents a very real problem for Thoreau. Ironically, then, it is precisely what he admires most about Native Americans—their closeness to Nature—that ultimately compels Thoreau to anxiously exclude them. The Indians, in the final analysis, must be removed from the discursive landscape in order for Thoreau to imaginatively construct himself as a "*native* American."

It is not enough, however, simply to erase the physical presence of Indians from the imagined community of the nation. Thoreau must ultimately go one step further and actually occupy the cultural subject position of the "Native American." This moment occurs at the end of the seventh chapter, when Thoreau describes "the fishermen and hunters, poets and philosophers" who come out to visit Walden Pond as being "all honest Pilgrims" and greets them with the words "Welcome, Englishmen! welcome, Englishmen!" (219)—words historically attributed to Samoset, who taught the Pilgrims indigenous farming techniques.[25] Thoreau here boldly rewrites the origins of the nation, producing a monocultural version of "American" history that casts himself in the role of Samoset, the "Native American" who will show the first Europeans how to survive in the New World.

White appropriation of Native American culture, as Philip J. Deloria has shown in *Playing Indian*, can be traced back to the cultural origins of "American" identity, to such events as the Boston Tea Party. "Americans," Deloria writes, "wanted to feel a national affinity with the continent, and it was Indians who could teach them such aboriginal closeness. Yet, in order to control the landscape they had to destroy the original inhabitants."[26] Certainly this paradigm helps to explain Thoreau's decision to constantly depict Indians as "extinct," even though there were more than two hundred thousand Native Americans living within the geographic boundaries of the United States at this time. My intent is not, however, to document and denounce the hegemonic politics of the American Renaissance. Instead, the purpose of this multicultural analysis is to instigate a theoretical inversion. In response to Thoreau's cry for "simplicity, simplicity, simplicity!" (173), *Ruthless Democracy* issues the call for "complexity, complexity, complexity!" Turning Thoreau's philosophical strategy upside down, this exegesis demonstrates not how the cultural diversity of the nation comes to be reduced to a transcendental Oneness embodied in a white, male, Protestant New Englander. Rather, the goal is to demonstrate how this seemingly monological Oneness is actually riven through with other cultural influences which, ironically, Thoreau appears deeply invested in repressing.

Reading *Walden* in a historical multicultural context reveals how Indian culture implicitly, yet profoundly, shapes Thoreau's conception of transcendentalism. In "Sounds," for example, Thoreau writes that "My days were not days of the week . . . nor were they minced into hours and fretted by the ticking of the clock; for I lived like the Puri Indians, of whom it is said that for yesterday, to-day, and to-morrow they have only one word" (188). Having used the demands of the economic sphere to exile Indians in the first chapter, Thoreau here returns to Native American culture to help escape the anxiety of being "fretted by the ticking of the clock" in that same capitalist society. As in "The Ponds," where he uses an "Indian fable" to enrich "the poverty of our [white] nomenclature" (240, 250), Thoreau utilizes the Puri conception of transcendental temporality to overcome the "poverty" of Western and capitalist conceptions of time.

It is critically important not to collapse the theoretical complexity of this multilayered discourse, with its conflicting levels of meaning, into a more manageable simplicity. For the contradictions between Thoreau's seemingly all-inclusive transcendental rhetoric, his nativist subtext, and the sub-subtext of multicultural hybridity exposes the ideological conflict within the nation itself during the age of Indian Removal. The interplay of these three levels—inseparable yet always at odds—captures the nation's seemingly never-ending struggle to resolve the conflict between its commitment to democratic equality and its deep-seated fear of the its own multicultural identity.

The Evanescence of African Americans

Like his literary inscription of Native Americans, Thoreau's depiction of African Americans constitutes a strange mélange of "real" individuals, abstractions, and figures of absence. The only bodily representation of an African American in *Walden* occurs in "Visitors," where Thoreau receives "guests" from those groups "not recognized commonly among the town's poor, but who should be" (217).

> Men of almost every degree of wit called on me in the migrating season . . . runaway slaves with plantation manners, who listened from time to time, like the fox in the fable, as if they heard the hounds a-baying on their tracks, as much as to say,—
>
> "O Christian, will you send me back?"
>
> One real runaway slave, among the rest, whom I helped toward the northstar. (217–18)

This peculiar description—"One real runaway slave, among the rest"—inadvertently calls into question whether the previously mentioned "runaway slaves with plantation manners" are "real" or just nameless, fictive foils designed to call attention to Thoreau's transcendental commitment to freedom.

The problem of slavery was, of course, all too real at the time that Thoreau was writing. The admission of California as a "free" state in 1850 upset the delicate balance between North and South and led to the passage of the Fugitive Slave Law, which gave slaveholders the legal right to recapture and return runaway slaves hiding in the North. The area in and around Boston witnessed some of the most vehement and violent protests of the Compromise of 1850. In 1851, for example, a group of fifty abolitionists burst into a courtroom in Boston and rescued a runaway slave by the name of Shadrach, who was being tried under the Fugitive Slave Act. Shadrach was liberated and transported to Concord, where he was hidden until he could be safely spirited away to Canada.[27] In the spring of 1854, the trial of Anthony Burns, another fugitive slave, galvanized the abolitionist cause throughout New England. An armed "negro mob" stormed the courthouse where Burns was being held, breaking down the door with a battering ram and then openly engaging U.S. federal marshals—one of whom, James Batchelder, was killed in the assault. Accompanied by more than fifteen hundred militia troops, Burns was marched past thousands of abolitionist supporters to a steamer in Boston harbor, to be sent back to his master in Virginia.[28] In "Slavery in Massachusetts," Thoreau wrote that the trial of Anthony Burns "was really the trial of Massachusetts. Every moment that she hesitated to set this man free—every moment that she now hesitates to atone for her crime, she is convicted."[29]

There can be no question of Thoreau's commitment to the cause of immediate abolition. In "Civil Disobedience," he places the end of slavery above the preservation of the Union: "This people must cease to hold slaves . . . though it cost them their existence as a people."[30] And yet the fleeting representations of blacks in *Walden* seems to contradict, or at least query, Thoreau's professed devotion to abolition. As Robert F. Sayre has noted of Thoreau's commitment to antislavery activities, "In his abolitionism and refusal to pay taxes, his hiding of escaped slaves and championing of John Brown, he indeed did help slaves. But the near absence of anything in his writing *about* the slaves [whom] he helped reveals how little interest he had in them. Their pathos called on his manhood, but they were not his manly equals."[31] It is interesting, in this regard, to compare the journals to *Walden*. Whereas in *Walden* the one "real" runaway slave remains faceless and nameless; in the journals Thoreau writes in much greater detail of "a fugitive slave, who has taken the name of Henry Williams," recently "escaped from Stafford County, Virginia," who "had been corresponding through an agent with his master, who was also his father, about buying himself."[32] Details like these, that would bring the discursive black figure to life, are carefully omitted from *Walden*, to keep the narrative focus on Thoreau's passionate dedication to freedom.

The clear and defiant tone of Thoreau's antislavery rhetoric should, therefore, be examined more carefully. As we will see in the next chapter, on Harriet Beecher Stowe, abolitionist sentiments often disguised a deep-seated ambivalence about whether African Americans could be fully considered part of the constitutional "We, the People." In October 1845, for example, the New Bedford (Mass.) Lyceum, whose stated mission was to "remove many of the prejudices which ignorance or partial acquaintance [with blacks] fostered," voted to exclude African Americans from their regular membership.[33] A similar ambivalence haunted the Free Soil movement, whose leader, David Wilmot, insisted that "a fundamental condition to the acquisition of any territory" gained as a result of the Mexican-American War was that "neither slavery nor involuntary servitude shall ever exist in any part of said territory." Wilmot's antislavery sentiments, however, had nothing to do with a concern for African Americans' constitutional rights. "I have no . . . morbid sensitivity for the slave," Wilmot declared. His goal was, instead, to establish "a fair country, a rich inheritance where the sons of . . . my own race and color can live without the disgrace associated with negro slavery."[34]

The hesitancy that underlies Thoreau's description of blacks in *Walden* is, however, much more subtle and complicated than the explicit racism that Wilmot's statement demonstrates. Thoreau encodes his ambivalence in a complex dialectic of revealing and concealing: he appears to make a conscientious effort to acknowledge African Americans as an important, though often overlooked, part of "American" history, only to suggest elsewhere that they are a "race departed" (299). The interplay of transcendentalism and nativism is extremely subtle in Thoreau's representation of African Americans, and it is critically important not to collapse the delicate ambiguity which the literary text, much more than the didactic rhetoric of Thoreau's political essays, effectively enacts.

This ambivalence can be seen most clearly in the chapter entitled "Former Inhabitants; and Winter Visitors," where Thoreau places himself in the rhetorical position of a transcendental chronicler who sets out to write a revisionist account of the local history. In explaining the names of the hills and "locations" in and around Walden Pond, Thoreau writes, for example, of "ground famous for the pranks of a demon [alcohol] not distinctly named in old mythology, who has acted a prominent and astounding part in our New England life, and deserves, as much as any mythological character, to have his biography written one day" (296). Self-consciously working to recover the repressed demons and lives "not distinctly named" by the official discourse of "history," Thoreau includes the "biographies" of three African Americans. Cato Ingraham is described as "a slave of Duncan Ingraham" who lived in a house built by his master in a "little patch among the walnuts" (295). Thoreau also tells the story of Zilpha, a "colored woman . . . [who] spun linen for the townsfolk" and whose house was burned down by the British in the War of 1812. "She led a hard life," Thoreau observes, "and somewhat inhumane" (295). And, finally, he recounts the life of "Brister Freeman, 'a handy Negro,' slave of Squire Cummings." Thoreau reads Freeman's epitaph in the old Lincoln burying-ground and comments wryly, "he is styled 'Sippio Brister,'—Scipio Africanus he had some title to be called,—'a man of color,' as if he were discolored" (295).

Thoreau concludes this historical section of *Walden* with the image of a subterranean spring that symbolically embodies the place of blacks in America. The dialectical interplay of revealing and concealing here offers a telling insight into the conflict between Thoreau's political allegiance to abolition and his philosophical commitment to transcendental Oneness.

> Sometimes the well dent is visible, where once a spring oozed; not dry and tearless grass; or it was covered deep,—not to be discovered till some late day,—with flat stone under the sod, when the last of the race departed. What a sorrowful act that must be,—the covering up of wells! coincident with the opening of wells of tears. . . . But all I can learn of their conclusions amounts to this, that "Cato and Brister pulled wool." (299)

On the one hand, Thoreau's image of the "covering up of wells" and "the opening of wells of tears" is a beautifully crafted metaphor of the reservoir of black sorrow that lies hidden beneath the discursive landscape of white "history," from which African Americans have been excluded. And yet, on the other hand, his insinuation that this revelation can occur only "when the last of the race departed" implicitly suggests that blacks have somehow already disappeared.

It is possible, of course, that Thoreau's choice of the adjective "departed" can be read as a historical reference to the underground railroad and the flight of fugitive slaves like Shadrach. In his journal, Thoreau tells of helping to hide and raise money for a number of runaway slaves on their way to Canada.[35] To label blacks a "race departed," however, ignores the historical reality of African American presence in Boston. As James Oliver Horton and Lois Horton document in *Black Bostonians*, the census of 1850 indicates that there were two thousand African Americans living in Boston, 54.5 percent of whom had been born in New England.[36] During the time that Thoreau was writing and revising *Walden*, blacks in the city were engaged in a highly visible struggle to desegregate Boston's schools. In 1846, the Boston school committee announced that segregation was founded on a "distinction . . . which the Almighty has seen fit to establish." After an eleven-year boycott and petition campaign, Boston's schools were finally integrated in 1855, when Governor Henry Gardner signed the legislation into law.[37]

Black Americans do not, however, completely vanish from the pages of *Walden*. Like his depiction of Indians (whom Thoreau also refers to in his journal as a "departed race"), African Americans come to be subsumed by Nature. Cato Ingraham's historical presence is transformed into a "half-obliterated cellar hole . . . filled with smooth sumach" (295). Zilpha becomes a "sweet-scented black-birch," growing where her doorstep once lay (299). And Brister Freeman is known to Thoreau by a grove of "apple-trees which Brister planted and tended; large old trees now, but their fruit still wild and ciderish to my taste" (295). "Now only a dent in the earth"—a deconstructive "trace" indicating the presence of black absence—"marks the site of these dwellings with buried cellar stones, and strawberries, raspberries, thimble-berries, hazel-bushes, and sumachs growing in the sunny sward there" (299). Like the "lone Indian woman" of Thoreau's journals, African Americans have been "absorbed into the elements again"—a complicated metaphorical act which, strangely, suggests a thoroughly multicultural conception of Nature while at the same moment buttressing Thoreau's distinctly monocultural conception of the transcendental Oneness of national identity.

Significantly, Thoreau immediately follows the discursive "disappearance" of African Americans with a reassertion of his own narcissistically fragile claim to being the original occupant of the soil. He concludes the section on "Former Inhabitants" by writing, "Again, perhaps, Nature will try, with me for a first settler, and my house raised last spring to be the oldest in the hamlet" (300). It is a peculiarly ahistorical image with which to conclude a self-consciously historical section of the book. Thoreau (inadvertently?) obliterates the African American historical presence he has worked so hard to reconstruct by representing himself as "a first settler" and his newly raised house as "the oldest in the hamlet." Here again Nature becomes the agency which justifies and enacts Thoreau's transcendental monoculturalism ("Nature will try . . ."). Although this narcissistic fantasy of white indigenity represents a distorted construction of the nation's multicultural origins, it is nevertheless a very "American" representation of the country's past, this idea that "history" begins with the "first" white settler, an Adamic figure in a vast wilderness.

Despite this erasure, the historical presence of African Americans plays an important (though understated) role in shaping Thoreau's conception of "the only true America." For although he disingenuously suggests that African Americans are a "race departed," black culture and the struggle for freedom deeply influenced Thoreau's transcendental idealism. In the

opening chapter of *Walden*, for example, Thoreau writes: "It is by a mathe-
matical point only that we are wise, as the sailor or the fugitive slave keeps
the polestar in his eye; but that is sufficient guidance for all our life. We
may not arrive at our port within a calculable period, but we would preserve the true course" (158). Throughout the narrative the "north star"
functions as an important and enduring symbol of freedom and the endpoint of Thoreau's abolitionist struggle. Just as the fight to eradicate slavery invigorates and empowers Thoreau's voice in essays such as "Civil Disobedience" and "Slavery in Massachusetts," so too in *Walden* does the
figure of the fugitive slave and his quest for freedom indicate "the true
course" and provide "sufficient guidance for all [Thoreau's] life."

The Manliest Relations to Men

What distinguishes Thoreau's representation of women from his depiction
of either Native Americans or African Americans is the lack of any vestige
of reformist rhetoric to gloss over the forces of cultural exclusion. Whereas
Thoreau is clearly deeply invested in the abolitionist cause and the ethno-
graphic exploration of Native American culture, his literary narrative
makes no mention of the women's movement, which, after the Seneca
Falls convention in 1848, had taken its place upon the national stage.
There are, in fact, almost no women in the narrative at all. And yet Thoreau's complicated construction of his social position as outside of the
economic sphere yet representative of the nation is anxiously close to the
place assigned to white, middle-class women. This similarity creates a crisis
of masculinity that threatens Thoreau's narcissistically fragile sense of
himself as possessing "the manliest relations to men" (109).

To recover the role of sentimental women's culture in shaping Thoreau's conception of "the only true America" presents a distinct challenge,
given that any traces of the women in his life have been carefully eradicated
from the literary text. As Richard Lebeaux notes in *Thoreau's Seasons*,
women played an important, behind-the-scenes role in many aspects of
Thoreau's philosophical venture beside Walden Pond. Although not recorded in the narrative, Thoreau's mother visited him almost every Satur-
day, bringing food to augment his spartan diet of Indian huckleberries.
One neighbor speculated that "he would have starved, if . . . his sisters
and mother [hadn't] cooked up pies and doughnuts and sent them to him
in a basket."[38] In 1846, much to Thoreau's chagrin, a woman whom literary historians believe to be his aunt Maria paid his poll tax and thus cut
short his famous act of "civil disobedience" (the jailer reported that the
next morning Thoreau was "mad as hell" when he discovered that he had
been bailed out against his will). Despite Thoreau's protests, his aunt

Maria and other members of the family continued to pay his poll tax for years to come.[39] And, finally, when it came time to leave Walden and return to the reality of a market-driven economy, Thoreau avoided the necessity of taking a regular paying job by moving in with Lidian Emerson while her husband was away in England.[40] By expunging any trace of his mother, his aunt Maria, and Lidian Emerson from the textual surface of his narrative, Thoreau buttresses his imperiled sense of transcendental self-reliance and his literary persona of a man living "a primitive and frontier life, though in the midst of outward civilization" (113).

In the very few instances where Thoreau does represent women in *Walden*, his attitudes are mostly negative, at times even openly hostile. In "Where I Lived, and What I Lived For," for example, Thoreau notes that his attempt to purchase a farm from a neighbor named Hollowell is abruptly terminated when "his wife . . . changed her mind and wished to keep it"—to which Thoreau tacks on the acerbic addendum, "every man has such a wife" (166). In *Thoreau's Wild Rhetoric*, Henry L. Golemba argues that Thoreau's decision to publish this chapter as a preview of *Walden* suggests that he believed that "an aristocratic tone of snooty no-shoes prejudice sold then as delicious Americana."[41] (Interestingly, the other chapter Thoreau published in advance, "Baker's Farm," contains some of the book's most vehemently anti-Irish passages).[42] Golemba's blunt assessment of Thoreau's misogyny does not, however, address fully enough the complicated and deeply conflicted nature of his relationship to women's culture and the tenets of sentimentalism.

Thoreau's harsh assessment of wives as inherently limiting belies the rhetorically effective chiasma produced by the crossing of transcendental and sentimental discourses in *Walden*. Thoreau's complex use of the nineteenth century's gendered spheres can be seen in his negotiations to purchase "James Collins' shanty" in the opening chapter. His confrontation with Mrs. Collins constitutes one of the very few bodily representations of women in the text. In keeping with the nativist hierarchy that informs the narrative, Thoreau condemns the Irishwoman's home as "dank, clammy, and aguish" (137). Beneath this nativist subtext, however, lies the sub-subtext of multicultural hybridity. That is to say, this nativist jeer covers over an act of cultural appropriation whereby Thoreau metaphorically and literally takes possession of the domestic sphere. As feminist critics such as Cathy Davidson and Lora Romero have recently observed, the notion that men's and women's cultures were consigned to "separate spheres" in the nineteenth century is a theoretical misnomer.[43] Thoreau's proud proclamation that "I live in a tight, light, and clean house" a few chapters later invokes the purity of the domestic sphere and provides a meaningful insight into how sentimental discourse implicitly structures his transcendental project.

Like sentimental treatises on household management, Thoreau advocates a carefully planned domestic routine. "I got up early and bathed in the pond;" Thoreau writes, "that was a religious exercise, and one of the best things which I did" (171). "Instead of three meals a day, if it be necessary eat but one; instead of a hundred dishes, five; and reduce other things in proportion" (173). As Philip Fisher observes in *Hard Facts*, Thoreau's prescribed regime shares many goals with Catherine Beecher's *A Treatise on the Domestic Economy.* "In *Walden*," Fisher notes, "the possibility of independence and full selfhood are linked to the discovery and description of a simple and rational house and a round of tasks that permit self-sufficiency and even poetry. . . . the political significance of the smallest repeatable unit—the self-sufficient household—joins Thoreau's philosophical experiment to Beecher's more commonplace utopia of pots and pans."[44] This discursive echo, while puzzling, becomes clearer when one considers Thoreau's vexed relationship to the economy.

As many critics have noted, Thoreau's attitudes toward the economic realm are difficult to understand, even at times contradictory.[45] On the one hand, as we have seen, he trumpets his interest in the developing capitalist economy: "I have always endeavored to acquire strict business habits; they are indispensable to every man" (119). At other times, however, he seems to actively disavow any interaction with the marketplace, proclaiming his freedom from "all trade and barter" (153). Whereas he earlier used the "strolling Indian" to define "the other without," to mark the racial boundaries of the imagined economic community, he utilizes white women as "the other within," to help situate himself at the moral center of the national imaginary while remaining free from the inherent evils of the market economy.[46]

The discourse of "true womanhood," propounded by both the women's popular press and the male clergy, held that the moral health of the nation depended upon the "purity" of women, which in turn depended on their sequestration from the corrupting influences of the marketplace. *The Lady at Home*, for example, counseled women to remain within the sanctuary of the domestic sphere and not to "look away from her own little family circle for the means of producing moral and social reforms, but begin at home."[47] In *Uncle Tom's Cabin*, Harriet Beecher Stowe cannily played upon antebellum notions of prescribed gender roles to enhance the importance of women's place in American society. In the scene, for example, where a runaway slave, seeking refuge, knocks on the door of the Bird home, it is Mrs. Bird, rather than her husband, who possesses the moral authority to offer shelter, precisely because Senator Bird has been morally tainted by his association with the Fugitive Slave Law in Congress.[48] As Gillian Brown trenchantly observes, "*Uncle Tom's Cabin* reinterprets domesticity as a double agentry in which women simultaneously act within society as its exemplars . . . and at the boundaries of society as its critics and revolutionaries."[49] This rhetorical strategy of "double agentry" is very close to Thoreau's perception of himself as both an exemplar of "the only true America" and a critic of "the state which buys and sells men, women, and children, like cattle at the door of its senate-house" (232).

The problem for Thoreau is that his avoidance of "all trade and barter" would have been perceived, in the parlance of the mid–nineteenth century, as a withdrawal from the "masculine sphere."[50] As E. Anthony Rotundo points out in *American Manhood*, social constructions of masculinity were undergoing dramatic changes at the time Thoreau was writing. Prior to 1800, Rotundo observes, manhood was understood in terms of the duties a citizen owed to his community. As America moved headlong toward industrialization in the first decades of the nineteenth century, this "communal form of manhood" came to be eclipsed by a "self-made manhood" that stressed "ambition, rivalry, and aggression." Avoidance of the economic sphere "not only meant a withdrawal from the central male activity of work," Rotundo writes, "but it also involved a rejection of fundamental manly virtues—achievement, ambition, [and] dominance." As an example of this "self-made manhood," Rotundo quotes a young gentleman who wrote in 1836 that the American man "is never . . . so uneasy as when seated by his own fireside; for he feels . . . that he is making no money."[51]

This aggressive, market-driven conception of masculinity constitutes almost the exact antithesis of Thoreau's transcendental ideal. Thoreau's carefully constructed pose of philosophical authority does not allow him to address such fears openly in the text of *Walden*. In the privacy of his journal, however, his anxiety is more apparent (albeit, even here, indirectly). Worrying about his friend Amos Bronson Alcott, for example, Thoreau writes: "Alcott . . . knew of nothing which he could do for which men would pay him. He could not compete with the Irish in cradling grain. His early education had not fitted him for a clerkship. He had offered his services to the Abolition Society, to go about the country and speak for freedom as their agent, but they declined him."[52] Thoreau wrote this entry in August 1853, just one year before he would leave Walden Pond to confront an uncertain future. Although subtly misdirected, the anxieties he articulates on behalf of his friend Alcott are palpable and clearly weigh heavily on Thoreau's mind.

Thoreau attempts to resolve this tension between his reliance upon the sentimental construction of the domestic sphere and nineteenth-century conceptions of self-made masculinity by inventing what might be termed the rhetoric of transcendental "true manhood." "Actually, the laboring man has not leisure for a true integrity day by day; he cannot afford to sustain the manliest relations to men; his labor would be depreciated in the market"(109). "True integrity," for Thoreau (and Stowe), is a condition which depends on freeing oneself from "the market." And yet Thoreau self-consciously works to avoid any suggestion that he is out of touch with the "masculine sphere" by cloaking his withdrawal in the linguistic guise of "the manliest relations to men." Having appropriated the moral high ground hitherto held by "true womanhood," Thoreau here discursively erases any association with sentimentalism by disguising his rhetorical construction of moral "integrity" in the discourse of "true" masculinity.

An important difference, however, between Thoreau's position and that of Harriet Beecher Stowe is their perceived place in the gendered hierarchy of mid-nineteenth-century American society. Stowe, for example, accepts (at least on the rhetorical surface of her text) the subordinate position which the patriarchal society dictates for females: Mrs. Bird's moral authority in the domestic sphere is directly tied to her acceptance of the fact that she does not "trouble her head with what was going on in the house of the state."[53] Thoreau, on the other hand, absolutely disavows any notion that his social position as an outsider to the economic sphere entails subordination. Instead, he struggles to convince the reader of his vigorous masculinity and pictures himself in philosophical ascendancy, standing atop the hierarchical structure of society. Peering down from the transcendental heights of "true manhood" on those laborers who become trapped within the economic sphere, Thoreau writes: "Look at the teamster on the highway, wending to market by day or night. . . . What is his destiny to him compared with the shipping interests? Does not he drive for Squire Make-a-stir? How godlike, how immortal is he?" (110). Thoreau, in contrast, fashions himself as being "one of the elect" and compares himself to "the gods of Troy" (138). The narcissistic grandeur of his rhetoric, however, belies the crisis of masculinity that underlies such bold claims. Moreover, this "manly" stance implicitly disavows the cultural hybridity that informs Thoreau's conception of "the only true America," denying his indebtedness to sentimental literature's brilliant reversal of the industrial economy's hierarchy of values.

The "Boggy Ways" of the Irish

In stark contrast to Native Americans (who are "almost exterminated"), African Americans (a "race departed"), and women (who are simply invisible), the Irish are everywhere throughout *Walden*. During the winter months beside the pond, "literally, a hundred Irishmen, with Yankee overseers, came from Cambridge to get out the ice" (323). Thoreau buys his shanty from James Collins, "an Irishman who worked on the Fitchburg railroad" (137). When caught in the rain while fishing, he finds shelter under the leaky roof of John Field. And, finally, in response to his comment on the railroads—"that a few are riding, but the rest are run over"—"a million Irishmen starting up from shanties in the land" answer him back, crying "'is not this railroad we have built a good thing?' " To which Thoreau responds, "I wish, as you are brothers of mine, that you could have spent your time better than digging in this dirt" (145).

A hostile and palpable nativism, however, undercuts this filial relationship and ultimately leads Thoreau to distance himself from the Irish. At times the Irish who work for the railroads are sympathetically portrayed: "Did you ever think what those sleepers are that underlie the railroad? Each one is a man, an Irishman. . . . The rails are laid on them" (174). And yet as he sits with John Field, waiting for the rain to stop, Thoreau muses to himself that "the culture of an Irishman is an enterprise to be undertaken with a sort of moral bog hoe" (258). Thoreau concludes that John Field is "a poor man, born to be poor, with his inherited Irish poverty . . . and boggy ways" and that he is destined "not to rise in this world, he nor his posterity, till their wading webbed bog-trotting feet get talaria to their heels" (260). The Irish may play a large part in Thoreau's literary construction of the imagined community of the nation; nevertheless, they appear predestined to remain mired at the muddy bottom of society, with no real chance to become part of "the only true America."

The uncertainty that underlies these contradictory representations of the Irish mirrors, in some respects, the historical ambivalence of those whites who saw themselves as "native" New Englanders. When the potato blight first hit Ireland late in 1845, the people of Boston responded with genuine concern and charity. The Catholic community, responding to the bishop of Boston's call to his flock to share their "last loaf of bread" with their Irish brethren, raised more than $150,000 in famine relief. Non-Catholics made substantial contributions as well. In March 1847, for example, Boston merchants convinced the United States Congress to allow them to use the *Jamestown*, a sloop of war moored at the Charleston Navy Yard, to transport provisions to the victims of the famine in Ireland.[54]

As the Irish poured into Boston harbor—thirty-seven thousand came in 1847 alone—the attitudes of "native" whites quickly began to change.[55] Theodore Parker complained that Suffolk County, Massachusetts had become "a New England 'County Cork,' " while Boston had been transformed into "the Dublin of America."[56] In 1850, the mayor of Boston declared that "Foreign paupers are rapidly accumulating on our hands" and warned taxpayers to be wary of "aged, blind, paralytic, and lunatic immigrants who have become charges on our public charities."[57] And yet despite nativist resentment, the Irish quickly integrated into the new capitalist economy and became a driving force of the growing industrial revolution. When a business recession in 1848 threw hundreds of mill operatives out of work in Lowell, companies began to replace Yankee women with Irish laborers, who were willing to work for cheaper wages and who did not have to be housed and supervised in specially built dormitories. In 1851, the Prescott Corporation in Lowell institutionalized the hiring of Irish labor for the first time, justifying their controversial decision by arguing that "the Irish girls, having no friends in this country, would remain at their posts in all seasons."[58]

As critics like David R. Roediger and Noel Ignatiev have skillfully demonstrated, the Irish self-consciously and effectively played upon their racial whiteness to create a place for themselves in the nation's political and economic realms.[59] The bishop of Boston, John Bernard Fitzpatrick, urged the Irish community to help newly arrived immigrants immediately register for naturalization (immigration laws at the time required only a five-year waiting period before naturalized citizens were allowed to vote). "We should make ourselves Americans as much as we can," Bishop Fitzpatrick wrote in the Irish newspaper *The Pilot*. "This is our country now. Ireland is only a recollection." In 1853, the Irish vote played an important role in defeating proposed changes to the Massachusetts Constitution which would have taken power away from the urban centers, where the Irish were quickly gaining political strength.[60] In 1854, the Know-Nothing party, rallying under the banner of "Americans must rule America," answered back by sweeping the state elections. The newly elected governor and lieutenant governor of Massachusetts were nativists, as were 11 U.S. congressmen, every county commissioner, every state senator, and 326 state representatives.[61] It is telling, however, of the implicit power of the Irish community's racial whiteness that the new nativist legislature did not attempt to halt Irish immigration but merely to extend the period of naturalization to twenty-one years (the same amount of time, they reasoned, that it took for "native" Americans to be eligible to vote).[62]

The familiarity of a shared sense of whiteness almost certainly plays a repressed part in Thoreau's willingness to represent the Irish, in contrast to the noted absence or imminent vanishing of Native Americans and African Americans. In the opening chapter, where Thoreau is discussing how "the poor *minority* fare," he refers to the Irish as "one of the white or enlightened spots on the map," which he contrasts with "the North American Indian . . . or any other savage race" (131). And yet the question of who gets represented and why in Thoreau's literary construction of the national imaginary cannot ultimately be reduced to simply a matter of race (as Thoreau's exclusion of white, middle-class women makes clear). Instead, the forces of inclusion and exclusion that shape Thoreau's imagined community of "America" need to be theorized as an aporia defined by a multiplicity of cultural relations, of which race is but a single (albeit important) factor.

The intricate complexity of Thoreau's relationship to the Irish can be seen in his confrontation with John Field. Immediately following his dismissal of Irish culture as "an enterprise to be undertaken with a sort of moral bog hoe" (258), Thoreau writes:

> I told him, that as he worked so hard at bogging, he required thick boots, and stout clothing . . . but I wore light shoes and thin clothing, which cost not half so much, though he might think that I was dressed like a gentleman, (which, however, was not the case,) and in an hour or two, without labor, but as a recreation, I could, if I wished, catch as many fish as I should want for two days, or earn enough money to support me a week. If he and his family would live simply, they might all go a-huckleberrying in the summer for their amusement. (258)

On the one hand, John Field's struggle to support his family in a new country provides Thoreau an opportunity to delineate the important philosophical difference between "labor" and "recreation" which is fundamental to his transcendental project to "live simply."[63] On the other hand, the Irishman's "poverty" calls attention to Thoreau's "light shoes and thin clothing," which mark him as a "gentleman." The comparison proves problematic precisely because it raises serious questions about the degree to which Thoreau's ability to avoid "labor" is dependent upon his unacknowledged status as a member of the middle class. Although Thoreau quickly denies that he is a "gentleman," his philosophy of "self-reliance" remains haunted by the question of class privilege.

Throughout the opening chapter of *Walden*, Thoreau works self-consciously to disavow his middle-class standing. In describing his relationship to the land he writes, "I put no manure whatever on this land, not being the owner, but a squatter" (145). After a carefully detailed list of "the exact cost of my house," Thoreau adds, "These are all the materials excepting the timber, stones and sand, which I claimed by squatter's right" (141). What Thoreau does not reveal anywhere in his narrative is that he is living on the property of his good friend and mentor, Ralph Waldo Emerson, who bought the land around Walden Pond in 1844.[64] Thoreau's description of himself as "a squatter," like his claim to being the "first settler" or a "native American," is thus revealed to be a carefully crafted fiction which disguises the kind of class privilege that allowed him to go from "squatting" among the Irish in Walden Woods to living in Emerson's spacious home on Lexington Road when his "experiment" was over.[65]

Looking back, we can now see that Thoreau's acquisition of Mrs. Collins's "shanty" constitutes the appropriation not only of the domestic sphere but of the Irish family's class status as well. Thoreau's comparison of the Collins's shack to a "compost heap" (137) augments the illusion that he is part of "the poor *minority*," living just above the poverty line (130). The fundamental importance of the Irish is that their proximity confers upon Thoreau the authority to speak for the working class, so that when he writes, "the luxury of one class is counterbalanced by the indigence of another," he clearly means for himself to be seen as one of the "silent poor" (130). Purchasing the Collins's shack allows Thoreau to ally himself with the economically oppressed, even though Emerson's solidly middle-class status implicitly supports Thoreau's "experiment" at Walden Pond.

Ironically, whereas the Irish have a textual presence denied to Indians, blacks, and women, Thoreau seems to be less interested in the actual workings of Irish culture. Thoreau does not depict the historically rich ethnic identity of the Irish but instead employs them as a kind of literary foil, whose function in the narrative is to reaffirm Thoreau's complicated social position as both a squatter and a philosophical pioneer. As Thoreau dismantles the Collins's shanty, for example, "a young Patrick" whispers "treacherously" that Seeley, an Irishman standing nearby and chatting amiably, is "transfer[ing] the still tolerable, straight, and driveable nails, staples, and spikes to his pocket" (138) whenever Thoreau departs to cart away the lumber. Seeley, at first glance, is a fairly well-defined character, albeit a stereotypical nineteenth-century representation of the "shiftless" Irish. And yet Thoreau empties out his character by writing that "he was there to represent spectatordom, and help make this seemingly insignificant event one with the removal of the gods of Troy" (138). The Irish "represent," in this case, nothing more than "spectatordom," a hollow presence whose role in the transcendental drama of Thoreau's narrative is to transform a "seemingly insignificant event" into a heroic act, thus elevating Thoreau's quest to the level of the Homeric epic.

Having carefully situated himself in close physical proximity to the working-class Irish in the opening chapters of his narrative, Thoreau then precedes in subsequent chapters to methodically distance himself from the Irish. In "Bakers Farm" Thoreau writes, "As I walked along on the railroad causeway, I used to wonder at the halo of light around my shadow, and would fain fancy myself as one of the elect. One who visited me declared that the shadows of some Irishmen before him had no halo about them, that it was only the natives that were so distinguished" (255). Thoreau here tacitly reinscribes the cultural boundaries of "the only true America," leaving the Irish textually present yet stranded at the boggy bottom of American society. Moreover, this passage explains why the Irish are so prevalent throughout the text of *Walden*. Whereas the Indians and blacks who lived in Walden woods must be discursively *erased* in order for Thoreau to see himself as "the first settler," it is the *presence* of the Irish as newly arrived white immigrants that provides the cultural contrast necessary for Thoreau to construe himself as a "native." And, finally, the precarious position of the Irish in Thoreau's conception of "the only true America"—as racially white though culturally other—supplies him with a liminal point of reference which allows him (and a long line of Americanists) to see himself as "one of the elect."

. . . . .

My intent in the first half of *Ruthless Democracy* has been to use the works of Hawthorne, Ridge, and Thoreau to create a new, multicultural conception of the American Renaissance, to redraw the racial, ethnic, and regional boundaries of Matthiessen's "America." The first three chapters have taken us across the continent from Massachusetts to the heart of the Cherokee nation in the South, to Indian Territory in what is now Oklahoma, to the hills of California, and finally back to Walden Pond. This continental, multicultural perspective has set the voices of white New Englanders in dialogue with Cherokee nationalists, Digger Indians, Mexicanos, Irish laborers, Chinese Americans, fugitive black slaves, and white women. The first half of my study has been devoted to recovering the voices of those groups who were not *of* "America" (the "chosen people") but who nevertheless lived *in* the United States. The second half, in turn, will concentrate on recovering the voices of those people who lived *beyond* the borders of the United States but who nevertheless were still part of the imagined community of the nation. Using the works of Harriet Beecher Stowe, William Wells Brown, and Herman Melville as a literary window into antebellum society, this section will study carefully the ambivalent nature of U.S. "colonization," the lives of fugitive slaves in the "American Diaspora," and the international work force of the whaling industry. By mapping and incorporating these undertheorized extraterritorial regions I will work toward inscribing a new, transnational multicultural understanding of "American" identity.

PART II

TOWARD A TRANSNATIONAL

UNDERSTANDING OF

"AMERICAN" IDENTITY

HISTORICAL INTERLUDE

"A LITTLE BLACK AMERICA" IN AFRICA

On January 3, 1848, four years before Harriet Beecher Stowe concluded *Uncle Tom's Cabin* by sending virtually every surviving black character to Liberia, thousands of people assembled in a dusty central square on the west coast of Africa to celebrate the birth of the Republic of Liberia and the inauguration of the first black President, Joseph Jenkins Roberts. White representatives from the American Colonization Society, which had founded the "colony" in 1820, turned the country over to President Roberts as shouts of joy and spontaneous celebrations broke out among the more than three thousand repatriated black Americans.[1] Also present were several hundred Dahome and Ibo who had been rescued from the holds of slave ships, as well as members of the Vai, Dei, Gola, and Bassa kingdoms who had originally occupied the land on which the Republic of Liberia was founded.[2] Together they watched with very different emotions as the flag, a single white star on a field of blue with eleven red and white stripes, was raised above the capital in Monrovia—named for President James Monroe, who provided the initial funding for the colony and pronounced Liberia "a little black America destined to shine gemlike in the darkness of vast Africa."[3]

Based on American ideals of democracy, the constitution of the Republic of Liberia declared that "All men are born equally free and independent, and have certain natural, inherent, and inalienable rights."[4] And just as the United States denied African Americans the rights of citizenship, so too did the Liberian constitution of 1847 refuse to recognize "native" Africans as citizens (even though Africans, like repatriated black Americans, paid taxes).[5] The question of whether the founding of the Republic of Liberia constituted a triumphant return of African Americans to their ancestral homeland, a unique instance of American imperialism, or the partial realization of the white colonizationists' dream of "ridding" the United States of its black population depends largely on which historical voices one accepts as definitive or representative.

The founding of Liberia is like a many-faceted historical mirror. Its different surfaces reflect an array of cultural perspectives whose sheer multiplicity utterly deconstructs any singular sense of either "black" or "American" identity. Within the geographic boundaries of Liberia, for example, where "no white person, under any circumstances, [was] allowed to become a citizen,"[6] the establishment of a black republic elicited widely different responses. To Lott Cary, who had led a revolt to depose the white

ACS leadership of Liberia, independence meant the fulfillment of a long, protracted struggle for self-rule. To black Africans from the Bassa, Kru, Dei, Grebo, and Gola kingdoms, whose lands had been "absorbed" by the aggressive colony of Liberia, Americo-Liberians were Kwee, or "white" people, and Monrovia was known as "the American place."[7]

In the United States, the project to return African Americans to their "fatherland" was a source of bitter contention within the white abolitionist community. Supporters of African colonization proclaimed Liberia to be a nation "founded in wisdom, under the direction of an overruling Providence, and adapted to place the free colored people of the United States in a position in which they can enjoy all the privileges and blessings of freedom."[8] To white radical abolitionists like William Lloyd Garrison, who led a campaign to condemn the American Colonization Society, Liberia was "conceived in blood, and its footsteps will be marked with . . . the blood of the poor natives."[9]

The African American community was similarly divided. Free blacks in the north openly questioned the motives of the American Colonization Society and its "colony," Liberia. Frederick Douglass, in a speech entitled "Henry Clay and Colonization Cant, Sophistry, and Falsehood," declared that "The object is, *to get rid of us*. Our presence is an offense to [Clay], and to the whole herd of colonizationists, and they are determined to have us out of the country if they can."[10] The National Colored Convention of 1847 issued a statement that "Among the many oppressive schemes . . . we view the American Colonization Society as the most deceptive and hypocritical . . . with President Roberts, of Liberia, a Colored Man, for its leader."[11] And yet to other African Americans the idea of a black republic in Africa, free not only of slavery but of white racism, held a powerful appeal. As the National Emigration Convention of 1854 declared: "*Resolved*, That we believe that Liberia offers to the oppressed children of Africa a home where they may be free: and that it is the only place where we can establish a nationality, and be acknowledged as men by the nations of the earth."[12]

This dialogic complexity provides a unique insight into the unresolved conflict at the heart of antebellum America regarding the question of whether African Americans could ever be incorporated into the imagined community of "We, the People." "Liberia," in this sense, can be read as a site where the discourses of abolition, white racism, sentimental benevolence, and black nationalism all intersect. To theorize this nexus of competing rhetorical constructions it is first necessary to understand what "American colonization" means in this context. This conflicted desire to simultaneously "rid" the United States of its African American population and to establish a "little black America" in the "colony" of Liberia is replete with contradictions. Rather than trying to resolve these contradictions by dismissing Stowe's pro-colonizationist conclusion as a literary oversight, I want to study the "colony" of Liberia at length. The discursive construct of "Liberia" can thus be read as an important and undertheorized opening into both the United States' conflicted will to empire and Harriet Beecher Stowe's anxiety about the place of blacks in postabolition America.

CHAPTER FOUR

HARRIET BEECHER STOWE:
UNCLE TOM'S CABIN AND THE QUESTION OF
THE AMERICAN COLONIZATION SOCIETY

> The utility of a plan for colonizing the free people of color,
> with whom our country abounds, . . . [is] its tendency to
> confer a benefit on ourselves, by ridding us of a population
> for the most part idle and useless, and too often vicious.
> (First Annual Report, *American Colonization Society*)

> I have no wish to pass for an American, or to identify myself
> with them. . . . The desire and yearning of my
> soul is for an African *nationality.*
> (George Harris, at conclusion of *Uncle Tom's Cabin*, 1852)

> I could see that things were changed [after the enactment of
> the Fugitive Slave Law], and frequently I would be sent in
> the kitchen to eat my meals when traveling. I was once
> ordered out of the first-class car to take a seat in the Jim
> Crow car. These things galled me, and after many
> years reflection on the subject, I came to the conclusion,
> if there was a free spot in all God's earth, I would seek
> that place. . . . I wanted a home where I could be free.
> (Rev. Samuel Williams, *Four Years in Liberia* [1857])

THE ENDING of Harriet Beecher Stowe's *Uncle Tom's Cabin*, in which virtually every surviving black character departs for Liberia, reads like the literary realization of the American Colonization Society's mission to "promote and execute a plan for colonizing (with their consent) the free people of color residing in our country [to] Africa."[1] One of the characters, George Harris, states, amid much rhetorical flourish, "On the shores of Africa I see a republic,—a republic formed of picked men, who by energy and self-educating force . . . raised themselves above a condition of slavery."[2] In the closing pages of the novel, George Harris departs with his entire extended family to the "splendid continent of Africa" (461). Topsy, after being taken back to New England as "an odd

and unnecessary addition to their well-trained domestic establishment,"
departs ("by her own request") for Liberia, where "she is now employed
. . . in teaching the children of her country" (463). Cassy too repents her
formerly wild ways and "yield[s] . . . with her whole soul, to every good
influence, and [becomes] a devout and tender Christian"—before she exits
as a missionary to Liberia. And, finally, Cassy's son, who appears in Stowe's
narrative only to disappear into the dark continent, is "educated by friends
of the oppressed in the north" and reported to be leaving "soon [to]
follow his family to Africa" (463). In all, eight of Stowe's black characters
depart for Africa at the end of the novel.[3]

The intertextual echoes between Stowe's clearly contrived ending and
the goals of the American Colonization Society (ACS) raise a number of
perplexing theoretical questions.[4] Is the ending an anomaly? Joan Hedrick, in her biography of Stowe, writes that the novel as a whole is more
interesting than its colonizationist conclusion.[5] Or does George Harris's
letter at the conclusion of the novel provide a fleeting, though meaningful,
glimpse into the ambivalence that lies buried beneath Stowe's rhetoric of
sentimental benevolence? If so, does this ambivalence call into question
the newly attained status of *Uncle Tom's Cabin*, which won its way into
the canon of American literature in the mid-1980s because of Stowe's
commitment to abolition and the sentimental values of domesticity?

It is disconcerting that neither of the two critical works most responsi-
ble for the novel's canonization ever fully engaged the role that the American Colonization Society played in shaping her vision of the national imaginary. In *Sensational Designs* (1985), Jane Tompkins argued that "the
political purpose" of Stowe's novel was to "turn the socio-political order
upside down" and "to bring in the day when the meek—which is to say,
women—will inherit the earth."[6] Philip Fisher, in *Hard Facts* (1985), buttressed Tompkins's call for greater critical attention to sentimental women
novelists by asserting that *Uncle Tom's Cabin* performed the "cultural
work" of changing "what the census of the human world looks like," by
"redesign[ing] the boundary between the categories of man and thing"
and establishing "human representability for black Americans."[7] And
while I strongly agree that *Uncle Tom's Cabin* provides a culturally important representation of the central role that white women played in constructing the imagined community of "America," I believe that the second
wave of Stowe criticism needs to explore the multicultural perplexities of
her sentimental "masterpiece" more fully. To reintroduce the question of
Stowe's colonizationist sympathies, for example, productively complicates
the conclusions of both Tompkins and Fisher. Given the racist subtext of
so much ACS rhetoric, it must be asked whether part of the "cultural
work" of the novel is to enact the discursive exile of the free black community from the United States. In which case, it would appear that Stowe has

neither turned "the socio-political order upside down" nor significantly altered the "census" of the imagined community of "America."

Whereas Tompkins and Fisher may have ignored Stowe's advocacy of colonization in the final pages of her novel, her African American contemporaries were all too well aware of it. Martin Delany, a prominent black nationalist, responded angrily in the black press: "I demand [to know] . . . is not Mrs. Stowe a *Colonizationist*? . . . we should reject the proffers of Mrs. Stowe as readily as those of any other colonizationist. What! Have our children tutored under colonization measures? God forbid!"[8] In the months following the publication of Stowe's best-selling novel, a bitter dispute broke out between Delany and Frederick Douglass about whether the black community should support Stowe, in the face of the procolonizationist conclusion to her novel. Although Douglass himself vehemently opposed Stowe's views on African colonization ("The truth is, dear madam," Douglass wrote to Stowe, "we are *here*, and here we are likely to remain. Individuals emigrate—nations never"),[9] he nevertheless defended her. The debate between Delany and Douglass provides an important insight into how the black community struggled to come to terms with a literary text that was, without a doubt, the most powerful and effective argument for immediate abolition in the years leading up to the Civil War and yet, at the same time, seemed to suggest that even the most sympathetic whites did not imagine a place for blacks in an "America" free, at long last, of the curse of slavery.[10]

Stowe's conclusion, however, not only mirrors the rhetoric of the American Colonization Society but the political views of the more than eleven thousand African Americans who did emigrate to Liberia before the Civil War. Could it be, then, that George Harris is simply speaking for a significant portion of the antebellum black community who have not yet received sufficient scholarly attention?[11] It is a complicated and volatile question. On the one hand, many black Americans who favored emigration despised Liberia, because of its association with the American Colonization Society. Martin Delany, for example, advocated black repatriation to Africa but vehemently opposed going to Liberia. He accused the ACS of having "selected the tide-swamp of the coast of Guinea . . . and [having] designedly established a national Potter's Field, into which the carcass of every emigrant who ventured there, would most assuredly molder in death."[12] (More than one thousand newly arrived immigrants died of "African fever" before 1843.)[13] On the other hand, there are certain distinct resemblances between George Harris's longing for an "African *nationality*" and the views of some repatriated black Americans, like Samuel Williams, who went to Liberia to find "a home where I could be free."[14]

To critically plot the ideological complexity of Stowe's conclusion requires a highly nuanced theoretical paradigm. Before undertaking this difficult hermeneutic challenge, it will be necessary to invent several new analytical terms specifically designed to help map this complicated and contradictory literary/cultural terrain. In particular, I am interested in the relationship between what I will call fear of "miscege-nation" and America's "sentimental imperialism." By fear of "miscege-nation" I mean not only the hysterical reaction to blacks and whites intermarrying but also the intense anxiety surrounding the question of whether African Americans could ever be included as fully constituted democratic citizens in the "family of nations."[15] I will argue that the "sentimental imperialism" advocated by both Stowe and the American Colonization Society is shaped in part by this fear of "miscege-nation."[16] Although I will examine carefully the question of whether Stowe's pro-colonization conclusion is racist, by studying the biographical and historical roots of the ambivalence that underlies her sentimentalism, my larger project is to complete the "multicultural turn" begun in chapter 3. That is to say, instead of simply *deconstructing* Stowe's exclusion of African Americans, I will continue the process of *reconstructing* the American Renaissance, by working to include George Harris and the "colony" of Liberia in a new, transnational conception of the imagined community of "America."

"Colonization" in an American Context

To define "colonization" as it was used with regard to Liberia is a challenging hermeneutic undertaking. White Americans were (and still are) reluctant to see themselves as "colonizers." The Declaration of Independence, of course, eloquently argues the case that white Americans were the "colonized." By the time Harriet Beecher Stowe completed *Uncle Tom's Cabin* in 1852, however, this self-perception had been called into doubt by the fact that the United States had pushed the boundaries of its "empire for liberty" all the way across the continent. Before addressing the question of how Stowe's novel participates in the discourse of "sentimental imperialism," we must first try to understand more fully the way in which racism, democracy, fear of "miscege-nation," expansionism, and evangelism intertwine to give "American colonization" its unique and contradictory character.

The "colonization" of Liberia is part of a tradition of United States imperialism that can be traced back to two distinct yet interrelated patterns of expansion.[17] The first constitutes what I will call America's conflicted will to empire. It is possible to argue, as Bernard DeVoto has suggested, that the United States was an empire before it was a nation.[18] As early as 1754, at the Albany Conference, Benjamin Franklin articulated a plan for the "colonists" to expand westward into Indian territory.[19] Certainly with the conclusion of the Mexican-American War in 1848 the United States established itself as one of the world's great imperial powers.[20]

The plan to found a "colony" on the west coast of Africa was, in part, an extension of this will to empire and ACS supporters could on occasion be quite explicit about their dreams of economic expansion. In an address entitled "Colonization and Commerce," for example, Frank Blair announced: "All that is required to develop untold wealth is a race of men capable of enduring the [tropical] climate. . . . I have spoken of this plan of colonizing our slaves as a means of . . . propagat[ing] our power and influence as England has done."[21] Because white Americans were deeply invested in an image of themselves as a group of former colonies that came into being as a nation through a revolutionary act of independence, such comparisons to the British empire were perplexing. American statesmen justified continental imperialism by arguing that the Constitution allowed for contiguous expansion.[22] The case of Liberia, however, called into question the very essence of "American" identity as it had been constructed by the founding fathers. (John Quincy Adams, for example, vehemently opposed the funding of the ACS on the grounds that overseas colonies were unconstitutional).[23] The ACS attempted to deflect such concerns by carefully dressing the plan to "colonize" Liberia in the language of sentimental benevolence: "the introduction of the Christian religion . . . to Africa," wrote one ACS supporter, "[will lead to] the annihilation of the slave trade, and the diffusion of freedom and happiness over a continent in degradation."[24]

The second tradition of imperialism that the ACS comes out of is the United States' history of internal colonization. This tradition includes Indian reservations (initially called "colonies"), *colonias* of Mexican American workers in antebellum Texas, and the internment camps where Japanese Americans were held during World War II.[25] Unlike the economic or political imperialism of the British empire, which sought to expand England's power to global dimensions, U.S. internal colonization was driven by the dominant white society's will to monoculturalism and was primarily directed toward institutionally isolating people of color in the name of preserving national "unity." The Indian Removal Bill of 1830, which provided for "the removal of the Indian Tribes within any of the States and Territories, and for their permanent settlement West of the river Mississippi,"[26] provides a telling example of internal colonization in an American context. Although Liberia was an overseas "colony," the ACS's goal to rid the United States of its black population clearly links this plan to Indian Removal and other forms of internal colonization. Like America's continental imperialism, this internal variation cloaked itself in the rhetoric of sentimental benevolence. In his annual address of 1835, for example, President Andrew Jackson sought to justify the Indian Removal Act by arguing that "no one can doubt the moral duty of the Government of the United States to protect and if possible to preserve and perpetuate the scattered remnants of this race which are left within our borders."[27]

In the case of the American Colonization Society, these two impulses, the will to empire and the will to monoculturalism, came together in a unique but distinctly "American" fashion to create the "colony" of Liberia. Like the rhetoric of Manifest Destiny and Indian Removal, Stowe's pro-colonization conclusion and the ACS's writings are carefully and elegantly adorned in the language of divine providence and sentimental benevolence. "I trust that the development of Africa is to be essentially a Christian one," George Harris declares in the novel's closing pages. "As a Christian patriot, as a teacher of Christianity, I go to my country,—my chosen, my glorious Africa!" (462). This benevolent mission to spread the gospel to the unenlightened was, however, intertwined with a tremulous fear of miscege-nation. In an attempt to be fair to Stowe, I will analyze in careful detail both the intertextual connections between ACS rhetoric and *Uncle Tom's Cabin* and Stowe's insistent denial that she ever meant to advocate colonization. My hermeneutic intent is not to answer definitively the question of whether Stowe was a colonizationist. Instead, I want to study the rhetorical crossing between Stowe's sentimental imperialism, the discourse of the American Colonization Society, and the letters of black Americans who emigrated to Liberia in order to map the irreducible complexities of "American colonization."

.   .   .   .   .

The scheme to "return" black Americans to Africa can be traced back to the founding fathers. "The slave, when made free [in ancient Rome], might mix with, without staining the blood of his master," wrote Thomas Jefferson in 1781. "But with us a second [step] is necessary . . . when freed, he is to be removed beyond the reach of mixture."[28] This plan was adopted by the Reverend Robert Finley, who founded the American Colonization Society in 1816. Finley's colonizationist vision intended a threefold effect: "We should be rid of them"; Africa would receive "partially civilized and Christianized" settlers; and African Americans would be afforded a "better situation." Much of the ACS rhetoric was adorned with Christian majesty: "I know this scheme is from God!" Finley declared. Finley firmly believed that colonization would bring about the end of slavery and save society from "the intermixture of the different colours."[29]

The success of the ACS can be attributed to its ability to appeal both to the nation's moral anxiety about slavery and to its conflicted will to empire. Finley was able to enlist the aid of some of the most powerful politicians in the country to serve on the first ACS board, including Bushrod Washington, Secretary of the Treasury William Crawford, Speaker of the House Henry Clay, and General Andrew Jackson. The United States, Finley argued, was destined to "extend the empire of liberty and Christian blessings to surrounding nations." By linking the scheme of colonization to U.S. concerns with policing the west coast of Africa, the ACS secured an initial grant of one hundred thousand dollars as part of the Slave Trade Act of 1819. Secretary of State John Quincy Adams, however, opposed the plan and argued forcefully to President James Monroe that nothing in the Constitution warranted the "establishment of a colonial system of government subordinate to and dependent upon that of the United States."[30] To avoid the appearance of imperial design, the federal government funded the search for land on the western coast of Africa, with the agreement that the "colony" would be established in the name of the American Colonization Society rather than the United States of America.

The African American community responded immediately. In the summer of 1817, James Forten called a protest meeting, attended by three thousand blacks, at the Bethel Church in Philadelphia. Forten and other black leaders denounced the scheme of the American Colonization Society as a plan to exile free blacks "into the savage wilds of Africa." Forten challenged the fundamental assumption of the ACS that only in the "land of their fathers" could "Africans" (as Finley insistently referred to blacks in the United States) find freedom and equality. Such a charge, Forten stated, was an "unmerited stigma . . . cast upon the reputation of the free people of color."[31] The meeting, organized by Forten, Richard Allen, and Absalom Jones, published a series of resolutions among which was this declaration: "Whereas our ancestors (not of choice) were the first successful cultivators of the wilds of America, we their descendants feel ourselves entitled to participate in the blessings of her luxuriant soil, which their blood and sweat manured."[32]

In spite of such protests the ACS was able to find a significant number of African Americans willing to risk the unknown in Africa to escape what many felt to be intractable racism in the United States. In 1820, after a six-week voyage across the Atlantic, the first black colonists arrived in Africa. The first venture, however, proved to be a dismal failure. The site which the ACS selected was in the middle of a marsh. Within a month all of the white ACS agents were dead, and most of the eighty black colonists had been afflicted with a mysterious sickness that came to be known as "African fever." But the struggle to establish a colony continued, and the following year the ACS sent new agents, accompanied by a U.S. naval officer, Lieutenant Robert Field Stockton, who had been given absolute authority by the ACS to purchase a strip of African territory.[33] The problem was, of course, that the indigenous African kingdoms did not conceive of their relationship to the land in terms of private property.[34] After several unsuccessful attempts to buy land on Cape Mesurado in the Bassa country, Stockton finally procured a deed by holding a pistol to King Peter's head and announcing that the Americans came as benefactors, not enemies. The small colony was named "Liberia" after the Latin *liber*, or freeman.[35]

The following year, 1822, a confederation of eight chiefs of the Dei, Gola, and Mandingo kingdoms rose up in an attempt to destroy the colony.[36] A history of the ACS published by the Massachusetts Colonization Society recounts that "the colonists were attacked by about 800 natives. . . . Two weeks after, they were again attacked by double the former number."[37] The ACS agent who was in charge of the colony, Jehudi Ashmun, described the ensuing battle in the *African Repository*, noting that "the ground was drenched considerable" from "the quantities of blood."[38] Thus, while white ACS members sought to define "American colonization" in terms of "the virtues of the gospel, defended by the Almighty from the influences of paganism," to black Africans the struggle to found Liberia was as bloody and repressive as British or Spanish imperialism.[39]

Black Americans who chose to repatriate to Liberia likewise had powerful feelings about the white invasion of Africa that often belied the benevolent rhetoric of the American Colonization Society. In March 1824, Lott Cary led a black Americo-Liberian revolt against Jehudi Ashmun and white ACS rule. Ashmun had tried to induce repatriated black Americans to work harder by threatening to cut off the colonists' food rations, arguing that the subsidies encouraged indolence and pauperism. Cary and his followers seized control of the food and weapons, temporarily deposing Ashmun, who fled to sea. The insurrection lasted three months and ended when the ACS capitulated by rewriting the constitution to permit black colonists to hold certain appointive offices under the white colonial agent.[40]

In 1825, Ashmun was restored to power in Liberia and quickly began to expand the colony and to pursue his dream of a vast tropical empire on the west coast of Africa. Supported by gunships of the U.S. navy and with a militia subsidized by the federal government, Ashmun waged war on King Peter to the north and the Basa to the south, extending the colony by 150 miles. Accusing French and Spanish traders of "piratical depredations" on American shipping, he invaded and demolished their towns, thus solidifying the American monopoly of trade along the coast. Ashmun established trading posts at key sites and boldly predicted that the area of Cape Mount alone, which he had wrested away from King Peter, would be worth fifty thousand dollars a year to the United States in trade. Thrilled by Ashmun's success, William M. Blackford of Fredericksburg, Virginia declared in the *African Repository* that "the germ of an Americo-African empire has been planted" which would "flourish and expand until it overshadows a continent."[41]

One must be careful, however, of imposing overly simplistic binaries such as colonizer/colonized or black/white onto the Liberian situation.[42] The meaning of "race," "nationality," and "colonization" were extremely complex and fluid in Liberia at this time. One African man, for example, who had been sold into slavery, liberated from a slaver, and then returned to Liberia by the U.S. government was asked if he would prefer to be returned to his original home. He responded, "No, if I go back to my country they make me slave—I am here free. . . . I got my land—my wife—my children learn book—I am here a *white man*."[43] To many Africans, "whiteness" was not a function of race but of the colonial power conferred by Liberian citizenship. Black Americans, ironically, were thus perceived by indigenous Africans not as "brothers" but as "white." A historically accurate and theoretically nuanced paradigm thus needs to account for black Americans as both the colonizers and the colonized.[44]

The complexity of the relationship between the "colony" of Liberia and the United States is formidable. On the one hand, the U.S. government proved instrumental in the founding of Liberia, providing the initial funding and later supplying gunboats to protect the colony.[45] The ambivalence that underlies "American colonization" can be seen, however, in the federal government's refusal to recognize the Republic of Liberia after it declared independence in 1847. The reason, in part, was that America did not feel it could recognize a republican government of former slaves while slavery was still legal in the United States.[46] The ACS, on the other hand, remained deeply invested in its "colony" even after independence. Despite relinquishing direct control, the society continued to actively support Liberia. From 1848 to 1854, for example, the ACS chartered forty-one ships and sent nearly four thousand black Americans to the new republic.[47] The complexity of "American colonization" can be seen in the *African Repository*'s description of the newly established Republic of Liberia as being "another star set on the sable brow of night, [that] flashes along the coast of [African Americans'] fatherland! Yes, it is a child of our country!—outcast it may be—but still a child!"[48] This double consciousness—Liberia as both a "child" who shared a familial bond and an "outcast" exiled by race—maps the emotionally conflicted terrain of what I am calling America's "sentimental imperialism."

Stowe and the American Colonization Society

Harriet Beecher Stowe's pro-colonization conclusion to *Uncle Tom's Cabin* is historically puzzling, given that the ACS had come under withering attack by abolitionists in the Northeast as early as 1832. William Lloyd Garrison exposed the dark underside of ACS rhetoric in *Thoughts on African Colonization* (1832), which brought together excerpts from the *African Repository* (the official publication of the ACS) and written statements by blacks opposed to colonization. "The free people of color," Garrison quoted from the *African Repository*, "are by far . . . the MOST CORRUPT, DEPRAVED, AND ABANDONED [class of Americans]. They have no home, no country, no kindred, no friends. . . . Let them be maltreated ever so much."[49] Because Stowe did not address the question of colonization at any significant length in either her letters or *The Key to Uncle Tom's Cabin*, it is difficult to know precisely why she thought it was appropriate to deport nearly all of her surviving black characters to Africa. The most explicit connection between Stowe and the ACS can be traced back to her father, who advocated African colonization throughout his lifetime, and to his difficulties as the president of Lane Seminary in Cincinnati, Ohio.

At the annual meeting of the Colonization Society in Cincinnati in January 1833, Lyman Beecher called the efforts of the ACS "wise and successful" and "approved of Heaven, to facilitate the education and emancipation of slaves, and the abolition of slavery, at home."[50] One year later, however, Beecher's colonizationist views embroiled him in a heated debate with the students of Lane over the issue of immediate abolition. Infuriated by Beecher's support of the ACS and its plan to gradually do away with not only slavery but the black population of America, the students, led by Theodore Weld, issued a declaration of principles which called for "social intercourse according to character, irrespective of color." The trustees of Lane, as well as whites in Cincinnati, were outraged at the sight of students walking with blacks, both male and female, through the streets of Cincinnati. Beecher warned the students that "If you will visit in colored families, and walk with them in the streets, you will be overwhelmed."[51]

Lyman Beecher and Stowe's husband, Calvin, sought to appease the trustees and townspeople by delivering sermons reaffirming their commitment to African colonization.[52] In protest, the students staged a walkout, which became known as the "Lane rebellion," and left en masse for Oberlin College: to study with Charles Grandison Finney. Garrison labeled Lane Seminary "a Bastille of oppression" in the pages of the *Liberator*, and Beecher's reputation was badly damaged. Between 1836 and 1840 the average class size dwindled to five students. In 1845 there were no students at all. Beecher struggled to keep the doors of Lane open until 1851, when he finally retired, the same year that *Uncle Tom's Cabin* began appearing in serialized form in the *National Era*.[53]

Harriet Beecher Stowe remained loyal to her father and supported his views throughout the crisis at Lane and beyond. Although Stowe was sympathetic to the cause of immediate abolition, especially after angry mobs attacked James Birney's newspaper office in 1835 for printing proabolitionist editorials,[54] she nevertheless continued to support her father's colonizationist views well after they had been discredited by most people in abolitionist circles. (The year of the "Lane rebellion," the Reverend Robert J. Breckinridge reported from Boston that "Colonization is dead, in all the region; and the principles of our parent society, will never revive here anymore.")[55] In 1853, Stowe vehemently defended her father's reputation when Wendell Phillips wrote in the *Liberator* that Beecher's role in the Lane Debates demonstrated that "the weight of his hand had always been felt against the slave." In an effort to rehabilitate her father's reputation, Stowe utilized the profits that she had made from *Uncle Tom's Cabin* to organize, in collaboration with William Lloyd Garrison, an abolitionist lecture series bearing the name of her father and husband.[56]

Stowe's support for African colonization, however, clearly goes well beyond being simply a deeply felt sympathy for her father's beleaguered reputation. On July 9, 1851, one month after *Uncle Tom's Cabin* had begun appearing in weekly installments in the *National Era*, Stowe wrote to Frederick Douglass soliciting "information from one who has actually been a laborer" on a cotton plantation. Stowe asked Douglass if he could put her in touch with Henry Bibb and offered to contribute "something" to his newspaper "at some time when less occupied." She then remarked, "with regret," Douglass's "sentiment on two subjects,—the church and African colonization." Arguing defensively on behalf of her father, Stowe noted that her "father's sermons and prayers" on the Missouri question made "the strongest and deepest impressions" on her mind and assured Douglass of "the anguish of [her father's] soul for the poor slave at that time." She also made sharply clear her own position on African colonization, telling Douglass, "I would willingly, if I could, modify your views" on that issue.[57]

It may be that Stowe's faith in African colonization was buttressed when Liberia gained its independence in 1847 and when the fortunes of the ACS improved steadily throughout the early 1850s. Weakened by mounting debts and internal dissent over the leadership of Ralph R. Gurley, the ACS had stumbled through the 1840s. Unable to protect Liberia from British merchants in Sierre Leone and unable to convince the U.S. government to claim sovereignty over the colony, the directors of the ACS ordered the Liberians to proclaim their independence. Once the republic established independence, however, the fortunes of the ACS began to turn. In 1850, the Virginia legislature appropriated thirty thousand dollars a year for five years to support and encourage emigration.[58] The colonization movement also gained strength at this time when Ohio, Iowa, Michigan, and Illinois enacted so-called "Black Codes" and set aside money from their state treasuries to fund the removal of free blacks. This support for African colonization was, however, driven by a deeply racist impulse. Isaac Newton Blackford, an Indiana Supreme Court judge, warned that "a low, ignorant, degraded multitude of free blacks" would swarm into Indiana unless the colonizationist movement was supported. In response to such fears, the Indiana constitution barred African Americans from settling in the state and empowered the legislature to appropriate funds for the colonization of blacks. The *New York Tribune*, in turn, remarked that the Indiana constitution's declaration "all men are created equal" really meant "all men are created equal—except niggers."[59]

Given the racist subtext of so much of the colonizationist rhetoric, Stowe's support for the movement remains a historically puzzling and critically disturbing aspect of her newly canonized novel and needs to be explored more fully. *Uncle Tom's Cabin* is a text of profound contradictions—a novel that has been credited by white scholars with achieving "human representability for black Americans"[60] and yet whose main character, Uncle Tom, remains a powerful symbol of racism and obsequious behavior for contemporary blacks. These conflicting cultural legacies suggest that the "cultural work" of *Uncle Tom's Cabin* has still not yet been fully explained. In the next section I will attempt to navigate the critical vortex created when the two powerful discursive currents of colonization and sentimentalism collide.

"America Is the White Man's Home; God Has So Ordered It"

Mapping the intersections between Harriet Beecher Stowe's *Uncle Tom's Cabin* and the rhetoric of the American Colonization Society reveals a complex pattern of conjunctures and disjunctures. Although both Stowe and the ACS shared a fundamental belief in the Christian mission to colonize Africa, their views on issues such as racism and the ability of whites to learn to accept blacks in their midst were quite different, at least on the textual surface. By setting the discourse of the Colonization Society in dialogic relation to Stowe's views, as expressed in the novel and in *The Key to Uncle Tom's Cabin*, it becomes possible to see beneath the polished rhetorical surface of Stowe's canonical text. To do so requires a critical archeology that digs down beneath Stowe's benevolent intent to the level where repressed fears of miscege-nation ultimately compel her to send the vast majority of her surviving black characters to Liberia at the end of *Uncle Tom's Cabin*, in an act of sentimental imperialism.

The American Colonization Society's plan to repatriate free blacks to Liberia was based on a conception of national essentialism: blacks and whites were fundamentally different, and national identity was determined by racial identity. The First Annual Report of the ACS remarked, for example, that "You may manumit the slave, but you cannot make him a white

man. He still remains a negro or a mulatto. The mark and recollection of
his origin and his former state still adhere to him."[61] The essentialist logic
of racial nationalism can be seen here in the implicit argument that blacks
could not become "Americans" because, quite simply, they could not become "white." This myopically ahistorical argument simply refused to recognize that black and white Americans shared a common language, culture, and history dating back to the year before the Pilgrims landed at
Plymouth Rock. Despite the long and inextricably intertwined history of
black and white Americans, the first volume of the *African Repository* is
replete with reference to blacks as "alien enemies" and to Africa as their
"native shores."[62] This logic of racial nationalism was still prevalent at the
time Stowe was writing. In a letter published by the ACS in 1851, for
example, J. H. B. Latrobe wrote that "America is the white man's home;
God has so ordered it."[63]

The racial essentialism of the ACS not only rigidly categorized "Africans" as possessing certain indelible characteristics but stigmatized whites
as well. As one writer in the first volume of the *African Repository* wrote,
"Let us recollect that our fathers have placed them here; and that our
prejudices, prejudices too deep to be eradicated while they remain among
us, have produced the standard of their morals."[64] The statement is interesting in two respects. On the one hand, it inadvertently undermines the
essentialist argument that blacks were by nature a "degraded" race by acknowledging that whites played a significant role in shaping "the standard
of their morals." And, on the other hand, it reveals a belief that racism was
endemic to the white race ("while they remain among us"). The idea that
prejudice against blacks was intractable runs throughout the ACS rhetoric
and strangely justifies the racism and white self-interest that lay just beneath the ACS's pretense of evangelism and abolitionism. "As bitter an
enemy as I am to slavery," one supporter of the society wrote, "I cannot
greatly desire that . . . slavery should be abolished, unless its unfortunate
and degraded subjects can be removed from the country."[65]

By the early 1850s, when Stowe began writing *Uncle Tom's Cabin*, the
rhetoric of the ACS (particularly in the Northeast) had changed, in response to Garrison's attacks, Liberia's attainment of independence, and
the inescapable realization that America had become significantly more
multicultural in terms of its population and identity. (In 1825, 11 percent
of the American population was foreign-born; by 1845 the figure had
risen to 35 percent, and by 1855 to over 50 percent).[66] The struggle within
the ACS to maintain its rigidly monocultural vision of national identity
at a time when international immigration was diversifying the country's
population at an unprecedented rate can be seen in a speech presented by
the Reverend John Orcutt to the Massachusetts Colonization Society in
1852. Orcutt begins his oration by noting that "immigrants are flocking

from other nations, and they can be assimilated. All except this one [black] race, can intermingle and become one with us." Upholding the principle of racial nationalism outlined by the founders of the ACS, Orcutt insists that "these two races [cannot] be common citizens of this republic." And yet, instead of attacking blacks as a "vicious" race, as earlier ACS writers often did, Orcutt concentrates on the apprehensions of his white listeners, reminding them that "the slave population of the South doubles once in thirty years" and demanding to know, given "the terrible state of things," how the "white population [can] sleep at night, in the midst of them." Orcutt knowingly plays upon the fear of miscege-nation that was a mainstay of ACS rhetoric by arguing that "the impossibility of intermarriage renders *their* assimilation, and their standing upon an equality with us, impossible." A multiracial conception of "America" in which blacks and whites would be recognized as equals and compatriots is, Orcutt maintains, prohibited by God: "Providence has *decreed* that it cannot be." And thus the only possible solution is "for the black man to return to his original home."[67]

Like the ACS, Stowe's support for African colonization was predicated on a conception of racial nationalism that was covered over by a heartfelt evangelical fervor to spread Christianity to "heathen" Africa. Near the end of *Uncle Tom's Cabin* she writes that "It is the statement of missionaries, that, of all races of the earth, none have received the Gospel with such eager docility as the African. The principle of reliance and unquestioning faith, which is its foundation, is more a *native element* in this race than any other" (421, my emphasis). In *The Key to Uncle Tom's Cabin*, Stowe observed of "the negro race" that "the divine graces of love and faith, when in-breathed by the Holy Spirit, find in their *natural temperament* a more congenial atmosphere" (my emphasis).[68] For Stowe, this "native" receptivity to religion not only made blacks "naturally" open to Christian teachings but also meant that they were especially well suited as missionaries. The racial essentialism that forms the basis of Stowe's sentimental imperialism is clearly illustrated in Topsy's decision to leave the United States as a "missionary to one of the stations in Africa" and to teach "the children of *her own country*" (463, my emphasis).

Like many ACS writers, Stowe construed black Americans as being fundamentally different from white ones. In the preface to the novel she describes African Americans as "an exotic race, whose ancestors, born beneath a tropic sun, brought with them, and perpetuated to their descendants, a character so essentially unlike the hard and dominant Anglo-Saxon race, as for many years to have won from it only misunderstanding and contempt" (v). The colonizationist conclusion is thus foreshadowed in the opening pages of the novel. Because the slaves' ancestors were "born beneath a tropic sun"—an essentialist identity "perpetuated" from one generation to the next—they are fundamentally "unlike . . . [the] Anglo-Saxon race" and thus must return to their "exotic" homeland. This belief that race determines national identity runs throughout the novel. Stowe, for example, describes Uncle Tom as having "truly African features" (32). When George Harris discusses the plight of black Americans, he refers to them as "despairing African fugitives" (216). And in discussing the domestic skills of African American women, Stowe writes of Dinah, "She was a native and essential cook, as much as Aunt Chloe,— cooking being an indigenous talent of the African race" (225). Like the writings of the ACS, Stowe's sentimental imperialism represents blacks as indelibly marked "Africans" and as "essentially unlike" the "dominant" white race.

And yet Stowe's vision of African colonization has a noticeably softer edge than that of contemporary ACS writers like J. H. B. Latrobe or John Orcutt. One striking difference, at least on the surface, is Stowe's belief that racial prejudice could be overcome. She uses the triangular relationship between Topsy, Ophelia, and Little Eva to demonstrate how the "evil" of racism could be undone. When St. Clare gives Topsy to Ophelia, he confronts her with the accusation that "You loathe [blacks] as you would a snake or a toad. . . . You would not have them abused; but you don't want to have anything to do with them yourselves. You would send them to Africa, out of your sight and smell, and then send a missionary or two to do up all the self-denial of elevating them compendiously"; to which Ophelia is forced to admit, "there may be some truth in this" (195). After Little Eva tells Topsy on her deathbed that she loves her, Miss Ophelia sheds a sentimental tear and implores Topsy, "don't give up! I can love you, though I am not like that dear little child. I hope I've learnt something of the love of Christ from her. . . . I'll try to help you grow up a good Christian girl" (321).

In *The Key to Uncle Tom's Cabin*, Stowe observes that "Miss Ophelia . . . represents one great sin, of which, unconsciously, American Christians have allowed themselves to be guilty . . . the prejudice of caste and color."[69] Unlike many ACS writers who held that "here invincible prejudices exclude [blacks] . . . the bar, the pulpit, and our legislative halls are shut to them by an irresistible force of public sentiment,"[70] Stowe does not view racism as intractable but seems to make a self-conscious effort to suggest that these "invincible prejudices" could be overcome. In *The Key*, Stowe credits "the gentle Eva, who is an impersonation in childish form of the love of Christ," with "solv[ing] . . . the problem which Ophelia has long been unable to solve by dint of utmost hammering and vehement effort."[71]

And yet a closer examination of the way in which Stowe's implicit fear of miscege-nation drives her sentimental imperialism calls into question just how different Stowe's views really were from those of the American Colonization Society. In the same chapter on "Miss Ophelia" in *The Key*, Stowe writes that those "who keep up this prejudice may be said to be, in a certain sense, slaveholders." And yet she follows this observation with the qualification: "It is not meant by this that all distinctions of society should be broken over, and that people should be obliged to choose their intimate associates from a class unfitted by education and habits to sympathize with them." Here the limits to Stowe's attack on "prejudice" begin to become clear. Stowe denounces racism as the "most baneful feature" of slavery but stops well short of calling for complete equality. Like Orcutt, she seems to maintain that the two races should not intermarry—that "not all distinctions" should be done away with and that whites should not "choose their intimate associates" from the black race (although she softens the blow by describing African Americans in terms of "class" instead of race). Indeed, in the next paragraph she goes on to comment that "The negro should not be lifted out of his sphere of life because he is a negro; but he should be treated with Christian courtesy *in* his sphere."[72]

This problematic notion that blacks should occupy a separate but equal sphere (reminiscent of the rhetoric that was used to keep women from complete social equality at this time) reveals an underlying dimension of class essentialism that further complicates the question of Stowe's commitment to overcoming racism. As she notes in *The Key to Uncle Tom's Cabin*, "*true* socialism . . . comes from the spirit of Christ . . . without breaking down existing orders of society."

> Men would break up all ranks of society, and throw all property into a common stock; but Christ would inspire the higher class with [a] Divine Spirit. . . . In this way, and not by an outward and physical division of property, shall all things be had in common. And when the white race shall regard their superiority over the coloured one only as a talent intrusted for the advantage of their weaker brother, *then* will the prejudice of caste melt away in the light of Christianity.[73]

The relationship between race, class, and benevolence is exceedingly complicated here. On the one hand, it appears that Stowe advocates a form of benevolent socialism, where "all things [shall] be had in common." And yet, upon closer analysis, it becomes evident that her Christian rhetoric merely papers over a rigid belief in the status quo of a class system defined along racial lines. For Stowe explicitly states that her kind of "*true* socialism" does not advocate breaking up "all ranks of society" or throwing "all property into a common stock." Instead, she advocates a form of benevolent domination whereby "the higher class," inspired by a "Divine Spirit," will watch over the lower ones, "their weaker brother." In doing so, Stowe justifies the "superiority" of the "white race" by imagining a divinely sanctioned system in which "the prejudice of caste [will] melt away in the light of Christianity," without disturbing the racial or class hierarchies that work to keep blacks "weaker."

This essentialist view of race and class is highly problematic in terms of Stowe's ideological commitment to both abolition and the women's movement. Jane Tompkins credited Stowe with "turn[ing] the socio-political order upside down";[74] and yet in light of Stowe's belief that blacks were "native" to Africa and that the class structure could not be changed, the idea that she advocated radical social change must be critically reevaluated. As Karen Sánchez-Eppler has insightfully observed, the first generation of feminist scholars working on Stowe often conflated her views of race and "true womanhood." By deconstructing the "presumed alliance between abolitionist goals and domestic values," Sánchez-Eppler writes, we uncover a "rhetorical crossing . . . fraught with asymmetries and contradictions."[75]

The "asymmetries and contradictions" that undergird Stowe's views on African colonization can be clearly seen in the case of Topsy. Stowe carefully describes Topsy's domestic training, which at first glance seems to prepare her for a life of "true womanhood" in a postabolition America. "Miss Ophelia began with Topsy," Stowe writes, "by taking her into her chamber . . . and solemnly commencing a course of instruction of the art and mystery of bed-making." Stowe goes on to describe Ophelia's "martyrdom": "With a self-sacrifice that some of our readers will appreciate, [Ophelia] resolved, instead of comfortably making her own bed, sweeping and dusting her own chamber . . . to condemn herself to the martyrdom of instructing Topsy to perform these operations" (263). According to the tenets of Stowe's domestic philosophy, Ophelia is initiating Topsy into "the *science* and *training*" of the "high and sacred duties" of womanhood.[76]

The class and racial hierarchies that underlie Stowe's apparently democratic construction of "true womanhood" begin to come into view, however, when Topsy arrives in New England and the question of where she fits into the "existing order of society" must be answered. Stowe writes that Topsy is perceived to be "an odd and unnecessary addition" to the "well-trained domestic establishment" in New England (463). As Jacqueline Jones's well-documented study *Labor of Love, Labor of Sorrow* amply demonstrates, Topsy's sentimental education in "the art and mystery of bed-making" would in all likelihood have prepared her not for a place in the "Cult of True Womanhood" but for a life of domestic servitude. (By 1900, for example, nine out of ten servants in the South were black.)[77] Given Stowe's racial and class essentialism, then, there is no place for Topsy to go, finally, but to "her country" in Liberia. Stowe's sentimental imperialism, which constructs blacks as "naturally" suited for missionary work, thus conveniently circumvents the problems of miscege-nation and class mobility by simply sending all of the surviving African American characters to Liberia at the end of the novel.

Harriet Beecher Stowe's Response

The intertextual echoes between *Uncle Tom's Cabin* and the statements of the American Colonization Society raise haunting questions that go to the heart of the arguments used in the mid-1980s to bring Harriet Beecher Stowe into the canon of American literature. Does Stowe's ambivalence about the place of blacks in a postabolition America constitute racism? Is George Harris's final argument nothing more than a literary minstrel show, a blackface rendition of the ideology of the American Colonization Society? Does Stowe's celebration of the sentimental virtues of true womanhood disguise a white, middle-class, Eurocentric view of national identity? These are perplexing critical questions that, though compelling, may be misleading in both their directness and their simplicity. By way of answering them, I will examine more carefully Stowe's own response to the charge of being pro-colonizationist in the years immediately following the publication of *Uncle Tom's Cabin*.

Stowe made several notable and explicit attempts to disassociate herself from the ACS. Thomas F. Gossett's research shows that in 1853 Stowe wrote a letter to the American and Foreign Anti-Slavery Society in New York denying any connection to the ACS. Although the letter itself has not survived, a summation of Stowe's retraction was recorded in the minutes of the meeting: "Stowe had no sympathy with the coercive policy of the Colonization Society, but she thought Liberia now a 'fixed fact,' and that the opportunity there afforded of sustaining a republican government of free people of color ought not to be disregarded by them or their friends." Stowe concluded her letter with the assurance that she was "not a Colonizationist." Leonard Bacon, a close friend of the Beecher family, then is reported by the secretary to have stood and declared, "Mrs. Stowe had told him that if she were to write 'Uncle Tom' again, she would not send George Harris to Liberia."[78]

Stowe's letter, in all likelihood, reveals more about her response to the criticism she received after writing the novel than her thoughts as she penned George Harris's declaration that "the whole splendid continent of Africa opens before us. . . . *Our nation* shall . . . plant there mighty republics" (461). The Reverend Henry Clarke Wright, for example, wrote of Stowe's novel that the pro-colonization passages were "but the echoes of the arguments by which the negro haters of this republic have for thirty years been seeking to drive the free colored people from this land." The

Provincial Freeman, a black antislavery journal published in Canada, was even harsher: "Uncle Tom must be killed, George Harris exiled! Heaven for dead Negroes! Liberia for living mulattoes. Neither one can live on the American continent. . . . Death or banishment is our doom[,] say the Slaveocrats, the Colonizationists, and Mrs. Stowe."[79]

Perhaps the most telling evidence that these attacks caused Stowe to modify her views on colonization is the conclusion to her next novel, *Dred* (1856). Dred, unlike Uncle Tom, is a strong black figure, a man of "herculean strength" and "an imperial air." Anything but obsequious, Dred "yearn[s] for liberty"; he kills a white man and then flees to the dismal swamps. Rather than constructing this violence as being a "natural" feature of the "African race," Stowe carefully frames Dred's rebellion in terms of "the more successful [revolution] which purchased for our fathers a national existence." The conclusion of the novel also demonstrates that she had substantially modified her views on colonization in the four years since completing *Uncle Tom's Cabin.* In the closing pages some of the surviving black characters emigrate to a "colony" in Canada. Others, however, move to New York, where Milly says of her Sunday school congregation, composed of "white, black, and foreign" children, "I don't make no distinctions of color,—I just don't believe in them. White chil'en, when they 'haves themselves, is jest as good as black, and I loves 'em jest as well."[80]

These ideological shifts, to Stowe's credit, seem to indicate that she listened carefully to black abolitionists like Frederick Douglass and Martin Delany, who criticized the pro-colonization passages in *Uncle Tom's Cabin.* The conclusion of *Dred* does not, however, change the fact that the ending to her sentimental "masterpiece" appears deeply problematic when judged by the very standards that were used to admit her to the canon. A close analysis of George Harris's final letter suggests that Stowe was more attuned to the ideological implications of African colonization than she later admitted. George Harris states, "I grant that this Liberia may have subserved all sorts of purposes, by being played off, in the hands of our oppressors, against us" (460). Stowe thus works carefully to negotiate a distinction between the ACS and the colony of Liberia which distances her from the more controversial aspects of the society's history. Rather than openly condemning the racism of the ACS (which she was ostensibly trying to overcome), Stowe invokes the Christian rhetoric of sentimental imperialism to simplistically dismiss the fact that Liberia had been founded at gunpoint. "But the question to me is," George Harris concludes, "Is there not a God above all man's schemes? May he not have overruled their [the ACS's] designs, and founded for us a nation by them?" (460).

The carefully crafted rhetorical complexity of George Harris's letter demonstrates that Stowe was well informed of the most common criticisms leveled against African colonization. One of the most frequent and powerful attacks was the argument that emigrating to Liberia meant abandoning the four million African Americans still enslaved in the United States. Henry Foster, a black abolitionist, wrote, "we look upon the man of color that would be influenced by the Society to emigrate to Liberia, as an enemy to the cause and a traitor to his brethren."[81] Another frequent criticism was eloquently articulated by Frederick Douglass in his speech "The Free Negro's Place Is in America" (1851). "Simultaneously with the landing of the pilgrims," Douglass noted, "there landed slaves on the shores of this continent. . . . We have grown up with you, we have watered your soil with our tears, nourished it with our blood, tilled it with our hands."[82]

Stowe responds carefully to each of these arguments in the conclusion to *Uncle Tom's Cabin*. George Harris asks rhetorically, "Do you say that I am deserting my enslaved brethren?" To which he answers, "What can I do for them here?. . . A nation has a right to argue, remonstrate, implore, and present the case of its race,—which an individual has not" (461). The more difficult question to answer, however, was the one posed by Frederick Douglass about the multicultural origins of the nation. This query proved particularly nettlesome when posed by abolitionists of mixed race, such as Douglass, William Wells Brown, or Henry Bibb, whose interraciality served as a powerful metaphor for the cultural hybridity of the nation's history. George Harris's response provides a telling insight into the racial essentialism that links Stowe's monocultural conception of "American" identity to that of the ACS. "Full half the blood in my veins is the hot and hasty Saxon" (462), George Harris writes. Having acknowledged the interracial hybridity of American identity, however, Harris immediately moves to disavow it. "I have no wish to pass for an American, or to identify myself with them. It is with the oppressed, enslaved African race that I cast in my lot and, if I wished anything, I would wish myself two shades darker, rather than one lighter. The desire and yearning of my soul is for an African *nationality*" (460). Stowe's novel thus concludes with the assertion of a distinctly monocultural vision of "American" identity, self-consciously invoking the racial and national essentialism that links her sentimental imperialism to the ACS's view of "American colonization."

This one-dimensional view of the historical complexity of black masculinity (Uncle Tom) and American identity (George Harris) has given *Uncle Tom's Cabin* a long and controversial cultural history. Langston Hughes called the novel "the most cussed and discussed book of its time."[83] The debates that raged in the mid–nineteenth century were played out again in the 1980s, when Tompkins, Fisher, and others succeeded in getting

Stowe admitted into the canon of American literature. In response to Fisher's claim that Stowe had changed the "census" of American letters, Richard Yarborough condemned the "tragic failure of imagination [that] prevented her from envisioning blacks . . . as viable members of American society."[84] Hortense J. Spillers answered white feminists like Tompkins, who claimed that *Uncle Tom's Cabin* "turned the socio-political order upside down," by attacking the foundations of Stowe's sentimental vision: "If the 'blueprint' for 'colonizing' the 'world' in the name of the 'family state,' under the leadership of Christian women, is prefigured in this novel, then I know precisely where I belong in its domestic economies, and I want no part of it."[85]

Perhaps one of the most blistering attacks on Stowe came three decades earlier, from James Baldwin in *Notes from a Native Son.* "*Uncle Tom's Cabin*," wrote Baldwin, "is a very bad novel."

> Sentimentality, the ostentatious parading of excessive and spurious emotion . . . is always the signal of secret and virulent inhumanity, the mask of cruelty. *Uncle Tom's Cabin* . . . is a catalogue of violence. . . . One can hardly claim for the protest novels the lofty purpose they claim for themselves. . . . They emerge for what they are: a mirror of our confusion, dishonesty, panic, trapped and immobilized in the sunlit prison of the American Dream.[86]

Baldwin here strips away the veneer of sentimentality to uncover the discursive violence of Stowe's literary removal of the novel's entire "census" of free blacks. The question is: Now that the violence of sentimental imperialism and "American colonization" has been exposed, where do we go from here? To become entangled in the bitter debate about the racism and nativism that underlies Stowe's benevolent call to bring Christianity to Africa risks an internecine war between white feminists and African American critics. "Within this web of lust and fury," Baldwin writes, "black and white can only thrust and counter-thrust . . . so that they go down into the pit together."[87]

Rather than becoming caught up in an endless, mutually destructive cycle, I want to try to steer the debate in a new direction by negotiating what I am calling the "multicultural turn." This new hermeneutic strategy is indebted to Eve Kosofsky Sedgwick's call for "reparative criticism." After nearly twenty years, Kosofsky points out, "the detection of hidden patterns of violence and their exposure . . . have become the common currency of cultural and historicist studies."[88] In her introduction to *Novel Gazing*, Sedgwick calls for a more affirmative, less paranoid style of criticism for queer theory. My goal is to embrace the spirit of Sedgwick's challenge and to articulate a reparative model for multicultural studies. Thus, rather than focusing (once again) on racial exclusion and the hegemonic politics of canonical literature, thereby reifying the power of monoculturalism even as it comes under attack, I want to work toward developing a new, radically *inclusive* critical paradigm.

This is not to say that the racist subtext of Stowe's novel should be ignored in the name of affirming "American" values. God forbid that we go backward. The first step in the multicultural turn must still be a discursive archeology, to uncover the myriad of ways in which nativism wraps itself in the mantle of democracy and/or sentimental benevolence. Having fully exposed the racial nationalism that underlies Stowe's sentimental imperialism, however, I want to initiate the "turn" toward *re*incorporating African Americans living in Liberia. Rather than seeing blacks as an "alien race" or, in Stowe's words, as "essentially unlike the hard and dominant Anglo-Saxon race," we need to theorize the "colony" of Liberia as part of what I will call "the American Diaspora"—an integral, if not yet well-understood, dimension of the transnational scope of "American" identity in the mid–nineteenth century.

Letters from Liberia

To initiate the critical turn away from focusing solely on the forces of exclusion toward constructing a more radically inclusive vision of the imagined community of "America" requires reading George Harris not simply as a reflection of Stowe's ideology but as a historical referent. What this hermeneutic shift reveals, interestingly, is that George Harris's views constitute a historically accurate depiction of nineteenth-century black nationalism.[89] He states, for example, "I have no wish to pass for an American or to identify myself with them. . . . On the shores of Africa, I see a republic. . . . There it is my wish to go to find myself a people." (460). Strikingly, Harris's words echo those of Lott Cary, who was one of the first black settlers to emigrate to Liberia in the 1820s. "I am an African," Cary wrote shortly before leaving for Liberia, "and in this my country, however meritorious my conduct, and respectable my character, I cannot receive the credit due to either. I wish to go to a country where I shall be estimated by my merits, not by my complexion; and I feel bound to labor for my suffering race."[90] Cary went on to become one of the most fervent and effective advocates of black nationalism in Liberia, leading the revolt against white ACS rule in 1824.

A historically accurate critical reconstruction of America's transnational identity, however, needs to engage as fully as possible the dialogical complexity of black perspectives on Liberia. Certainly not all visitors to Liberia saw in it, as Harris did, a great "republic of picked men" (460). In *Four Months in Liberia* (1855), William Nesbit openly condemned Liberia: "On stepping ashore, I found that we had been completely gulled and done for. The statements generally circulated in [the United States] by the Colonization agents, respecting the thrift and prosperity of that country, are most egregious falsehoods. . . . The whole country presents the most woe begone and hopeless aspect."[91] And yet to many other African Americans, Liberia offered a haven from white racism at a time when the enactment of the Fugitive Slave Law seemed to legally sanction the institution of slavery even in the so-called "Free States." The Reverend Samuel Williams, for example, in the introduction to his book *Four Years in Liberia*, explains that he decided to go to Liberia after being prohibited from voting in Pennsylvania on an amendment to the state constitution intended to revoke African American suffrage. Williams, like Stowe, argued that a distinction should be made between the American Colonization Society and Liberia. "When we oppose the colonization cause," Williams wrote, "we oppose Liberia . . . [but] I believe that the time is not far off when many who now oppose the operations of Liberia will either come to her embrace themselves or will send their children to enjoy the blessings of liberty and equality, that the government holds out to all the oppressed sons of our race in every clime."[92]

Historically, the plight of black emigrants to Liberia proved far more difficult than either Stowe or Williams was willing to acknowledge. The letters of Peyton Skipwith, who emigrated to Liberia in 1833 and lived there until his death thirteen years later, expose a dark historical underside to George Harris's fantasy of "mighty republics, that, growing with the rapidity of tropical vegetation, shall be for all coming ages" (461). Skipwith was freed along with his wife and children by his white master, John Cocke, an adamant supporter of the ACS, on the condition that they leave the country to repatriate in Liberia. Skipwith's first letter from Liberia is, however, utterly devoid of the ideological zeal of a glorious return to his "native land." "After fifty Six days on the ocean," Skipwith writes to his former master, "we all landed Safe on new years day and hav all had the fever and I hav lost [my six-year-old daughter,] Felicia." The next letter, dated March 6, 1835, opens: "I embrace this opportunity to write you these few lines to inform you that I am not well with a blindness of nights so I cannot see."[93] Within the first year, Skipwith would lose his wife, Lydia, and two of his six children to "African fever." (Statistical analysis shows that before 1843, 22 percent of all immigrants died within the first year of their arrival.)[94]

Skipwith's letters also provide insight into how Christian rhetoric and American imperialism were intertwined in the founding of the "colony" of Liberia. Like George Harris's, Skipwith's writing is filled with evangelical imagery and the fervor of nationalism. "I believe," Skipwith writes, "I shall have more help in this dark benighted land, to try and civilize the heathens and bring them to know life and life eternal." Shortly before

Liberia gained its independence, Skipwith wrote to Cocke, "Sir, I am in hopes that when the Constitution [of Liberia] is presented that the Eyes of the blind will become opened."[95] Skipwith's heartfelt evangelical mission thus reveals that Stowe's benevolent rhetoric was not simply a rhetorical ruse but an accurate reflection of the mid-nineteenth-century's faith in the power of Christian reform.

And yet just as Skipwith's letters provide historical context for Stowe's evangelism, so too does the epistolary evidence give credence to the argument that there was an imperialistic subtext to George Harris's stated intent "to conquer . . . the continent of Africa" (462). In a letter dated April 22, 1840, Skipwith describes "the greatest war that was ever fought" in which "three americans" held off "about four Hundred men." At the end of the battle, Skipwith writes, the three men returned to Monrovia bearing the head of the leader of the indigenous African kingdom, to be "made an ornament in the Hands of Governor Buchanan."[96] Such barbarism, committed in the name of bringing the light of the gospel to the dark continent, foretells the imperialistic "horror" that Joseph Conrad would recount half a century later in *Heart of Darkness*.

Skipwith's letters, furthermore, belie Stowe's vision of a monolithic "African" identity and the notion that black settlers gave up their "American" identity once they set foot on African soil. Read in a transnational multicultural context, Skipwith's writings reveal that the cultural and familial ties between Americo-Liberians and the land of their birth were not so easily severed. During his thirteen years in Liberia, Peyton Skipwith never stopped writing to his master or the family he had left behind in America. Moreover, Skipwith's description of the relationships between black repatriates and indigenous Africans—"those [repatriated black Americans] that are well off hav the nativs as Slavs"—underscores the need for far more ideologically complex and racially nuanced critical paradigms to make sense of the transnational complexities of Liberia as, in President Monroe's words, "a little black America destined to shine gemlike in the darkness of vast Africa."

.   .   .   .   .

To answer, by way of conclusion, the question of how Stowe's intertextual connections to the American Colonization Society problematize her newly attained canonical status, let me invoke Jane Tompkins's argument from *Sensational Designs*. The purpose of the American Renaissance, Tompkins writes, is to "provide people with an image of themselves and of their history, with conceptions of justice, and . . . attitudes towards, race, class, sex, and nationality."[97] I agree with James Baldwin that *Uncle Tom's Cabin* is "a mirror of our confusion."[98] Beneath its critically important representation of the central place of white women in the domestic sphere, Stowe's novel inadvertently reveals the conflict within the dominant white society between the benevolent impulse to abolish slavery and the innermost fears of miscege-nation. *Uncle Tom's Cabin* also provides a historically accurate (though critically underappreciated) insight into the ambivalence within the African American community about whether blacks would ever achieve democratic freedom in the United States. In this sense Stowe's sentimental narrative gives us "an image of [our]selves and of [our] history" in all of its transnational, multicultural complexity. *Uncle Tom's Cabin* thus deserves its place in the new, more ideologically nuanced, multicultural canon of American literature.

HISTORICAL INTERLUDE

DIS-FIGURING BLACK BODIES ON THE WHITE PAGE

The federal census of 1840 first enumerated the mentally ill or, as they were then officially classified, the "insane and idiots." The statistics gathered by the government revealed a startling discrepancy between northern and southern blacks which became part of the acrimonious debate slowly tearing the nation apart in the decades prior to the Civil War. While the census indicated no appreciable difference between whites living in the North and those in the South, the incidence of insanity among African Americans in the free states appeared to be nearly ten times greater (1 in 162.4 in the North compared to 1 in 1,558 in the slaveholding states). Moreover, the statistics documented a significant decrease from Maine to the Mason-Dixon line. In Maine, the census showed, every fourteenth black was found to be either "insane" or an "idiot"; in New Hampshire, every twenty-eighth; in Massachusetts, every forty-third; in New Jersey, every two hundred and ninety-seventh. In neighboring Delaware, just across the Mason-Dixon line, the rate suddenly dropped by half—leading one writer in the *Southern Literary Messenger* to conclude that blacks grew "more vicious in a state of freedom."[1]

The accuracy of the Census of 1840 came under sharp attack from statistician and physician Edward Jarvis and African American physician James McCune Smith. Jarvis noticed that according to federal figures the town of Scarboro, Maine was home to six insane blacks, although the state census showed that the town had no African American residents. In Worcester, Massachusetts the federal census maintained that a remarkable 133 of 151 blacks were insane. Jarvis published his findings in two separate articles in the *American Journal of Insanity* and went before the U.S. Senate to report on the discrepancies between the state and federal censuses. James McCune Smith also petitioned Congress to investigate the Census of 1840. Smith's findings revealed that in 116 towns in the North that had no black residents whatsoever, the federal census listed 36 blacks who were deaf and dumb, 38 who were blind, and 186 who suffered from mental illness.[2]

In spite of Smith and Jarvis's extensive documentation of the errors of the Census of 1840, proslavery advocates continued to trumpet the statistics as proof that African Americans could not survive in a condition of freedom. In response to Jarvis's findings, Secretary of State John C. Calhoun read a statement on the floor of the U.S. Senate attributing the attack not to "gross and glaring errors [in] the late census" but to the fact that "[the census] exhibits the condition of the free negroes of the non-slaveholding States to be so much worse than that of the slaves of the other States, in reference to the far greater prevalence of insanity, blindness, deafness, and dumbness." Calhoun argued that rather than "bettering [the] condition of the negro or African race, by changing . . . the slaveholding States, [abolition] would render [blacks] far worse." Freedom, Calhoun concluded, "would be a curse instead of a blessing."[3]

Robert Walker likewise utilized the disputed figures of the federal census to support his call for the annexation of Texas. In an open letter to "the public" published in 1844, Walker argued that "the free black is (as the census proves) much more wretched in condition, and debased in morals, than the slave." Walker went on to observe that "the negroes, however equal in law, are not equal in fact. They are nowhere found in the colleges or universities, upon the bench or at the bar, in the muster, or the jury-box, in legislative or executive stations; nor does marriage, the great bond of society, unite the white with the negro, except in the rare occurrence of such unnatural alliance, to call forth the scorn or disgust of the whole community." In response to the question "is slavery never to disappear from the Union?" Walker advocated the balm of Manifest Destiny. Walker believed that by "open[ing] Texas as a safety-valve" slavery would "slowly and gradually recede, and finally disappear into the boundless regions of Mexico, and Central and Southern America."[4] For Walker, the "degradation" of blacks in freedom, as demonstrated by the census figures, suggested that "America" would attain its Manifest Destiny not when slavery was abolished but only when African Americans had disappeared.

The Census of 1840 provides a powerful illustration of the way in which black bodies were routinely dis-figured within the margins of the white page. These forces of discursive mutilation need to be carefully theorized when reading the first African American novel, William Wells Brown's *Clotel; or, The President's Daughter* (1853). Brown's novel—like the discursive bodies of blacks rendered deaf, dumb, blind, and insane by the Census of 1840—is textually dis-figured. Self-consciously fragmenting the narrative, Brown continuously disrupts his own black voice by inserting a vast array of white voices into the novel. In doing so, he makes painfully clear the historical forces that openly challenge his ability to freely imagine "America." And yet, by formally incorporating these disruptive white voices into his narrative, Brown constructs exactly the kind of hybrid conception of the nation that these forces of exclusion worked so fervently to prevent.

CHAPTER FIVE

WILLIAM WELLS BROWN:

MAPPING THE AMERICAN DIASPORA

"*You* have a country; but what country have *I*, or any one
like me, born of slave mothers? . . Sir, I have n't any
country, any more than I have any father but I'm going to
have one. I don't want anything of *your* country,
except to be let alone."
(Harriet Beecher Stowe, *Uncle Tom's Cabin*, 1852)

"Let's send them to Liberia," said Carlton.
"Why should they go to Africa, any more than to the Free
States or to Canada?" asked the wife.
"They would be in their native land," he answered.
"Is not this their native land? What right have we, more
than the Negro, to the soil here, or to style ourselves native
Americans? Indeed it is as much their home as ours, and I
have sometimes thought it was more theirs."
(William Wells Brown, *Clotel*, 1853)

WILLIAM WELLS BROWN'S *Clotel; or, The President's Daughter* offers an important dialogic response to Harriet Beecher Stowe's
pro-colonization conclusion in *Uncle Tom's Cabin*. Writing in
the midst of the intense excitement surrounding the unprecedented sales
of Stowe's abolitionist masterpiece, Brown cannily copies and challenges
Stowe's sentimental vision. Whereas Stowe's character George Harris insists that he has neither a country nor a father, Brown's story of Thomas
Jefferson's unacknowledged, interracial offspring argues insistently that
African Americans were indeed part of the "family of nations."[1] And yet,
as in *Uncle Tom's Cabin*, all of Brown's surviving black characters end up
in exile, living outside the geographic boundaries of the United States.
Taken together, these two novels provide a critically important insight
into the cultural conflict at the heart of the nation in the volatile period
just before the Civil War and show us the country struggling to answer
the question of whether blacks could ever be fully constituted members
of the imagined community of "America."

The relationship between *Uncle Tom's Cabin* and *Clotel* is exceedingly
complicated. Both novels were written in direct response to the Fugitive

Slave Law of 1850, which extended the property rights of southern slave-holders over runaway slaves in the "free states." Brown clearly knew and admired Stowe's novel, remarking in the introduction to *Clotel* that he hoped the extraordinary commercial success of *Uncle Tom's Cabin* would "prepare the public of Great Britain and America" for a novel written "by a real fugitive slave."[2] Brown's angry response to George Harris's declaration that "I have no wish to pass for an American"[3] was no doubt exacerbated by forced political exile. Brown had been traveling in Europe when the fugitive slave laws were enacted. As a runaway slave, he discovered he could not return to the United States without the threat of once again becoming a slave. Like the characters in his novel, Brown found freedom only by living abroad. And yet despite his rage at American politics, Brown always vehemently insisted that the United States was his "native land."

Setting Brown's novel in dialogic relation with Harriet Beecher Stowe's *Uncle Tom's Cabin* thus productively complicates our understanding of the "American Diaspora." Whereas repatriated black Americans like George Harris voluntarily emigrated to Liberia, William Wells Brown's exile was externally imposed. The inclusion of *Clotel* in this new multicultural conception of the American Renaissance thus meaningfully extends the transnational borders of the imagined community of the nation. By incorporating the "colonies" of fugitive slaves living in Europe, Canada, and Haiti, a much more complex and historically accurate portrait of the multicultural expanse of "American" identity begins to come into focus. The irony inherent in the fact that Brown composed the first African American novel while living in exile outside the geographical borders of the United States adds yet another layer of meaning to the phrase "ruthless democracy" and provides an important critical opportunity for better understanding national identity as seen from the farthest reaches of the American Diaspora.

Like the juxtaposition of Hawthorne and Ridge, the inclusion of William Wells Brown's novel raises intriguing yet difficult questions about aesthetics and form (even in comparison to Harriet Beecher Stowe's "popular" sentimental novel). The hermeneutic challenge of reading the first African American novel is to make sense of the complicated array of newspaper clippings, poems, passages from the Declaration of Independence, plagiarized stories, and other discursive miscellanea that continually intrude into and interrupt the narrative. Given that Brown was writing at a time when fugitive slaves were denied the right to speak in court on their own behalf, I want to approach *Clotel*'s fragmented narrative not as a poorly executed example of the novel form but as a sophisticated discursive strategy, designed to comment on Brown's plight as an exiled writer living in the American Diaspora. While Benedict Anderson has insightfully analyzed the important role that novels play in constructing the imagined community of the nation, he never explicitly addresses the question of whether an author's freedom to imagine the nation in his or her own image is limited by race.[4] It is instructive, in this regard, to contrast the constraints that shackle Brown's imaginative freedom with Hawthorne's ability to imaginatively erase "the original occupant[s] of the soil" in *The House of the Seven Gables* and Harriet Beecher Stowe's power to remove African Americans to Liberia in the concluding pages of *Uncle Tom's Cabin*.

As William Andrews notes in *To Tell a Free Story*, slave narratives written during this period wrestled with similar restraints. Because slave narratives were compelled to recount the "truth" about slavery, any suggestion of "fiction" was carefully avoided. And yet because the facts of slavery were so horrifying, this "truth" had to be carefully edited. "White acceptance of a slave narrative as truth," Andrews argues, "depended on how judiciously the slave had censored the facts of his life into something other than the whole truth."[5] William Wells Brown, however, brilliantly complicates the relationship between "truth" and "fiction" inherited from the slave narrative form by placing the "fictive" figure of Clotel, Thomas Jefferson's daughter by a black slave, at the center of his narrative. In doing so Brown challenges his white readers, conditioned to think of black writing as "truth stranger than fiction," to confront the persistent rumors that Jefferson had fathered several children by Sally Heming and, on a deeper level, to rethink the meaning(s) of the phrase "founding fathers."

And yet, despite the sheer bravado of Brown's opening gambit, he never breaks completely free of the imaginative constraints that haunted the slave narrative form. In the preface to *Clotel*, for example, Brown writes that "The great aim of the true friends of the slave should be to lay bare the institution, so that the gaze of the world may be upon it" (16). Brown's "aim" of "lay[ing] bare" the nation's miscegenated past went straight to the heart of one of the dominant white society's greatest anxieties. "Amalgamation," Charles Brown stated on the floor of the House of Representatives, "is not to be desired by any sane member of the European branch of the American family. It is too monstrous to think of, and would lead to a degeneracy of the whole people of this country."[6] As an interracial author working to expose the cultural hybridity of the nation's historical origins, Brown thus confronted the formidable literary challenge of persuading his readers to try to think the unthinkable.

Black Words on the White Page

The central narrative dilemma facing William Wells Brown can be clearly seen on the first page of the novel. Brown announces his intent to probe the historical depths of the nation's miscegenated past by quoting John Randolph, "a distinguished slaveholder of Virginia, and a prominent statesmen," who wrote that " 'the blood of the first American statesmen coursed through the veins of the slave of the South.' "[7] Brown goes on to argue for the nation's inescapably miscegenated future, again using a white voice to make his point, noting that "the late Henry Clay, some years since, predicted that the abolition of Negro slavery would be brought about by the amalgamation of the races" (59). On the one hand, Brown's rhetorical strategy represents an important departure from the slave narratives. By self-consciously doing away with the "authenticating documents" that invariably preceded the slave narratives, Brown works to strengthen the authorial black voice.[8] And yet he continues to rely upon white authorities in the opening pages of his novel, thereby refracting and obfuscating his own voice. (To invoke the figure of Henry Clay, for example, who at the time of his death in 1852 was the president of the American Colonization Society, unintentionally complicates Brown's argument that blacks were "native" to America.)

Brown's novel is remarkably heteroglot: there are no less than seven different white voices in the first chapter alone. Brown fractures his narrative of Thomas Jefferson selling his miscegenated family into slavery by inserting an advertisement for a slave auction from a Richmond newspaper, long passages from slave laws asserting that "the slave is entirely subject to the will of his master" (60), and fragments from the Shiloh Baptist Association's report arguing that laws governing marriage should not apply to enslaved blacks. Further complicating the critical endeavor of sorting through this pastiche of white legal, literary, and popular texts is the fact that Brown borrowed much of the central narrative from Lydia Maria Child's story "The Quadroons."[9] (In the conclusion to *Clotel* he openly acknowledges his "indebted[ness]" to Child "for part of a short story," [245].)

Given the support which the abolitionist movement received from women like Child and Stowe, Brown's use of sentimental themes to structure his novel is understandable. In the opening chapter, for example, Brown attempts to establish the sentimental trope of marriage as the central thematic structure for *Clotel*. As Nina Baym has noted, the marriage of the main character to a sympathetic male figure comprised a standard device for resolving narrative conflicts in sentimental literature.[10] "Marriage is, indeed," Brown writes, "the first and most important institution of human existence—the foundation of all civilization and culture—the root of church and state" (61). In *Beyond Ethnicity*, Werner Sollors observes that marriage has traditionally been used as a powerful tool for ethnic inclusion, because it combines "the language of consent and descent. . . to create a sense of Americanness among heterogeneous inhabitants of this country."[11] And yet, as Brown was all too well aware, the sentimental power of marriage to bring black slaves into the "American family" was impaired by the fact that "the marriage relation, the oldest and most sacred institution given to man by his Creator, is unknown and unrecognised in the slave laws of the United States" (60).

Brown boldly exposes and thematizes the failure of sentimentalism's "most sacred institution" by tracing three generations of interracial marital misfires. In doing so, Brown reveals both the way in which the genealogical roots of black and white Americans were inextricably intertwined and the forces of disavowal that worked to keep the races socially separate. Brown begins his shadow history of the nation with Thomas Jefferson's unacknowledged "marriage" to one of his slaves, Currer, with whom he has two children. Brown then effectively explores the inner workings of white shame, explicating Jefferson's rationale for selling his miscegenated family to slave dealers in order to pursue a career in politics. (Although self-consciously fictional, Brown's account of Jefferson's interracial affair played upon rumors that Jefferson's political rival John Quincy Adams believed to be true; Adams wrote of the rumor of red-headed slaves on Jefferson's plantation that "[miscegenation is] the natural and almost unavoidable consequence of that foul contagion in the human character, Negro slavery.")[12]

This conflict between interracial desire and white disavowal continues in the second generation, when both of Jefferson's daughters, Clotel and Althesa, marry white husbands. Once again external forces intervene, shattering their "marriages" and returning their children to slavery. The failure of the sentimental institution of marriage runs through the third interracial generation as well (even though by this time the color line has effectively been erased, for Jefferson's granddaughters are as "white as most white women in a southern clime" [206]). Like her mother and her grandmother, Althesa's daughter Jane dreams of the sentimental sanctity of marriage, but her dream is shattered by white fears of miscege-nation: Volney Lapuc, the young white Frenchman with whom she falls in love, is shot while trying to help her escape. Clotel's daughter Mary finally achieves a marriage forged in love, wedding another mixed-race fugitive slave in the closing pages of the novel. Tellingly, Mary and George Green's marriage succeeds only after they have escaped to France.

Unlike most slave narratives, Brown depicts these interracial relationships as being founded on love rather than the brutal sexual tyranny of the master-slave relationship. Brown describes Clotel's marriage to Horatio Green, who rescued her from the auction block, as "a marriage sanctioned by heaven, although unrecognised on earth" (84). Horatio and Clotel, Brown writes, "lived together in loving amity," although the "edicts of society had built up a wall of separation" which would not allow them to legally sanction their marital bond. Brown's depiction of this interracial relationship offers a stark contrast to the fragmented "family" depicted in the slave narratives of Frederick Douglass, Henry Bibb, and even Brown himself—all of whose white fathers disowned their enslaved mothers and their mixed-race children.[13] And yet any sense of hope that these interracial "marriages" hold out for a miscegenated vision of "America" is ultimately destroyed as, one after another, they shatter. (Brown depicts no less than six failed interracial marriages in the novel). Like Jefferson, a deep-seated sense of shame finally leads Horatio Green to abandon Clotel and his miscegenated family in order to pursue a career in politics.

The "edicts of society" that destroy Brown's imagined interracial bonds were, of course, historically real. Even among the most liberal thinkers of the antebellum age, miscegenation constituted an heinous offense. John Quincy Adams, for example, who argued brilliantly before the Supreme Court that the leaders of the slave revolt aboard the *Amistad* should be freed, wrote in an essay on Shakespeare's *Othello* that "black blood and white blood cannot be intermingled in marriage without a gross outrage upon the law of Nature."[14] The state of Massachusetts, widely regarded as the most liberal state in the Union, only abolished its miscegenation laws after a protracted and acrimonious debate. The committee convened by the state legislature to look into repealing the law reported that the sexual separation of the races was divinely sanctioned: "It recognizes the distinctions impressed on the families of the human race by that Infinite Wisdom, which nothing but the insanity of fanaticism dares to arraign." Only after a bitter twelve-year campaign, led in part by Lydia Maria Child, did Massachusetts finally, in 1843, repeal the law banning miscegenation.[15]

At the time Brown was writing, rampant fear of miscegenation directly contributed to the passage of the Black Laws throughout what is now the Midwest. At the Illinois Constitutional Convention in 1847, William Kinney argued fervently to restrict African American immigration, declaring that to admit blacks into the state was tantamount to allowing them "to make proposals to marry our daughters." Any leniency in regard to restrictions on immigration, one native southern Illinoisan warned, would cause the people in his part of the state to "take matters into their hands, and commence a war of extermination."[16] The 1845 Illinois statute prohibiting interracial marriage stated: "No person of color, negro or mulatto, of either sex, shall be joined in marriage with any white person, male or female, in this state; and all marriages . . . entered into between such colored person and white person, shall be null and void in law." Those violating the law "shall be liable to pay a fine, be whipped, in not exceeding thirty-nine lashes, and be imprisoned not less than one year."[17]

"Mulattoes," in the mid–nineteenth century, were deemed to be an inferior, bastardized race. As clearly demonstrated by Josiah C. Nott's "The Mulatto a Hybrid—Probable Extermination of the Two Races if the

Whites and Blacks are Allowed to Intermarry," published in one of the most respected medical journals of its day, miscegenation was perceived as having potentially apocalyptic consequences. Basing his findings in part on the Census of 1840, Nott wrote that mulattoes were "subject to many chronic diseases" and hence were "bad breeders and bad nurses—many of them do not conceive at all—most are subject to abortions, and a large portion of their children die at an early age." Nott concluded that because the mulatto was a hybrid, the product of "two distinct species—as the mule from the horse and the ass," this new creature was "a degenerate, unnatural offspring, doomed by nature to work out its own destruction."[18]

Realizing that his literary project to construct a multiracial vision of "America" sanctioned by the sentimental institution of marriage was doomed to failure, Brown adopted the radical discursive strategy of making visible the historical forces that limited his imaginative freedom. The long passage from the Savannah River Association quoted in the first chapter, for example, concludes with the statement: "The slaves are not free agents" (61). In context, the white pro-slavery advocate who wrote these words meant to show why a slave should be compelled to remarry after his or her first spouse had run away (despite marriage laws which maintained that one could only remarry after the death of a spouse). Brown, however, cannily reconfigures the semantic implications of the statement by placing it within the miscegenated context of his novel, where white and black voices openly contest one another. "The slaves are not free agents" thus becomes a subtextual commentary, articulating the limitations not only of Clotel's freedom to marry but also of Brown's freedom to write. It encapsulates his plight as a runaway slave writing the first African American novel in exile because of the Fugitive Slave Law. In a brilliant, though ultimately highly problematic, example of what Homi Bhabha calls the subversive strategy of "mimicry" ("almost the same but not quite . . . almost the same but not white"), Brown appropriates the white voices that militate against his authorial freedom and puts them in the service of his own ideological vision.[19]

The Miscegenation of Form

Working within the historical and discursive constraints which rule the margins of the first African American novel, Brown ultimately fails to depict a marriage on U.S. soil which reflects his vision of the nation as an "amalgamation" of the black and white races. What Brown does accomplish, by juxtaposing white voices with his own black voice, is a hybridity of form that embodies his multiracial vision of "America." Brown forges this coming together of the races not in the depiction of a loving union but in his inherently fragmented, ceaselessly contentious depiction of the national imaginary.[20] And yet, while all of the mixed-race characters in the novel are either killed or forced to flee the country, the miscegenated form of his novel endures as a testimony to Brown's controversial view that the historical and discursive origins of the nation were inextricably interracial.

This hybridity of form can be seen on the title page of the novel, where Brown juxtaposes the title, *Clotel; or, The President's Daughter*, with Jefferson's famous quotation: "We hold these truths to be self-evident: that all men are created equal; that they are endowed by their Creator with certain inalienable rights, and that among these are LIFE, LIBERTY, and the PURSUIT OF HAPPINESS." Brown's rhetorical strategy figuratively places Thomas Jefferson's speech acts and his sexual acts side by side in order to expose the inherent ironies of the phrase "founding fathers" and to call attention to the invisible racial boundaries which exclude his protagonist from the "all" of "all men are created equal." In the chapter entitled "Retaliation," Brown juxtaposes a passage from Jefferson's *Notes on the State of Virginia* with his own fictional account of Clotel's daughter's plight as a slave. " 'I tremble for my country,' " Brown quotes Jefferson, " 'when I recollect that God is just and that His justice cannot sleep for ever' " (159). Attacking one of white America's most cherished heroes, Brown discursively enacts a unique form of "retaliation" by following Jefferson's words with his own conclusion: "But, sad to say, Jefferson is not the only American statesman who has spoken high-sounding words in favor of freedom, and then left his own children to die slaves" (160).

In his thoughtful and insightful reading of *Clotel* in *Fathering the Nation*, Russ Castronovo describes Brown's rhetorical strategy as "discursive passing."[21] I would suggest, however, that "discursive miscegenation" is a more useful term for describing Brown's exceedingly complicated experiment with the novel form.[22] Brown does not set out to pass Jefferson's voice off as his own but works instead to create a dialogic tension between the intrusive white voices and his own authorial black voice. In doing so he effectively attacks the historical forces of white America's will to monoculturalism. At the time Brown was writing, for example, the Indiana state legislature sought to keep blacks out of the state by not allowing African Americans to testify against whites in a court of law, or to serve as jurors, militiamen, voters, or officers of the state.[23] Brown's rhetorical strategy of "discursive miscegenation" thus allows him to "testify" against the white patriarchal authority that strictly controlled which voices were empowered to speak. In doing so, William Wells Brown brilliantly and radically reconfigures the national imaginary.

The problem with allowing so many contradictory white voices into his text, however, is that at times Brown seems to lose control of the narrative, thereby subverting his own authorial power. In the chapter entitled "Escape of Clotel," for example, Brown tells how Clotel escapes to Canada by dressing as a man, taking along her friend William, disguised as her "servant." Brown then follows his own fictive description with a lengthy excerpt from "one of the Southern newspapers" that he describes as "the most probable . . . account" (174). It is a thrice-told tale. The historical basis of the story was the escape of Brown's good friends William and Ellen Craft, who often lectured with him on abolitionist platforms. Brown retells the story of the Crafts' remarkable escape in *Clotel*, substituting Thomas Jefferson's daughter in the role of heroine. And yet by immediately retelling the story in the form of a needlessly long newspaper account, adopted almost verbatim from a report in the Newark, New Jersey *Daily Mercury*,[24] Brown inadvertently undercuts the power of the narrativeand reveals his own anxiety about too freely imagining the horrors of slavery, lest he be dismissed as writing mere "fiction." "This, reader, is not fiction," he writes shortly thereafter, "it actually occurred" (178). In this case Brown's reliance upon a more "probable" white voice to validate his own version of the Crafts' story calls into question the authority of the black author and ironically undermines Brown's own ability to utilize "fiction."

At other moments in the text, Brown utilizes this strategy of juxtaposing white and black voices to effectively represent the conflicted place of African Americans in the imagined community of the nation. Brown ends the third chapter of the novel, for example, with two vivid passages from southern newspapers. In the first, a white voice from the ironically (mis)-named Natchez *Free Trader* recounts: "the body [of a runaway slave] was taken and chained to a tree . . . set fire . . . [then] the sharp ringing of several rifles were heard: the body of the Negro fell a corpse on the ground. He was picked up . . . and again thrown into the fire, and consumed, not a vestige remaining to show that such a being ever existed" (81). The chapter concludes with a description from the *Vicksburgh Sentinel*: "A runaway's den [was] discovered . . . in a little patch of woods, where it had been for several months so artfully concealed under ground, that he was detected only by accident" (82). In the following chapter, entitled "The Quadroon's Home," Brown describes how Clotel and Horatio Green lived "*secluded* from the world" in a cottage "far retired from the public roads, and almost *hidden* among the trees" (82, 83). These newspaper accounts of black bodies burned to the point where "not a vestige remained to show that such a being ever existed" and fugitive slaves' underground hideouts that were "artfully concealed" serve to contextualize the historical forces that interrupt and destroy Clotel's "marriage" to Horatio Green. Brown thus "artfully conceal[s]" his own critique of these destructive forces by mimicking the white voices of southern journalists.

Brown's ability to bring to light the tortured lives of slaves, normally "hidden" to the larger white society, comprises a remarkable early instance of what Houston Baker has called the trope of the "black (w)hole" in African American literature. Only within black holes, Baker writes, could African American characters like Bigger Thomas "escape [the] incarcerating restraints of the white world"[25] to find a sense of wholeness. The (w)hole which William Wells Brown seeks to describe differs, however, from Richard Wright's conception. The sense of wholeness which Brown struggles to articulate and inscribe in the heteroglot jumble of *Clotel* always remains inescapably interracial: "Clotel had found a *sheltered* home in Horatio's heart." Unlike *Native Son*, where interracial desire is depicted in horrifyingly violent terms, Brown represents desire as a longing for a "loving amity" between the races. The forces of disavowal which flare up in reaction to miscegenation are, however, no less violent in *Clotel* than in Wright's novel.

It should be acknowledged that Brown's sense of the "black (w)hole" was not representative of the view of all or even most African Americans at this time. Even Frederick Douglass, who was committed to an interracial vision of national identity and who married a white woman later in his life, rarely addressed the issue of miscegenation directly in either his newspaper writings or his speeches in the years before the Civil War. Others in the black community were openly hostile to the idea. E. W. Blyden, a contemporary of Brown's who advocated a black nationalist agenda of returning to Africa, wrote that he did not want "people of mixed blood" in Liberia, because they "never get thorough sympathy with the work."[26] Brown explicitly addresses the forces of resistance within the black community when he has one "full-blooded" black character say, "dees white niggers always tink dey sef good as white folks" and acknowledges that "prejudice which is to be found among the Negroes, as well as among the whites of the Southern states" (158, 159).

For Brown, biracial African Americans were uniquely suited to carry out the fight for a multicultural society. In the closing pages of his novel, Brown writes: "The infusion of Anglo-Saxon with African blood has created an insurrectionary feeling among the slaves of America hitherto unknown. Aware of their blood connection with their owners, these mulattoes labour under the sense of their personal and social injuries" (212). At moments Brown unconsciously enacts in *Clotel* the prejudices which existed between light- and dark-skinned African Americans. And yet his belief in the essential unity of the "black" community is symbolized by the slave uprising near the end of the novel, led jointly by the interracial George Green and the "full-blooded Negro" Picquilo, who "claimed [Africa] as his native land" (213). Brown's literary aim was not that blacks would eventually become "white," and therefore "American," through generations of interracial marriage but rather that "America" would overcome its deep-seated fear of miscegenation and adopt an image of itself as a multiracial society. In the second edition of his novel, *Clotelle* (1864), Brown concluded his narrative with perhaps his clearest ideological formulation—calling for the elimination of "prejudice against color" and demanding, "Why should the white man be esteemed as better than the black?"[27]

Talking Back to Harriet Beecher Stowe

Brown's most successful use of the rhetorical strategy of "discursive miscegenation" is his dialogic response to the colonizationist conclusion of *Uncle Tom's Cabin*, published one year before *Clotel* (1853). While deeply respectful of Stowe's ability to engender support for the cause of abolition, Brown's anti-colonization stance differed sharply from Stowe's view that African Americans were "an exotic race, whose ancestors, born beneath a tropic sun, brought with them, and perpetuated to their descendants, a character . . . essentially unlike the hard and dominant Anglo-Saxon race."[28] Writing less than a year after the publication of *Uncle Tom's Cabin*, Brown devised a sophisticated rhetorical strategy of racial masking which allowed him to utilize the sentimental power of white women's voices while simultaneously subverting Stowe's colonizationist conclusion.

By the time *Clotel* was published in 1853, Stowe's novel had already sold more than three hundred thousand copies in the United States.[29] Clearly hoping to take advantage of the public's newfound interest in literature depicting the plight of African American slaves, Brown hurried his novel to press in London. Sincerely appreciative of the power of Stowe's sentimental novel to spread its abolitionist message to a wider audience, Brown praised it in glowing terms in the *Liberator*. "*Uncle Tom's Cabin* had come down upon the dark abodes of slavery like a morning's sunlight," Brown wrote, "unfolding to view its enormities in a manner which has fastened all eyes upon the 'peculiar institution' and awakening sympathy in the hearts that never before felt for the slave."[30]

Like many in the free black community in the North, Brown harbored a deeply felt resentment about the mass exodus of black characters to Africa in the concluding pages of Stowe's novel. Even before the Fugitive Slave Law compelled him to take up residence in Europe, Brown opposed the American Colonization Society's claim that African Americans could never live freely and peacefully in the land of their birth. In a collection of abolitionist songs that he compiled and published in 1848, entitled *The*

Anti-Slavery Harp, Brown included the "Colonization Song," which was written in the white slave master's voice:

> My religion is pure,
> And came from above,
> But I cannot consent
> The black negro to love.
> Will you, will you be colonized?
> Will you, will you be colonized?
>
> . . . .
>
> You're ignorant, I know,
> In this land of your birth,
> And religion though pure,
> Cannot move the curse.
> Will you, will you be colonized?
> Will you, will you be colonized?[31]

In *The Black Man, His Antecedents, His Genius, and His Achievements* (1865), Brown explicitly criticized "the idea of colonizing the slaves in some other country, outside of the United States," calling it "the height of folly."[32] Brown gives voice to his anti-colonization sentiments in *Clotel* as well, although because of his indebtedness to sentimental literature, and Stowe in particular, he disguises his ideological convictions behind a series of discursive masks.

Whereas Stowe appropriated the voice of a black slave by having George Harris state in *Uncle Tom's Cabin* that "I go to my country,—my chosen, my glorious Africa!"[33] Brown cannily reverses the literary power relations by having a white, female character, Georgiana, indirectly respond to Stowe. Georgiana explains to her slaves upon setting them free: "We think it wrong to send you from your native land. We did not wish to encourage the Colonization Society, for it originated in hatred of the free colored people. Its pretenses are false, its doctrines odious, its means contemptible" (190). Rather than sending her freed slaves to Liberia, as her southern neighbors would prefer, Georgiana buys land in Ohio for them, so that they may establish new lives within the geographic borders of what Brown insistently argues is "our country." Brown thus cannily revises the political and racial ideologies of Stowe: Georgianna's name is the feminine version of George, her skin white instead of black, her views anti-colonization instead of pro-. Her character allows Brown to take advantage of the sentimental logic of the day, which posited white, middle-class women as the embodiment of "American" virtue, while at the same time attacking Stowe's colonizationist conclusion.

Here again Brown risks compromising his own discursive authority by making the white voice more "credible" and leaving himself open to the charge of what Houston Baker calls "white-faced minstrelsy."[34] In a remarkable chapter entitled "Death of the Parson," Brown lifts the white mask for a fleeting moment to reveal the black vernacular voice underneath. Standing outside of the slave quarters on the night of her father's death, Georgiana hears the slaves singing inside. Her white, male companion warns her not to listen to these "unguarded expressions" but she insists upon doing so, noting that "we should learn a lesson." Led by Sam, one of the most obsequious blacks on the plantation, the slaves sing:

> Old master is dead, and left us at last,
>   And has gone at the Bar to appear.
> Old master has died, and lying in his grave,
>   And our blood will awhile cease to flow;
> He will no more trample on the neck of the slave;
>   For he's gone where the slaveholders go.
>
> . . .
>
> For his reign of oppression now is o'er.
> He no more will hang our children on the tree
>   To be ate by the carrion crow;
> He no more will send our wives to Tennessee;
>   For he's gone where the slaveholders go. (154–55)

In front of whites, Sam is alternately subservient and imbecilic. Indeed, when Georgiana sees him later that night, he looks "as solemn and as dignified as if he had never sung a song or laughed in his life" (156). By carefully constructing this discursive moment in which Georgiana inadvertently overhears the unguarded black vernacular voice, Brown brilliantly reverses the implicit power relations embedded in the dominant white discourse. Earlier, for example, a minister visiting Georgiana's plantation employs Christian rhetoric to justify the racial hierarchy of slavery, arguing that blacks have no "natural rights" because "they were condemned beings; they could have no rights, but by Christ's gift as King" (93). In Sam's song, however, the line "He no more will hang our children on the tree" metaphorically subverts the white minister's biblical rationale by transforming black children into Christ figures.

Despite this momentary triumph of depicting on the white page a black voice heralding that the "reign of oppression now is o'er," Brown's relentlessly fragmented narrative demonstrates that the power of the dominant white discourse cannot be so easily overthrown. Sam's brief uncensored speech is but a subplot of a narrative subplot. Clotel's tragic suicide in the shadow of the White House and the suppression of the slave insurrection

in the closing pages of the novel make it clear that the white power structure remains solidly in place in spite of Brown's rhetorical subversions.

The rage among both "full-blood" and "quadroon" slaves at the end of
the novel needs to be read, therefore, as yet another dimension of Brown's
dialogic response to Harriet Beecher Stowe's better-known novel. Signi-
fying on George Harris's renunciation of both his white father and his
American citizenship, Brown concludes his novel with a mixed-blood
character named George Green "testifying" in court that the reason "why
I joined the revolted Negroes" is that "I have heard my master read in the
Declaration of Independence 'that all men are created free and equal' "
(226). Brown's George, whose "father was an American statesmen,"
does not disavow his American identity but instead boldly argues for a
multiracial interpretation of the nation. And yet it is important to acknowledge that in *Clotel*, as in *Uncle Tom's Cabin*, the forces of white disavowal
ultimately prevail to enforce a monocultural construction of the imagined
community of the nation. In the end, George Green must flee to Europe
dressed as a white woman (subtly underscoring the freedom which Stowe
possessed to imagine the nation in her own image). In the concluding
pages of his novel, Brown works self-consciously to make it clear that
fugitive slaves did not have access to "American" citizenship either by
consent or descent. Like Brown himself, the two surviving mixed-race
characters find themselves condemned to exile. "We can but blush for our
country's shame," Brown concludes his novel, "when we recall to mind
the fact, that while George and Mary Green, and numbers of other fugitives from American slavery, can receive protection from any of the governments of Europe, they cannot return to their native land without becoming slaves" (244).

Mapping the "American Diaspora"

When William Wells Brown sailed from Boston harbor in the summer of
1849, his intention was to remain in Europe for approximately one year.
Traveling at his own expense as a delegate from the American Peace Society to attend the Peace Congress in Paris, Brown had arranged to tour
Great Britain and the continent giving lectures on the evils of American
slavery. His plans were dramatically altered, however, by the passage of the
Fugitive Slave Law in September 1850. Within the next two months reports of slave hunters tracking runaway slaves in the North and of free
blacks being kidnapped and sold at slave auctions began to reach Brown
in England. Because of his well-known status as a fugitive slave, reiterated
many times over on the abolitionist lecture circuit, Wendell Phillips and

other friends in the United States advised him to stay in Great Britain. Brown remained stranded in Europe until the spring of 1854, when Ellen Richardson of Newcastle upon Tyne purchased his freedom for three hundred dollars from his former master, Enoch Price.[35]

The Fugitive Slave Act was part of the Compromise of 1850, designed to hold together a nation deeply torn over the question of slavery in the new territories gained as a result of the Mexican-American War. In his speech of March 7, which turned the tide of support for the compromise in the Senate, Daniel Webster sought to articulate a sense of "American" nationalism that would bridge the chasm between North and South. "Mr. President, I wish to speak to-day," Webster began, "not as a Massachusetts man, nor as a Northern man, but as an American. . . . I speak to-day for the preservation of the Union." Addressing the Senate two days after a dying John C. Calhoun ominously predicted the collapse of the Union, Webster struggled desperately to articulate the magnitude of the issues at hand: "Peaceable secession!—peaceable secession! . . . Why, what would be the result? Where is the line to be drawn? . . . What is to remain American? What am I to be? An American no longer? . . . Heaven forbid!" In the concluding pages of his speech, Webster sought to find common ground between the two sides: "In my observations upon slavery . . . I have expressed no opinion of the mode of its extinguishment or melioration. I will say, however, . . . that if any gentleman from the South shall propose a scheme of colonization, to be carried on by this Government upon a large scale, for the transportation of free colored people to any colony or any place in the world, I should be quite disposed to incur almost any degree of expense to accomplish that object."[36] Playing upon the unspoken bond of whiteness between the North and South, Webster's invocation of colonization suggests that the "curse" haunting America was not the institution of slavery but the nation's multicultural population.

Because the colonization of four million black slaves was a fiscal impossibility, the Fugitive Slave Law became the crucial component of the Compromise of 1850, temporarily holding the slave states of the deep South in the Union. As David M. Potter notes in *The Impending Crisis*, "the Fugitive Slave Law, as enacted, contained a number of . . . obnoxious provisions." One of the most legally problematic aspects of the law was that it denied the accused fugitive slave any right to a jury trial, either in the state in which he or she was presently living or in the jurisdiction from which the runaway slave had allegedly escaped. Moreover, the act permitted these cases to be removed from the ordinary judicial tribunals and tried before a commissioner appointed by the courts. The commissioner received a ten-dollar fee in cases which returned the alleged fugitive to the slave master but only a five-dollar fee for decisions which set the accused free. The Fugitive Slave Law also empowered federal marshals to summon any citizen to aid in the enforcement of the act. In the eyes of many northerners this clause implicated the entire country in the unseemly business of southern slave catching.[37]

The Fugitive Slave Law set off a fire storm of protest in the northern states. In Christiana, Pennsylvania angry black mobs killed a slaveowner in a shootout to prevent a fugitive slave from being recaptured.[38] Charles Sumner, a senator from Massachusetts, declared that "the Fugitive Slave Bill [is] a flagrant violation of the Constitution, and of the most cherished human rights—shocking to Christian sentiments, insulting to humanity, and impudent in all its pretensions."[39] For better or worse, the Compromise of 1850 did manage to hold the country together for another decade. "It is the deliberate opinion of this Convention," members of the Georgia Convention asserted in 1850, "that upon faithful execution of the *Fugitive Slave Law* . . . depends the preservation of our much beloved Union."[40] The Fugitive Slave Law, which denied African Americans who had fled slavery in the South the right of habeas corpus, by not allowing them to confront or cross-examine their accusers, thus effectively held the Union together by excluding black Americans, thereby preserving a distinctly monocultural conception of the national imaginary.

Thrown into a state of turmoil, free black communities throughout the United States retreated in terror. "We are now . . . a people with nothing to protect us and truly at the mercy of the slaveholder," Frederick Douglass stated in a speech at Faneuil Hall attended by a crowd of more than five thousand people, overflowing into the streets.[41] The threat that the Fugitive Slave Law posed to Brown became painfully apparent after his good friends William and Ellen Craft had to be rescued from a southern slave catcher and then smuggled out of Boston.[42] In a letter to William Lloyd Garrison announcing that the Crafts had arrived safely in England, Brown wrote: "There is a general feeling of hatred here to the Fugitive Slave Bill, and every body, as far as I am able to hear, looks upon Mr. Webster as the originator of this most abominable law, and his connection with and support of it has brought a lasting shame upon him."[43]

The Fugitive Slave Law set off a mass exodus of black Americans, forced to flee the country to preserve their freedom. As William Wells Brown wrote from London, "Since the separation of the American provinces from the mother country in 1776, many thousands of slaves, escaping from the Southern States have sought a refuge and a home in Canada; and the 'Fugitive Slave Law,' recently enacted by the American Congress, has already added greatly to that number, so that the fugitive slave population is now estimated at about 30,000."[44] So many runaway slaves had come to England that in August 1851 Brown wrote to Frederick Douglass, in a letter that was published in the *Liberator*, "too many of our fugitive brethren . . . have set themselves up as lecturers, and . . . are in fact little less than beggars." Brown concluded the letter, "if you don't want to become beggars, don't come to England. If the climate in Canada is too cold, and you must leave the States, go to the West Indies. But by all means, don't come to England."[45] The routes by which African Americans could escape the new law were, however, both limited and perilous. Two months later Brown wrote again to the *Liberator*, with another warning: "I understand that a secret move is on foot in London to induce our unsuspecting people in Canada to go to the West Indies, and that agents are already in Canada for that purpose. . . . I take the earliest opportunity of warning all colored men to be on their guard, how they enter into agreements, no matter with whom, white or colored, to go to the West India Islands, lest they find themselves again wearing the chains of slavery."[46]

Brown's letters from England recalling the exodus of runaway slaves to the Caribbean, Canada, and Europe effectively map what I am calling the "American Diaspora." The flight of Brown's two surviving mixed-race characters in the closing pages of the novel likewise can be said to trace the transnational boundaries of the American Diaspora. After being convicted for his role in the slave uprising, George Green escapes from prison, only to discover that even in a "free state" like Ohio he is pursued by slave catchers. Forced into exile in Canada, "he imparted what he could to those of his fellow-fugitive slaves about him, of whom there were many" (231). After a brief stay Green departs for England, where, like Brown, he finds a sense of freedom that is denied to him in his own country. The flight of Clotel's daughter Mary likewise traces the patterns of migration resulting from the passage of the Fugitive Slave Law. After helping Green escape, Mary is sold at auction to a master in Louisiana. She eventually escapes, but this granddaughter of Thomas Jefferson does not find the liberty and equality promised by the Declaration of Independence until she flees to France and the farthest reaches of the American Diaspora.

This geographically deconstructed sense of cultural consciousness is, of course, usually associated with the "African Diaspora." Tellingly, Brown does not see either his characters or the fugitive slaves who arrived daily in England as dislocated from a "homeland" on the west coast of Africa. His denunciation of colonization in *Clotel* explicitly militates against such an interpretation. Instead, Brown clearly describes these displaced runaway slaves as part of an imagined community of "America" that extends beyond the country's geographical borders: "many of these people," he writes from London, "have . . . come to this country, seeking employment and that liberty and protection which are denied them in their *native* land."[47] Likewise, at the end of *Clotel*, Mary and George continue to think of America as their "native land." Instead of allowing national identity to be determined by citizenship—and thus seeing African Americans as *excluded* by the Fugitive Slave Law—a historical multicultural conception of national identity needs to theorize fugitive slaves living in Canada, the West Indies, or England as still *included* in "America."

HISTORICAL INTERLUDE

"THE ANSWER IS NEVER EXPRESSED IN WORDS"

In May 1852, the Reverend John Orcutt addressed the Massachusetts Colonization Society on the question "Why may not the whites and blacks dwell together?" Orcutt presented two possible solutions to the cultural dilemma that plagued the dominant white society in the years preceding the Civil War. The first, of course, given his audience, was to "open a door for the black man to his original home" by funding the American Colonization Society. The second, however, offers a meaningful hermeneutic preface to Melville's *Moby-Dick*. This "answer," Orcutt intimated, "*is never expressed in words. It never takes a visible shape. It is like the devil; a spirit of the power of the air.*" If it were possible to speak the "unspeakable" solution, Orcutt continued, "it would be this,—Remove the dangers by letting down the barriers. . . . This was the intent of the Cuban expedition, and of the Mexican war."[1] The notion that America's vast continental expanse would act as a "safety valve" for the explosive pressure of white racism and black rage generated by slavery can be found throughout the nineteenth century. What makes Orcutt's oration significant, in the context of the analysis that follows, is his reluctance or inability to name white America's will to empire.

Although an isolated, fleeting moment in U.S. history, the lacuna in Orcutt's speech provides a critically important opening into the inner workings of one of the fundamental contradictions of "American" identity. To understand the cultural aphasia that makes white America's hemispheric expansion "unspeakable" to Orcutt requires careful analysis of the complex interrelationship between U.S. imperialism, the nation's rhetorical commitment to democracy, and the "free" market. Having gained their independence from the "absolute tyranny" of England, America pursued its unique policy of postcolonial imperialism by purchasing 828,000 square miles of territory from France in 1803—effectively doubling the size of the country just twenty-seven years after the republic was founded. Unsure of whether the Constitution permitted the conquest or acquisition of new territories, Jefferson sought to justify his actions by calling this expansion an "empire for liberty."[2]

The intricate evasions inherent in the phrase "empire for liberty" allowed the United States to justify its imperial expansion throughout the nineteenth century. President James Monroe, for example, seized upon the rhetoric of anticolonial imperialism twenty years later to frame the

Monroe Doctrine. "American continents," he declared in 1823, "are no longer subjects of *any* new European colonial establishments." Extending a "sphere of influence" over an entire hemisphere in the name of protecting it from "colonization by European powers," the United States established its own unique form of anticolonial imperialism.[3] In 1842 President John Tyler used the Monroe Doctrine to justify seizing Texas, thus triggering the Mexican-American War.[4] In response to criticism that the Constitution prohibited wars of imperial expansion, the United States paid Mexico fifteen million dollars at the conclusion of the war (leading the *Whig Intelligencer* to remark that "we take nothing by conquest. . . . Thank God").[5] The economic principle of a "free" market, where virtually anything from black bodies to vast continental expanses could be purchased at a fair price, thus effectively worked to mask American imperialism in the nineteenth century. To break through the mask necessarily entails challenging one of the country's most cherished myths: that the nation was historically opposed to colonization and fundamentally committed to democratic equality.

Orcutt's cultural aphasia, like Ishmael's inability to name the "nameless horror" of the white whale, constitutes a hermeneutical puzzle whose "answer is never expressed in words." Only by struggling to come to terms with the psychological and historical origins of this cultural aphasia does it become possible to more fully understand the unique nature of American imperialism that lies cloaked behind Orcutt's willed silence. Likewise, only by considering carefully Ishmael's inability to articulate the meaning(s) of the whale's whiteness, by delving beneath his seemingly unconscious aphasia, can we begin to fathom the semantic depths of Melville's critique of white imperialism.

CHAPTER SIX

HERMAN MELVILLE: RUTHLESS DEMOCRACY

All evil, to crazy Ahab, were visibly personified, and made
practically assailable in Moby Dick. He piled upon the
whale's white hump the sum of all the general rage and hate
felt by his whole race.

What the white whale was to Ahab, has been hinted; what,
at times, he was to me, as yet remains unsaid. . . .
[T]here was . . . [such a] vague, nameless horror
concerning him . . . that I almost despair of putting it in a
comprehensible form. It was the whiteness of the whale
that above all things appalled me. But how can I hope to
explain myself.
(Herman Melville, *Moby-Dick*)

MORE than any other single work in the American Renaissance,
Herman Melville's *Moby-Dick* (1851) dramatizes the conflict
between the nation's will to empire, which exponentially increased the country's multicultural diversity, and the dominant white society's will to monoculturalism, which kept the imagined community of U.S. "citizenship" predominantly white.[1] Symbolically rendered in the figure of the vortex created by the collision between the destructive whiteness of the whale and the remarkable cultural diversity of the *Pequod*'s crew, Melville's novel takes us to the very heart of the conflict I have been addressing throughout this study. It is, however, a radically destabilized center, where meanings cannot be fixed but must be constantly constructed and reconstructed in the midst of ceaseless semantic flux. As the two passages above, contrasting Ahab and Ishmael's perspectives on the whiteness of the whale, succinctly demonstrate, Melville's literary text deconstructs itself to the point where it trails off into the silence of bottomless uncertainty.

In *Subversive Genealogy*, Michael Rogin writes that "those who see *Moby-Dick* as a political allegory choose one side or another in the political debates; *Moby-Dick* undercuts all." Rogin's historical overview of contrasting interpretations of *Moby-Dick* provides a fascinating demonstration of the uncanny ability of Melville's novel to function as a discursive mirror that reflects the ideological image of the literary critic looking at the text.

In 1960, for example, Willie T. Weathers argued in a southern journal that the white whale represented the Union and associated Ahab's assault on Moby-Dick with William Lloyd Garrison's abolitionist attack on the republic. Charles H. Foster, on the other hand, writing just one year later in the *New England Quarterly* and also identifying the white whale with the Union, saw Ahab as Daniel Webster, whose advocacy of the Fugitive Slave Law threatened to destroy the country. Rogin concludes his interpretive overview by clearly stating that Melville's novel "points to no fixed political truth above and outside its own story." And yet, some forty pages later, Rogin disregards his own hermeneutic caveat by writing that "Melville surely borrowed characterizations of Webster for the white whale"[2]—seemingly unable to resist the critical impulse to assign meaning to Melville's "unnameable imminglings."[3] My point is not, however, to criticize Rogin for attempting to impose a political meaning upon Melville's text; that is precisely what the work of being a cultural critic entails. To the contrary, my intent is to call attention to the fact that literary scholars working in different historical periods or from contrasting theoretical perspectives will invariably see very different ideological reflections in *Moby-Dick*.

To undertake a multicultural analysis of *Moby-Dick* at the end of the twentieth century, in an era that has witnessed the Rodney King decision, the collapse of the welfare state, and the dismantling of affirmative action programs in state universities across the country, the critic must once again reinterpret the whiteness of the whale. As Donald Pease insightfully observes in "Melville and Cultural Persuasion," readings of *Moby-Dick* have for the last fifty years been deeply influenced by the ideology of the Cold War. Pease notes that literary critics writing in the postwar era tended to see "Ishmael's survival as a sign of the free world's triumph over a totalitarian power."[4] My own historical multicultural interpretation of the novel radically reinterprets many of these Cold War associations. From this perspective, it is not the white whale who embodies the nation, as Foster and Weathers claim, but rather the culturally and racially diverse crew of the *Pequod*. And it is Ahab, not Ishmael, who is the heroic figure, as he struggles to kill off the destructive power of sheer whiteness.

To negotiate this critical turn, however, means confronting a myriad of perplexing and difficult questions. If the *Pequod* symbolizes the cultural complexity of the nation, for example, then what theoretical conception of nationalism encompasses a crew whose cultural origins range from the islands of New England to the islands of the Pacific and from the west coast of Africa to the east coast of China? Why do Ishmael and Ahab, both of whom are racially white, perceive the whiteness of the whale in such starkly different terms? Moreover, what nature of "despair" prevents Ishmael from expressing the "horror" of whiteness in "a comprehensible form"? And, finally, why does Melville destroy what he called, in a letter to Hawthorne, his "ruthless democracy" aboard the *Pequod* in the closing pages of the novel, so that Ishmael alone is left to tell the tale?[5]

In the first section of this chapter, "To Dive Deeper than Ishmael Can Go," I will explore the exceedingly complex narrative construction of Melville's novel. Much of the willed complexity of the text, it seems to me, derives from Melville's decision to strictly limit the reader's perspective by filtering the story of Ahab's vengeance through the eyes of Ishmael, who understands neither his "monomaniac commander's soul" nor the forces of racial rage that drive "the rushing *Pequod*, freighted with savages" (534). Like Melville's later novella "Benito Cereno" (1854), the real story of the racial conflict aboard the *Pequod* lies hidden behind the white veil of a narrator who only dimly and partially comprehends the clash of cultures unfolding everywhere around him. In order to uncover the contentious complexities of Melville's tale thus requires a careful and thoughtful rhetorical analysis of the silences that pervade Ishmael's narrative.

Having deconstructed the epistemological constraints that limit Ishmael's understanding of both American imperialism and Ahab's racial rage, I will then work toward explicating the transnational multicultural depiction of "American" identity embodied by the *Pequod*. The erratic voyage of the *Pequod*—from Nantucket across to the Azores, down to the whale grounds off the coast of South America, around the Cape of Good Hope, through the China Sea, and into the Pacific—traces the international boundaries of the United States' spheres of commerce.[6] The remarkable breadth of Melville's depiction of "American" identity utterly deconstructs the idea of the nation-state being defined solely by geographical boundaries. So diverse is Melville's vision that even one hundred and fifty years later adequate theoretical language remains elusive.[7] This international inscription, extending the geographical and cultural borders of national identity to include the vast global expanse of the U. S. whaling industry's international labor force, dramatically expands the imagined community of "America" and productively complicates received readings of the American Renaissance.

Melville's literary depiction of the transnational multiculturalism of the whaling industry thus provides a fitting conclusion for *Ruthless Democracy*. The first half of my study concentrated on challenging Matthiessen's monocultural conception of the American Renaissance by mapping the multicultural borders within the United States, from New England to the Cherokee Nation to Indian Territory to Sonora, Mexico to the "human menagerie" of California just after the gold rush. The second half of *Ruthless Democracy* has thus far charted the transnational boundaries of "America," from the repatriated black Americans who established the Republic of Liberia to the fugitive slaves living in exile on the outer reaches of the American Diaspora. The international crew of the *Pequod*, sailing under the American flag, gives new meaning to the concept of the American Diaspora. By returning to the canonical origins of the "American Renaissance" we have come full circle—but with a difference. Even a canonical work as critically familiar as Herman Melville's *Moby-Dick* comes to be seen in a new interpretive light in this historical multicultural context. Engaging the vast multiplicity of cultural and national identities "federated along one keel," this transnational exegesis embraces a dimension of "America" too often overlooked: workers, denied formal recognition of citizenship, who nevertheless powered one of the nation's most important industries from the seventeenth century through the nineteenth.[8] As the forces of whiteness embodied by Moby-Dick rise up out of the sea, in the final scene of the novel, to utterly annihilate the multicultural crew, we are left with the hermeneutic challenge, at the end of *Ruthless Democracy*, of reconstructing "American" identity out of the wreckage of the *Pequod*.

To Dive Deeper than Ishmael Can Go

Herman Melville's *Moby-Dick* constitutes one of the most unrelentingly multicultural depictions of "America" in all of U.S. literature. The novel is populated by Quakers from Nantucket, "Feegeans, Tongatabooans, Erromanggoans, Pannangians, and Brighggians" (125), "a gigantic, coal-black" African (216), "an unmixed Indian from Gay Head" (215), "Spanish sailor[s]" (274), "tiger-yellow . . . aboriginal natives of the Manillas" (318), as well as "green Vermonters and New Hampshire men" (125). Beginning with an interracial homosexual love affair and ending "as the last whelmings intermixingly poured themselves over the sunken head of the Indian at the mainmast" (685), Melville's masterpiece truly lives up to his description of the novel as a "ruthless democracy."

And yet the hermeneutic dilemma that every reader of *Moby-Dick* faces is to wrestle with the interpretive limitations of a white narrator who seems incapable of understanding Ahab's rage or his unique bond with the culturally diverse crew of the *Pequod*, particularly the harpooneers, who seem to share Ahab's vengefulness most fully. Melville visually depicts this interpretive dilemma in the form of the two whirlpools that appear in the closing pages of the novel, symbolizing the two competing hermeneutic circles at play in the narrative. In "The Chase—First Day," Ahab is swept overboard and sucked into a vortex caused by the white whale: "in the heart of such a whirlpool . . . helpless Ahab's head was seen" (660). This swirling vortex, with Ahab at its center, metaphorically embodies the hermeneutic circle that Melville depicts in greater detail in "The Quarter-deck," where Tashtego, Daggoo, and Queequeg cross their lances and

Ahab "touch[es] the axis" (264). (I will return to explore the meanings of the whiteness of the whale within this hermeneutic circle in the next section.) In the final chapter of the novel, Melville describes another hermeneutic "vortex," this time created by the sinking of the *Pequod* and recounted in Ishmael's narrative voice: "floating on the margin of the ensuing scene, and in full sight of it . . . I was then, but slowly, drawn towards the closing vortex . . . [until] gaining that vital centre . . . I floated on a soft and dirge-like main" (687). Thus, at the end of the novel, Ishmael moves from "the margin of the ensuing scene"—an itinerant oarsman, the 275th lay, who plays an unimportant and passive role in Ahab's quest for vengeance against the white whale—to the "vital centre" of the narrative.

To critically reconstruct the psychological origins of Ahab's rage and to more fully understand the "ruthless democracy" aboard the *Pequod* requires a thorough deconstruction of Ishmael's tacitly Eurocentric perspective. Like "Benito Cereno," the story of a slave mutiny aboard the *San Dominick* told from the perspective of a white American captain so blinded by ethnocentric prejudices that he remains oblivious to the fact that slaves have taken control of the ship, Melville constructs *Moby-Dick* as a double-layered narrative.[9] The difference, strikingly, between the narrative construction of "Benito Cereno" and *Moby-Dick* is that Ishmael never becomes aware of his own blindness. "Such a crew, so officered, seemed specially picked and packed by some infernal fatality to help [Ahab] to his monomaniac revenge," Ishmael recounts. "By what evil magic their souls were possessed . . . all this to explain, would be to dive deeper than Ishmael can go" (286).

Despite these ethnocentric shortcomings, Melville nevertheless depicts Ishmael as being a fundamental part of the "ruthless democracy" of the *Pequod*'s crew. Symbolically embraced in the opening chapters—"You gettee in," Queequeg orders him in "The Spouter Inn"(118)—Ishmael finds himself enmeshed in a world where the social hierarchies of race, sexuality, and class no longer adequately explain identity. As Eve Kosofsky Sedgwick notes in *Epistemology of the Closet*, the queering of the "heterosexual/homosexual binary" which "has been a presiding term . . . for all modern Western identity" uncovers the "irresolvably unstable" nature of the social construction of cultural identities.[10] Analogously, by beginning his novel with an interracial homosexual encounter, Melville effectively undermines entrenched political, social, and racial hierarchies and as such lays the intentionally unstable groundwork for his discursive inscription of the "ruthless democracy" on board the *Pequod*. And yet, given Melville's apparent aim to present a radically deconstructed transnational portrait of "America," why does he elect to tell the tale from Ishmael's exceedingly limited perspective? What results is a narrative riddled with conspicuous silences (or what might be termed "epistemological misfires") that make it difficult to explain the multicultural perplexities that abound aboard the *Pequod*.

The first instance in which Ishmael's narrative trails off into silence occurs in "The Counterpane," when he awakes to find "Queequeg's arm thrown over me in the most loving and affectionate manner" (118). Ishmael has no language, no epistemological framework, to make sense of either the interraciality or what we might now term the "exquisite queerness" of the moment. "I felt a shock running through all my frame," Ishmael tells his reader, "a supernatural hand seemed placed in mine . . . and the nameless, unimaginable, silent form or phantom, to which the hand belonged, seemed closely seated by my bedside" (120). Stunned into silence by Queequeg's presence or by his loving embrace, Ishmael's aphasia has its psychological and cultural roots in how he "knows" the world. Because an interracial homosexual encounter with a tattooed whaleman from the islands of the South Seas is "unimaginable" to Ishmael, Queequeg becomes "nameless . . . a silent form or phantom." Ishmael's inability to articulate the multicultural queerness of the moment does not constitute a temporary lapse; rather, his interpretive failures pervade the narrative. Thus, he confesses that "for days and weeks and months afterwards I lost myself in confounding attempts to explain the mystery. Nay, to this very hour, I often puzzle myself with it" (120). To see what is invisible to Ishmael requires a fuller exegesis of what Eve Sedgwick has called the "epistemological privilege of unknowing."[11]

The origins of Ishmael's "privilege of unknowing" can be traced back to his philosophy of universal humanism and its rhetoric of "eternal democracy," which allows him to systematically disavow any "prejudices." Before Ishmael meets Queequeg for the first time, he confesses to feeling "suspicious of this 'dark complexioned' harpooner" (106) and admits that he "abominated the thought of sleeping with him" (108). It then occurs to him that "I might be cherishing unwarrantable prejudices against this unknown harpooner" (109). Ishmael works self-consciously to dispel his acknowledged bigotry by invoking the tenets of transcendental humanism: "What's all this fuss I have been making . . . the man's a human being just as I am" (118). And yet beneath this humanist discourse lurks a deeply rooted ethnocentrism of which Ishmael (though not Melville) is unaware.

To make the silences of Ishmael's "epistemology of unknowing" speak, let us begin by looking more closely at what he considers to be "the truth" about Queequeg. "[A]n inkling of the truth occurred to me," Ishmael philosophizes. "I remembered a story of a white man—a whaleman too— who, falling among the cannibals, had been tattooed by them. I concluded that this harpooner, in the course of his distant voyages, must have met with a similar adventure" (114). Rather than attempting to understand Queequeg's tattoos in their cultural context, Ishmael can only make sense of his "dark complexioned" bedmate by telling himself that Queequeg is really a "white man" who has been tattooed against his will. Ishmael's conception of "the truth" about Queequeg thus reveals a profound Eurocentrism which will underlie and structure his (mis)understanding of the multicultural complexities aboard the *Pequod*.

Melville makes deft use of his double-layered narrative to deconstruct the complicated relationship between Ishmael's nativism and the novel's stridently democratic rhetoric. Ishmael's ecstatic assertion of "that democratic dignity which, on all hands, radiates without end from God; Himself!" (212) in the chapter entitled "Knights and Squires" has, of course, long been celebrated by Americanists.[12] Like Ishmael's transcendental philosophy, this democratic rhetoric pretends to overlook race by throwing "one royal mantle of humanity" over the "meanest mariners, and renegades and castaways," in the name of "thou just Spirit of Equality" (212). In the next chapter—also entitled "Knights and Squires," as if to call attention to the novel's double narrative—Melville reveals the nativism that lurks beneath Ishmael's democratic exclamations. Speaking in Ishmael's voice, Melville writes: "Herein it is the same with the American whale fishery as with the American army and military and merchant navies, and the engineering forces employed in the construction of the American Canals and Railroads. The same, I say, because in all these cases the native American liberally provides the brains, the rest of the world as generously supplying the muscles" (216). By juxtaposing Ishmael's rhetoric of the "just Spirit of Equality" with his nativist celebration of the dominance of the white "native Americans" over the "rest of the world," Melville subtly calls attention to the way in which Ishmael's democratic proclamations are founded on racial and imperialist hierarchies that silently structure his ethnocentric epistemology.

Ishmael's nativism and aggressive nationalism can be seen even more clearly in "Nantucket." In this chapter, Ishmael extols how whaling has allowed white Americans to "conquer the watery world like so many Alexanders; parcelling out among them the Atlantic, Pacific, and Indian oceans, as the three pirate powers did Poland" (158). "Let America add Mexico to Texas and pile Cuba upon Canada," Ishmael exclaims in support of the nation's imperial conquest of the hemisphere in the name of Manifest Destiny (159). Once again, Ishmael covers over his nationalistic zeal for imperial conquest by invoking the discourse of democracy. In "The Advocate," for example, Ishmael self-consciously strives to depict whaling as a force of democracy: "Until the whale fishery rounded Cape Horn, no commerce but colonial, scarcely any intercourse but colonial, was carried on between Europe and the long line of the opulent Spanish

provinces on the Pacific coast . . . whalemen at last eventuated the libera-
tion of Peru, Chili [sic], and Bolivia from the yoke of Old Spain, and
establish[ed] . . . eternal democracy in those parts" (206). Like the rhetorical crossings of the Monroe Doctrine—in which the United States extended their sphere of influence over the "American continents" in the
name of preventing "colonization by European powers"—Ishmael here
utilizes anticolonial rhetoric and the discourse of "eternal democracy" to
justify the United States' unique form of capitalist imperialism.[13]

Ishmael's ethnocentric nativism is not, however, an accurate reflection
of Melville's own views. To the contrary, the brilliant dialectical interplay
between blindness and insight in the novel's double-layered narrative
allows Melville to criticize the dominant white society without invoking
the editorial censorship that he encountered five years earlier when he
published his first novel, Typee (1846). In Typee, Melville openly condemned the destructive effects of commerce and missionizing on the Marquesas Islands. "The fiendlike skill we display in the invention of all manner of death-dealing engines . . . and the misery and desolation that follow
in their train," Melville wrote, "are enough of themselves to distinguish
the white civilized man as the most ferocious animal on the face of the
earth."[14] Having gone through the "fiery ordeal of Mr. Wiley's criticisms"[15] in seeing Typee through to publication, and still hoping at this
point in his career to be accepted as part of Evert Duyckinck's Young
America series, Melville works self-consciously to avoid editorial conflict
in Moby-Dick and carefully cloaks his criticisms of white imperialism in the
trappings of Ishmael's nationalist rhetoric.[16] Melville's characterization of
the destruction wrought upon the Marquesas by missionaries and
mariners are quite explicit in Typee: "among the islands of Polynesia, no
sooner are the . . . temples demolished and the idolators converted into
nominal Christians, than disease, vice, and premature death make their
appearance."[17] In contrast, Melville cautiously utilizes Ishmael's nativism
to disguise his own anti-imperial rhetoric in Moby-Dick. Ishmael's assertion that "The uncounted isles of all Polynesia confess the same truth, and
do commercial homage to the whale-ship, that cleared the way for the
missionary and the merchant" (206) reveals the sharp ideological differences between Melville's views, as expressed in Typee, and those of the
narrator of Moby-Dick.[18]

In Moby-Dick Melville disguises the focus of his attack on white imperialism so that "the most ferocious animal on the face of the earth" is not
"white civilized man" but the white whale. As with "Benito Cereno,"
misinterpreted for more than one hundred years as a "racist" tract,[19] it
has taken literary critics a long time to understand the carefully crafted
misdirection of Melville's sustained attack on the horrors of white imperialism, from Typee to Moby-Dick to "Benito Cereno" to "The Metaphysics

of Indian Hating" in *The Confidence Man*. Perhaps it is only with the emergence of critical white studies that it has become possible to theorize Melville's remarkable insights into the inner workings of cultural whiteness. In "The Possessive Investment in Whiteness," George Lipsitz analyzes what he calls "the 'White' problem" in American studies. Lipsitz notes that "Whiteness is everywhere in American culture, but it is very hard to see," because "as the unmarked category against which difference is constructed, whiteness never has to speak its name, never has to acknowledge its role as an organizing principle in social and cultural relations."[20] Likewise, Peter L. McLaren observes, in "White Terror and Oppositional Agency," that "perhaps white culture's most formidable attribute is its ability to mask itself."[21]

Melville's most sustained and brilliant exegesis of the ability of whiteness to mask itself comes in the chapter called "The Whiteness of the Whale," where Ishmael attempts to speak the name of whiteness and to confront the "vague, nameless horror" of his own possessive investment in whiteness. "How can I hope to explain myself here," Ishmael laments in the opening paragraphs of the chapter, "and yet, in some dim, random way, explain myself I must, else all these chapters might be naught" (287). Ishmael begins his narrative quest to articulate the meaning of whiteness by first cataloguing no less than twenty examples, from a wide range of cultures, illustrating how whiteness has archetypally been associated with purity and goodness:

> whiteness refiningly enhances *beauty*, . . . [as] it applies to the human race itself, [it gives] the white man *ideal mastership* over every dusky tribe; . . . among the Red Men of America the giving of the white belt of wampum was the deepest pledge of *honor*; . . . in many climes whiteness typifies the majesty of *Justice*; . . . in the Greek mythologies, *Great Jove himself* [was] made incarnate in a snow-white bull; . . . white is specially employed in the celebration of the *Passion of our Lord* . . . (287–88, my emphases)

Ishmael's invocation of cultures from all over the world to reify the idea that whiteness is universally associated with holiness, justice, and the "ideal mastership" of "every dusky tribe" exemplifies the worst kind of multiculturalism, where cultural differences collapse into a vast sameness that ultimately sanctifies Eurocentrism.[22] Significantly, this seemingly endless lexicon concludes with what appears to be acknowledgment of Ishmael's most honest and carefully guarded belief, that there is an "elusive something in the innermost idea of this hue, which strikes more of panic to the soul than that redness which affrights in the blood" (289).

Ishmael thus fails in his hermeneutic quest to explicate the "innermost idea of this hue." One way to critically "dive deeper than Ishmael can go," however, is to read "The Whiteness of the Whale" through the lens of

"Benito Cereno." One moment in particular from Melville's later novella seems to bring into focus both the psychological and cultural origins of Ishmael's "panic." The American captain, Amassa Delano, suspects that the Spanish captain, Don Benito, may be "in complicity with the blacks" who have seized control of the slave ship. Delano rejects this notion, however: "who ever heard of a white so far a renegade as to apostatize from his very species almost, by leaguing in against it with negroes?"[23] Like Delano, Ishmael's understanding of the racial rage exploding all around him is severely limited by the belief that to join the ongoing revolt would mean apostatizing from the white race. In order to explain his captain's rage against whiteness to himself, Ishmael describes Ahab as "black" (248) and notes that though "nominally included in the census of Christendom, he was still an alien to it" (250).

Precisely because of these epistemological limitations, Ishmael's voice finally trails off into silence, despite his opening resolution "to explain myself . . . else all these chapters may be naught" (287). At the end of "The Whiteness of the Whale," he says, "And of all these things the Albino whale was the symbol. Wonder ye then at the fiery hunt?" (296). Having weathered countless, contradictory examples of the meaning of whiteness from "the majesty of Justice" (288) to the "colorless, all-color of atheism from which we shrink" (296), the reader ironically seems no closer at the end of the chapter to understanding what the white whale means to Ishmael. All that is really clear, in the final analysis, is Ishmael's fear. As he says in the final paragraph of the chapter, "[whiteness] stabs us from behind with the thought of annihilation" (295). Given Ishmael's philosophy of transcendental humanism, which erases all forms of cultural difference, he immediately tries to abstract this terrifying quality of whiteness into the "voids and immensities of the universe" (295). Only by historicizing Ishmael's "thought of annihilation" does it become possible to understand what the whiteness of the whale means to Ahab and to reconstruct the multicultural origins of the racial rage that drives the *Pequod* on its quest to kill the white whale.

Ruthless Democracy

The interpretive challenge of *Moby-Dick* is to think beyond the epistemological limitations of Ishmael's narrative. By critically reconstructing the hermeneutic vortex that swirls around Ahab, it becomes possible to reinterpret the mission of the *Pequod*, the meaning(s) of the white whale, and the relationship between "native American[s]" and the "rest of the world." To do so, however, requires removing Ishmael from the "vital centre" of Melville's narrative back to "the margin of the ensuing scene" and historicizing the exceedingly complicated interracial bond between Ahab and his harpooneers. Unlike Ishmael's narrative, where ethnocentric nativism cloaks itself in the guise of democratic humanism, within the vortex of racial rage that revolves around Ahab's quest for vengeance the vast multiplicity of cultures aboard the *Pequod* come together in a contentious, often violent, nexus.

At the center of Melville's novel lies the aporia or unresolved tension between what I will call the "hermeneutics of whiteness" and the "hermeneutics of multiculturalism." This clash of competing vortices of meaning first becomes evident in "The Quarterdeck," when Ahab nails the Spanish dubloon to the mast and announces the *Pequod*'s quest. "It was Moby Dick that dismasted me," Ahab rages. "And this is what ye have shipped for, men! to chase that white whale on both sides of land, and over all sides of the earth, till he spouts black blood and rolls fin out" (261). To which Mr. Starbuck, the voice of New England prudence, replies: "I came here to hunt whales, not my commander's vengeance. How many barrels will thy vengeance yield thee even if thou gettest it, Captain Ahab? it will not fetch thee much in our Nantucket market" (261). Ahab's quest for revenge cannot, however, be measured by the standards of the "Nantucket market"; the value of the *Pequod*'s voyage will instead be determined by an economy of racial rage. "My vengeance," Ahab responds, "will fetch a great premium *here*!" Starbuck, whom Ishmael elsewhere describes as virtuous and "rightminded" (286), attempts to dismiss Ahab's quest as a mental aberration: "Madness! To be enraged with a dumb thing, Captain Ahab, seems blasphemous" (262). According to Ishmael's "hermeneutics of whiteness"—where whiteness is archetypally linked to "the Passion of our Lord"—Ahab's proposed assault is indeed a kind of "blasphemy."

In "The Quarterdeck" Melville hints for the first time that there exists another hermeneutic circle, one that revolves around Ahab and does not include Ishmael or Starbuck. As Ahab charges the crew of the *Pequod* with their mission, Ishmael notices that "Tashtego, Daggoo, and Queequeg . . . looked on with even more intense interest and surprise than the rest, and at [Ahab's] mention of the wrinkled brow and crooked jaw [of the white whale] they had started as if each was separately touched by some specific recollection" (260). By historically reconstructing Tashtego, Daggoo, and Queequeg's "specific recollection[s]" of "the most ferocious animal on the face of the earth," it becomes possible to critically reconstitute what the whiteness of the whale means to Ahab and his Native American, African, and Polynesian harpooneers.

Melville tells us, for example, that Tashtego is an "unmixed Indian from Gay Head" (215). The Indians of Gay Head were part of the Wampanoag nation, which, prior to white contact, inhabited more than thirty villages from Cape Cod to the Naragansett Bay and numbered approximately five thousand.[24] In 1675, led by King Philip, the Wampanoag staged the largest and most effective revolt in the colonial period of New England, destroying twelve frontier towns in a final effort to drive the white colonizers from their lands. The war ended with King Philip being cut into quarters and with his head impaled on a spike (where it would remain for the better part of a decade).[25] To escape the violence of white retribution, Wampanoag survivors fled to the Gay Head bluffs on the island of Martha's Vineyard,[26] where Tashtego was born and raised. In sharp contrast to Ishmael's belief that whiteness signifies "ideal mastership over every dusky tribe," a historical analysis of the Wampanoag's encounter with the destructive forces of white imperialism makes it clear why Tashtego would have joined Ahab in his "cries and maledictions against the white whale" (265).

Daggoo, a full-blooded African, would have surely shared Tashtego's sense of racial rage at the whiteness of the whale. To critically recover the historical origins of Daggoo's rage "it is only necessary," in the words of Frederick Douglass, "to lift up the hatchway of slavery's infernal hold, to uncover the bloody scenes of American thraldom, and . . . [take] a peep into its horrors."[27] Even as a free black seaman sailing on an American vessel Daggoo would have had a myriad of reasons to fear and detest the forces of whiteness. As W. Jeffrey Bolster points out in *Black Jacks*, after Denmark Vesey's failed revolt in 1822 southern states sought to extend their racial codes over ships and sailors. That same year the South Carolina legislature passed the "Act for the Better Regulation and Government of Free Negroes and Persons of Color," which stated that "if any vessel shall come into any port or harbor of this State . . . having on board any free negroes or persons of color . . . [they] shall be . . . confined in jail until said vessel shall clear out and depart from this State." After the British West Indian Revolt in 1838, Alabama, Louisiana, and the Spanish Caribbean passed laws similar to South Carolina's Negro Seamen Act. African and African American seamen became vulnerable targets for slave catchers, who kidnapped blacks off of merchant ships and sold them into slavery. In 1855 the British consul at Norfolk, G.P.R. James, wrote that the seizure of free blacks at sea had increased "frightfully." According to James, the U.S. district attorney in eastern Virginia believed that in 1854 alone more than two hundred free black sailors had been illegally captured and sold into slavery.[28]

Queequeg's cultural identity is more difficult to critically reconstruct. Ishmael tells us only that "Queequeg was a native of Kokovoko, an island far away to the West and South. It is not down in any map; true places never are" (150). Having already called into question Ishmael's Eurocentric conception of the "truth" about Queequeg, a more historically accurate reading of his identity can be gained by studying his tattoos. As

Queequeg undresses, Ishmael observes that "his chest and arms . . . were checkered with the same squares as his face; his back, too, was all over the same dark squares" (115). The color, pattern, and coverage of Queequeg's body would all seem to suggest a tattooing motif distinct to the Marquesas Islands (where, of course, Melville had lived and whose indigenous culture he had studied).[29] As Alfred Gell writes in *Wrapping in Images: Tattooing in Polynesia*, "the tattooing style of the Marquesas Isles was the most elaborate and extensive of any to be found in Polynesia. . . . all-over tattooing (*Pahu tiki* or 'wrapping in images') was a development unique to this area."[30]

The Marquesas Islands, as Melville well knew, had been devastated by an undeclared war of cultural conquest that reduced the population from one hundred thousand to twenty thousand by 1840, in what T. Walter Herbert calls "one of the principal horrors of Pacific history." The Marquesas Islands were also the site of one of the earliest instances of American imperial invasion abroad. In 1813 Captain David Porter conquered the Marquesas Islands in the name of the United States government. And although Porter's claim to the Marquesas was never ratified by the U.S. Congress, he did construct a fort on the island and assume the title of *haka-iki*, or tribal chieftain (although to the Marquesan people, Porter was known as the "demon of destruction").[31] Given that Porter used four whalers outfitted with cannons to conquer the Marquesas, Queequeg would have almost certainly had a very different interpretation of Ishmael's assertion that "whaling is imperial!" (207).

To historically reconstruct Ahab's rage at the whiteness of the whale requires careful comparative analysis. Unlike Ishmael, horrified by the idea of calling into question the "majesty" of the white race, Ahab experienced the mutilating forces of whiteness firsthand. As Toni Morrison argues in her insightful essay "Unspeakable Things Unspoken," Ahab may be "the only white male American heroic enough to try to slay the monster that was devouring the world as he knew it." The "idea of savagery" embodied in the white whale is not, Morrison observes, the missionary conception of being heathen or uncivilized; instead, Morrison reads "white racial ideology" as the "savage" force that destroys the *Pequod*. What distinguishes Ahab from Ishmael, according to Morrison's interpretive paradigm, is Ahab's ability to interpret whiteness in ideological rather than strictly biological terms. Given the singularity of Ahab's quest, a critical reconstruction of the specific historical "recollection[s]" that would have inspired Ahab's messianic zeal to kill the white whale proves difficult. As Morrison acknowledges, "a white, nineteenth-century, American male [who] took on not abolition, not the amelioration of racist institutions or their laws, but the very concept of whiteness as an inhuman idea . . . would be very alone, very desperate, very doomed."[32]

There are, however, analogous historical instances of white men and women standing up to and attacking the destructive forces of monocultural whiteness in the tumultuous years of the mid–nineteenthcentury.[33] Lydia Maria Child's decade-long struggle to rescind Massachusetts's law banning miscegenation provides a poignant example of one woman's war against monocultural whiteness.[34] Likewise, William Lloyd Garrison's protracted struggle against slavery led many to condemn him as a kind of traitor to the white race—to which Garrison responded: "[If to put] that most heart-rending and atrocious enactment, the Fugitive Slave Bill . . . beneath my feet, and to hold up those who are for executing it to the execration of the world . . . be treason, then I glory in being a traitor."[35] Finally, as Stephen B. Oates observes in his biography *To Purge This Land with Blood*, compelling similarities exist between Ahab and John Brown. Although Brown's raid on Harper's Ferry occurred a decade after Melville finished *Moby-Dick*, it is striking that Brown's friends and family tried to get him diagnosed as "monomaniacal" as he awaited trial.[36] The financial duress that Child suffered when her white readers boycotted her books because of her views on "amalgamation," the beatings that Garrison endured at the hands of antiabolitionist mobs, and Brown's execution are all meaningful examples of the ways in which those whites who challenged the powerful forces of monocultural whiteness were, like Ahab, left scarred and "dismasted" by the encounter.

Ahab, then, stands at the center of the hermeneutic vortex of Melville's "ruthless democracy." "Attend now, my braves," Ahab commands his harpooneers, "cross your lances full before me. Well done! Let me touch the axis. . . . And now, ye mates, I do appoint ye three cup-bearers to my three pagan kinsmen there—yon three most honorable gentlemen and noblemen, my valiant harpooneers" (264). Ahab here explicitly dismantles the racial hierarchies that underlie Ishmael's understanding of the world and so severely limit his ability to comprehend the meaning of the *Pequod*'s quest. Inverting the implicit relationship between race and rank, Ahab elevates Daggoo, Tashtego, and Queequeg to the rank of "noblemen" while subordinating the three white officers to them as their "cup-bearers." Melville then subtly but effectively remaps the familial borders of the imagined community of the nation by having Ahab embrace the harpooneers as "my three pagan *kinsmen*." The "axis"—created by the crossing of the lances of a Native American, an African, and a South Seas islander—defines the center of a multicultural hermeneutic circle within which whiteness comes to signify not "whatever is sweet, and honorable, and sublime" (288) but a destructive monocultural force that the harpooneers are deeply invested in eradicating.[37]

Melville's "ruthless democracy" should not be misconstrued as a simplistic form of liberal pluralism, however; his multicultural vision is considerably more complex. Just a few chapters after "The Quarterdeck,"in "Midnight, Forecastle," Melville depicts an incident of racial violence. A Spanish sailor taunts Daggoo: "Aye, harpooneer, thy race is the undeniable dark side of mankind—devilish dark at that" (274). Leaping at his tormentor, Daggoo responds: "White skin, white liver!" (275). Tellingly, Melville shifts to dramatic dialogue in "Midnight, Forecastle" as if to underscore Ishmael's inability to accurately represent the racism and racial conflict aboard the *Pequod*. Melville here reveals the dark underside of Ishmael's transcendental rhetoric of the "The great God absolute! The centre and circumference of all democracy!" who "hast spread one royal mantle of humanity" over the "meanest mariners, and renegades and castaways" (212). By engaging honestly and openly the historical violence that existed aboard the *Pequod*, Melville immeasurably complicates the simplistic liberal pluralism of Ishmael's "eternal democracy."

Melville's phrase "ruthless democracy" thus resonates on many different semantic levels. On the one hand, *Moby-Dick* offers meaningful insight into the "ruthless" racism that underlies the nation's rhetoric of "eternal democracy" by depicting the attack upon Daggoo in the forecastle. On another level, however, Melville's novel offers a critically important portrait of the "democracy" of the whaling industry. Just the cast of characters listed in "Midnight, Forecastle"—sailors from Nantucket, the Netherlands, France, Spain, Iceland, Africa, Malta, Sicily, the Azores, China, Lashkar, Tahiti, Portugal, Denmark, England, St. Jago's, and Belfast—provides a historically accurate representation of the unrelenting diversity of the international work force of the U.S. whaling industry. And on a still deeper level, by raising Queequeg, Daggoo, and Tashtego to the rank of "noblemen," Melville has inscribed a radical democracy in which the transnational workers have risen in a revolution against whiteness to assume positions of power.[38]

Toward a Transnational Conception of "America"

In *Nations and Nationalism since 1780: Programme, Myth, and Reality*, E. J. Hobsbawm writes, "That view from below, i.e., the nation as seen not by governments and the spokesmen and activists of nationalist movements, but by the ordinary persons who are the objects of their action and propaganda, is exceedingly difficult to discover."[39] What makes Herman Melville's *Moby-Dick* so valuable to this project to reconstruct "American" identity in a historical multicultural context is precisely this elusive "view from below"—a conception of the nation as seen by the Native American, African, and Pacific islanders who rowed the whaleboats and whose labor allowed the United States to dominate the world market in whaling throughout much of the nineteenth century. I want to conclude, then, by thinking carefully about what "America" might look like to the whalemen inside the forecastle of the *Pequod*. And yet a thoughtful historical multicultural analysis also needs to account for the final scene of the novel, in which the embodiment of monocultural whiteness rises up out of the "sullen white surf" to obliterate this multicultural community of workers. This conflict between America's dependence on its multicultural work force and the dominant white society's will to monoculturalism can be traced back, specifically in terms of the whaling industry, to the very origins of "American" identity.

. . . . .

The history of whaling and the history of the American nation are thoroughly intertwined; studied together, they provide an important insight into the country's deeply conflicted relationship to the multicultural work force that powered American industry. The first description of whaling in America dates back to 1605, two years before the settlement of Jamestown and twelve years before the Pilgrims landed at Plymouth Rock. Captain George Waymouth, an English navigator, described the Indians' method of capturing whales on the coast of what would become the New England colonies: "They go in company of their king with a multitude of boats; and strike him with a bone made in fashion of a harping iron fastened to a rope. . . . When they have killed him and dragged him to shore they . . . sing a song of joy . . . divide the spoil and give to every man a share."[40] Shore whaling began on Nantucket in the late seventeenth century. Because there were only seventy-five white males sixteen years or older according to the census of 1700, Nantucket whaleboat owners were compelled to hire the island's Indians to make up crews.[41] (Officer positions, however, remained the "exclusive preserve" of white Nantucket families.)[42] In the earliest years of the whale fishery—that is, before Captain Joseph Chase initiated a new era in 1738 by going off in his ship the *Diamond* to whale in "ye deep"—Native Americans provided the manpower that drove the whaling industry.[43] As Obed Macy, an early Nantucket historian, observed of this period, "nearly every boat was manned in part, many almost entirely by natives."[44] Between 1725 and 1734, historians estimate that 55 percent of the whaling crews were made up of Native Americans.

The whaling industry was unique in its inclusion of Native Americans at a time when they were being systematically excluded from almost every other segment of American society. This apparent "democratic" openness of the whaling industry did, however, have a "ruthless" underside. As legal documents from the early eighteenth century demonstrate, Native Americans were often taken into the economy of their conquerors against their will. As early as 1718 the Massachusetts General Court passed a bill intended to protect Indian labor: "A great wrong and injury happens to said Indians, natives of this country, by reason of their being drawn in by . . . small debts when they are in drink . . . [for] which [they] are soon sued and great charge brought upon them when they have no way to pay . . . but servitude." Jonas Cooper, for example, a Martha's Vineyard Indian living on Nantucket in the early 1720s, became indebted to the whaleboat owner John Clark, who used the courts to force Cooper to "seal, bind and oblige himself to go a-whaling for him both winter and summer voyages for the space of three years." Over the course of the eighteenth century, however, epidemics of small pox devastated the Indian nations of Nantucket and the New England coast. The population of Nantucket Indians shrank from fifteen hundred in 1675, to eight hundred in 1700, to 358 in 1763; at which time another outbreak of disease killed two out of three of those remaining.[45]

The dramatic reduction in the number of Native Americans available to row the whaleboats or to serve as lookouts opened new opportunities for black sailors. Having been set free by the Massachusetts Constitution of 1780, African Americans played an important role in the rapid expansion of the New England whale fishery in the nineteenth century.[46] Unlike most other industries in the United States, whaling and the merchant marine treated its black and white workers more or less equally. Beginning in 1796, for example, black sailors were offered Seamen's Protection Certificates, defining them as "citizens" of the United States and allowing them to interact freely with customs collectors in the United States and with consuls abroad. Whaleboats, in particular, tended to be more multiracial and more democratic. "There is not that nice distinction made in whaling as there is in the naval and merchant services," wrote a black boardinghouse master, "a colored man is only known and looked upon as a man, and is promoted in rank according to his ability and skill to perform the same duties as the white man." W. Jeffrey Bolster's research shows that black deckhands shipping from Liverpool and New York were paid as well as their white counterparts throughout the first half of the nineteenth century (the exception being voyages that originated in the South, where black mariners were paid less for doing the same work). African Americans, in a few rare though notable instances, were able to rise through the ranks to become ships' officers and captains. Absalom Boston, for example, gained notoriety in 1822 as the master of an all-black crew aboard the whaling schooner *Industry*. At the time of his death, Captain Boston owned three houses, a store, a garden lot, and a mowing field on Nantucket. And although the wealth and stability that Boston gained in the whaling industry were unusual, his personal success indicates the unique economic opportunities that the whale fishery provided to African Americans.[47]

This is not to say, of course, that racism did not exist aboard the whaleboats. William Allen, sailing on the *Samuel Roberts* in 1846, wrote in his diary of "a Nigger" who "was hauled out of his bunk by ½ dozen men on the deck halfway up the gangway [who] poured a bucket of cold water on a part of his body which shall be nameless which made the old Darkle kick and holler gor amighty."[48] J. Ross Browne, a white southerner on a New Bedford whaling ship during the 1840s, wrote that "it was . . . particularly galling to my feelings to be compelled to live in the forecastle with a brutal negro, who, conscious that he was upon an equality with the sailors, presumed upon his equality to a degree that was insufferable." Institutional racism also took its toll. In 1821 the U.S. attorney general, William Wirt, ruled that "free persons of color in Virginia are not citizens of the United States, within the intent and meaning of the acts regulating foreign and coasting trade, as to be qualified to command vessels." This ruling, coupled with the passage of the South Carolina Seamen Acts, which called for blacks to be imprisoned upon setting foot on South Carolina soil, marked the beginning of yet another shift in the racial composition of the whaling crews. The number of African Americans in the whaling industry declined steadily from 1820 to 1860, although at the time that Melville was writing historians estimate that some seven hundred men of color sailed as officers and harpooneers.[49]

Both the economic and cultural contours of the American whaling industry changed dramatically in the nineteenth century. In 1790, whaleboats rounded the Cape of Good Hope for the first time and discovered the rich whaling grounds of the Pacific. The once proud Nantucket fleet, nearly decimated by the War of 1812, rebounded and by 1822 boasted seventy-five ships and seven brigs. In 1820 a Nantucket ship, the *Maro*, discovered the most prolific of the Pacific's whaling grounds, what the whalers called "on Japan."[50] With the opening up of the Pacific, larger vessels were required, often reaching two hundred to three hundred tons, with three whaleboats and twenty-one-man crews.[51] To save money, whaling ships left New England with skeleton crews, recruiting extra sailors from island ports as they neared the killing grounds.[52]

In the mid–nineteenth century, the racial composition of the whaleboat crews thus changed once again. The three main ethnic groups that manned the whaleboats at this time were Azoreans, Cape Verdeans, and what were known as Kanakas or Pacific islanders. At the time Melville wrote *Moby-Dick*, Pacific islanders made up a significant portion of the whaling crews. In 1846, for example, the Hawaiian Ministry of the Interior estimated that some 3000 "Sandwich" islanders alone were at sea, 651 having left the islands officially in the preceding year (doubtless the actual numbers were considerably higher). Although paid substantially less than either black or white Americans, many islanders eagerly signed on to whalers; Cape Verdians, for example, frequently used whaling as a means of immigrating to the United States. By midcentury, Azoreans, Cape Verdeans, and Kanakas had developed a reputation as excellent sailors and whalers—although they rarely rose above the rank of boatsteerer.[53]

The opportunity which the whaleboats offered to Pacific islanders often came at a very dear price. As Samuel Browning testified to a Select Committee on Navigation Laws, "The American vessels are short-handed when they sail from their own coasts. . . . But they employ a great number of natives of the Sandwich Islands, the Marquesas, and also of Tahiti. . . . There is a good deal of desertion from American ships towards the end of the voyage . . . they are frequently very badly treated in order to make them desert . . . and they thereby forfeit their share of the oil." In 1852, a crew member of the *California* wrote in his diary that "Captain Wood to day made a cat of 15 lashes he struck a Kanaka while at the wheel 7 times drawing blood through his clothes the offense was nothing of consequence he let the sails shake when the captain told him to keep full."[54] No matter what their race, crew members were subject to brutal floggings while at sea. In the case of Pacific islanders, however, whaling captains had a vested interest in beating hands into desertion in order to increase their own share of the boat's profits. A significant number of islanders did, however, make it back to America and settled in the southwest section of Nantucket, in an area that eventually became known as "new Guiney." Originally separated from the rest of the town by a field, new Guiney was incorporated into the "new town" area south of the town center in the early 1820s. Native Americans, Portuguese from the Azores, Kanakas from the Pacific Islands, and blacks from both Africa and the mainland intermarried and increased the community's population of "free people of color" from 274 in 1820 to 571 in 1840. Still segregated, this interracial community supported its own Methodist and Baptist churches, an African school, and an abolitionist society.[55]

Finally, I would like to include one more group in this historical analysis of the "ruthless democracy" of the American whaling industry, even though Melville himself all but effaces them from his literary construction of the imagined community of the nation. As feminist historians like Margaret S. Creighton and Lisa Norling have argued, women played an integral (if often overlooked) role in the whaling industry.[56] Women's roles varied widely; seamstresses sewed the sailors' shirts, women married to whaling captains managed the family finances during their husbands' long absences, and native women of the South Pacific became concubines to

American sailors of whaling ships. Although the impact was complicated and uneven, the economy of whaling influenced the lives of thousands of women in the mid–nineteenth century. Caroline Gifford, for example, not only managed a farm while her husband was chasing leviathan but also invested the family's money: "I told [the banker]," she wrote to her husband at sea, "I wanted about $800 in your name and $800 in mine."[57] For women of the South Sea islands, their economic relationship to the whaling industry was considerably more complicated. As Charles Perkins wrote while working on the *Frances* at New Zealand's Bay of Islands in 1851, "I could not help pitying the miserable and unfortunate little girls who were compelled to give themselves up to . . . brutal sailors. . . . There seems to be no bounds to the licentiousness of the whites when they get among these poor benighted beings."[58] A decade later, Captain J. J. Fisher noted in his log that he had given a gun and eight jaws of whale, with three hundred and fifty teeth, in exchange for a girl "eleven and a half years and soft."[59]

This inextricably multicultural, transnational history of the American whaling industry needs to be carefully theorized. Donald Pease, in the introduction to *National Identities and Post-Americanist Narratives*, recently called for "a reconsideration of the crucial difference between the national narrative and the postnational narrative." I agree wholeheartedly with Pease that Americanists need to consider "race, class, and gender" (as well as sexuality, ethnicity, and regionality) more fully and to theorize national identity as "a permanent instability, an endless antagonism."[60] I do believe, however that Pease's theoretical construction of "postnationalism" is problematic. As Anne McClintock has insightfully observed about the term "postcolonialism": " 'Post-Colonial Studies' has set itself against this imperial idea of linear time . . . yet the *term* 'post-colonial' . . . is haunted by the very figure of linear 'development' that it sets out to dismantle."[61] Pease's conception of "postnationalism," analogously, suggests a linear progression in the development of the nation-state which needs to be more rigorously historicized. As the history of the U.S. whaling industry clearly demonstrates, "America" has *always* been an inherently multicultural society whose economic reach extended beyond its geographical borders. Well before "America" officially came into being as an internationally recognized nation, Americans had already begun their relentless pursuit of international markets and were deeply reliant upon a transnational labor force. While I agree that we need to move beyond "Americanist narratives" that limit "American literature" to one race, one gender, and one region, it is historically shortsighted to think that we can simply leave nationalism behind. Instead, nationalism and "American" identity need to be rethought in light of the country's long multicultural history.

Melville's novel provides a devastating example of why the historically interrelated forces of nationalism and monoculturalism cannot be dismissed on purely theoretical grounds. The ending of *Moby-Dick*, with its apocalyptic confrontation between the forces of transnational multiculturalism and monolithic whiteness, illustrates just how historically powerful the dominant white society's will to monoculturalism truly was. In the closing pages of the novel, Ahab galvanizes the multicultural crew of the *Pequod* for a final, all-out assault on the white whale. In "The Forge," Ahab calls on his harpooneers to baptize the barb that is to kill Moby Dick with their blood "in nomine diaboli" (600). "All your oaths to hunt the White Whale are as binding as mine," Ahab preaches, "heart, soul, and body, lungs and life, old Ahab is bound" (618). Before embarking on his fateful final voyage, Ahab intimates to Pip that "thou touchest my inmost centre" and bids the ship's blacksmith to "rivet these two hands together; the black one with the white" (631). Ishmael notes of Ahab's relationship with Fedallah, the Parsee, that it is "as if in the Parsee Ahab saw his forethrown shadow, in Ahab the Parsee his abandoned substance" (645). With one last wistful thought of his "widowed" wife, Ahab sets out with his crew of "tiger-yellow barbarians" (318) from the islands of Malaysia to hurl "the general rage and hate felt by his whole race" upon "the whale's white hump" (283).

Despite the strength of Ahab's multicultural alliance, the "malicious intelligence" of the white whale is in the end simply too powerful. With "retribution, swift vengeance, [and] eternal malice . . . the solid white buttress of his forehead smote the ship's starboard bow, till men and timbers reeled" (683). The harpoon rope wrapped around his neck—an ominous historical omen of how whiteness would maintain and reassert its power throughout the rest of the nineteenth century—Ahab is swept overboard. "Towards thee I roll, thou all-destroying but unconquering whale; to the last I grapple with thee; from hell's heart I stab at thee; for hate's sake I spit my last breath at thee" (684).

The annihilation of the multicultural crew of the *Pequod* and the triumph of "all-destroying but unconquering" whiteness at the end of the novel provides an ideologically perplexing conclusion to *Ruthless Democracy*. To understand why Melville would have gone to such lengths to offer a detailed and sympathetic depiction of the nation as seen from below the decks of an American whaler only in the end to destroy the *Pequod* requires a fuller understanding of the historical context within which Melville was writing. The forces of nationalism that worked to enforce a monocultural conception of "American" identity were formidable in the nineteenth century. In 1838, the year before Melville set off to sea for the first time on board a merchant marine ship, four thousand Cherokee men, women, and children died on the Trail of Tears, while under the supervision of federal troops.[62] Having sailed on a whaler and spent time as a deserter in the Marquesas Islands throughout the early 1840s, Melville witnessed first-hand the destruction of indigenous cultures in the Pacific because of white European and American commercial interventions.[63] And finally, as Melville was writing the final drafts of *Moby-Dick* in 1850, the Fugitive Slave Law extended the rights of white slaveowners across the entire country and confirmed the nation's commitment to the preservation of slavery.[64] In the tumultuous decades leading to the Civil War, the forces of mono-cultural whiteness were too historically powerful to allow the *Pequod* to triumph over the "white whale," even in an imaginative work of fiction.

The novel concludes, then, with Ishmael floating peacefully on "a soft and dirge-like main" (687). As the vortex of racial rage subsides, "car-r[ying] the smallest chip of the Pequod out of sight" (685), the dialogical complexity of the *Pequod*'s remarkably multicultural crew collapses into a single, white, monological voice. And so we are left to wonder whether this historical multicultural analysis of the American Renaissance ends where it began: with a monocultural fiction. As Nathaniel Hawthorne made a white New Englander "the original occupant of the soil," so his good friend Herman Melville seems to be picturing a white man as the sole survivor of the wreck of diversity—the last, if not the first, representa-tive of "American" identity. It is a distressing, albeit meaningful, pattern to consider. For despite the implicit progress here, from analyzing how Hawthorne's nativist fiction is "history imagined fantastically awry" to the reparative turn at the midpoint of *Ruthless Democracy* to the new trans-national understanding of the American Diaspora proposed in these final chapters, there is no corresponding linear progress in American race rela-tions. Perhaps, then, Melville's image of the vortex in the novel's closing pages offers us a more theoretically sophisticated and historically accurate paradigm by which to describe America's infinitely conflicted struggle to come to terms with its own multicultural history.

This figure of the vortex captures the unresolvable aporia created by the ceaseless conflict between the forces of multiculturalism and monocultur-alism that raged in the years leading up to the Civil War. And yet what this nonlinear image suggests, in the final analysis, is that, despite the dissolution of the "ruthless democracy" aboard the *Pequod*, the forces of whiteness do not completely triumph at the end of *Moby-Dick*. The white-ness of the whale is "all-destroying," Ahab shrieks above the tempest, but it is also ultimately "unconquering." Despite what appears to be the utter collapse of the dialogical complexity of the forecastle to the monocultural logic of Ishmael's narrative, an alternative history of the *Pequod*'s epic battle to destroy the forces of whiteness comes into sight in the novel's concluding pages. Out of the vortex emerges Queequeg's coffin, covered with "grotesque figures" copied from "the twisted tattooing" on his body.

According to Ishmael, these "hieroglyphic marks" encode "a complete theory of the heavens and the earth, and a mystical treatise on the art of attaining the truth" (593). And yet, tellingly, Ishmael admits that he cannot read the "grotesque figures."

Epilogue

In conclusion, it should be noted that every novel considered in *Ruthless Democracy* ends with the forces of monoculturalism apparently crushing or erasing the multicultural complexity of "American" identity. In chapter 1, despite having recovered the "lost Indian deed" at the heart of the House of the Seven Gables, Holgrave pronounces this final vestige of Native American existence to be "worthless" and goes off elated to live in a monocultural, middle-class utopia. Joaquín Murieta, his revolution crushed by white rangers, has his head cut off and displayed throughout California as a symbol of white supremacy. Although Thoreau remains deeply respectful of Native American culture and committed to abolition, Indians are represented as "extinct," blacks as a "vanishing" race, women as nearly invisible, and the Irish as "fated" to dwell at the "boggy" bottom of American society. At the end of Stowe's abolitionist masterpiece, the black slaves have been freed but are on their way, en masse, to Liberia. Despite William Wells Brown's insistence that African Americans are "native" to the United States, his characters (like Brown himself) only find freedom in the exile of the American Diaspora. And finally, in *Moby-Dick*, a community that is arguably the most multicultural depiction of the nation in all of American literature (if still all-male) is utterly annihilated by a gigantic "all-destroying" white whale.

And yet the way these novels end does not mean that "America" is, in the final analysis, a monocultural society. I have worked strenuously throughout this critical narrative to read against the linear narrative of white Manifest Destiny that dominated the mid–nineteenth century. What Melville's concluding image of the vortex teaches us is that the logic of the aporia never simply resolves itself into a binary solution, with one side winning, the other losing. Ishmael alone survives to tell the tale, but only because he floats atop Queequeg's coffin. There is *always*, as I have struggled to demonstrate, more than one tale to tell. Queequeg's coffin, like the "lost Indian deed," can be read as a deconstructive trace of the presence of absence. In calling for a *reconstructive* historical multicultural analysis of the American Renaissance, I am asking that, instead of focusing on the *absence* of "people of color" (thereby inadvertently reifying the tyranny of monocultural whiteness), we strive to critically recover the multicultural *presence* of those who have dropped out of sight: the Naumkeag, Joaquín Murieta, the Cherokee, Brister Freeman, Peyton Skipwith in Liberia, Thomas Jefferson's disinherited interracial daughters, and the transnational multicultural crew of the *Pequod*. By training our eyes to see the submerged coffin on which Ishmael floats and learning to read the hieroglyphs that encode Queequeg's interpretation of the whiteness of the whale, a new, more historically accurate representation of the multicultural perplexities of "America" begins to emerge. The "America" which *Ruthless Democracy* imagines stretches from Salem to Alta California, from Sonora to Indian Territory, from Walden Pond to Liberia, and around the world to the whaling grounds of the South Sea islands. Rather than seeing *Ruthless Democracy* as a definitive statement, I hope my work will encourage other scholars to pursue this historical multicultural line of analysis further and to continue to explore the transnational boundaries of "American" identity.

NOTES

HISTORICAL INTERLUDE
DEATH OF MONLUNTHA

1. Charles Gano Talbert, *Benjamin Logan: Kentucky Frontiersman* (Louisville: University of Kentucky Press, 1962), 210–13.

2. After Hugh McGary killed Moluntha, a fight broke out between McGary and Colonel Trotter. With considerable profanity, McGary announced that he would "chop down" Colonel Trotter or anyone else who tried to keep him from killing Indians whenever he liked. Talbert, *Benjamin Logan*, 212.

INTRODUCTION
THEORIZING RUTHLESS DEMOCRACY

1. Herman Melville, *Correspondence* (Chicago: Northwestern and Newberry Library, 1993), 190.

2. Leon Howard, "Historical Note," *Typee: A Peep at Polynesian Life*, Northwestern-Newberry edition, ed. Harrison Hayford, Hershel Parker, and G. Thomas Tanselle (Chicago: Northwestern University Press, 1968), 3.

3. Melville, *Correspondence*, 190.

4. For an insightful analysis of Melville's work in relation to Jefferson's conception of America as an "empire for liberty," see Wai-Chee Dimock, *Empire for Liberty: Melville and the Poetics of Individualism* (Princeton, N.J.: Princeton University Press, 1989).

5. The term "multiculturalism" can mean many different things and is often used so broadly that it means almost nothing at all. I realize that for journalists, the term "multiculturalism" can become a catch-all phrase applicable to any nonwhite culture. For the purposes of this work, I have taken the prefix "multi-" in a more literal sense. I will, therefore, define "multiculturalism" two ways. First, this analysis is dedicated to studying the complex interaction of a plurality of cultures. In the second chapter, for example, I will analyze John Rollin Ridge's novel, *The Life and Adventures of Joaquín Murieta*, in relation to Mexican-American, Native American, African-American, Asian-American, and the dominant white culture. Culture, however, should not be limited merely to race. I will, therefore, also look at regional, ethnic, and religious culture as well as divisions between eastern and western Indians. Second, "multiculturalism" also refers to the many cultures within one racial or ethnic group. In the fourth chapter, then, I will spend a good deal of time looking at the complexities of black identity. The groups considered will include free and enslaved blacks, assimilationists and nationalists, repatriated black Americans living in Africa, and Dei, Gola, and Bassa peoples indigenous to the territory named "Liberia." I would like to conclude by adding that a great deal more work needs to be done to define "multiculturalism" in scholarly terms. I hope that my attempt to define the field will begin a much needed debate and that my work, whether by means of inspiration or irritation, will generate more discussion about the meaning(s) of "multiculturalism."

6. F. O. Matthiessen, *American Renaissance* (New York: Oxford University Press, 1985), ix. For a fuller discussion of the historical context and political implications of Matthiessen's work, see William E. Cain, *F. O. Matthiessen and the Politics of Criticism* (Madison: University of Wisconsin, 1988).

7. Sacvan Bercovitch, *The American Jeremiad* (Madison: University of Wisconsin Press, 1978).

8. Jane Tompkins, "The Other American Renaissance," chapter 6 of *Sensational Designs* (New York: Oxford University Press, 1985).

9. David S. Reynolds, *Beneath the American Renaissance: The Subversive Imagination in the Age of Emerson and Melville* (Cambridge, Mass.: Harvard University Press, 1988), 10.

10. Donald E. Pease, "New Americanists: Revisionist Interventions into the Canon," *Revisionary Interventions into the Americanist Canon*, ed. Donald E. Pease (Durham, N.C.: Duke University Press, 1994), 16.

11. Arthur M. Schlesinger, *The Disuniting of America: Reflections on a Multicultural Society* (New York: W. W. Norton, 1992), 118.

12. William V. Flores and Rina Benmayor, "Constructing Cultural Citizenship," *Latino Cultural Citizenship: Claiming Identity, Space, and Rights*, ed. William V. Flores and Rina Benmayor (Boston: Beacon Press, 1997), 9.

13. For an overview of different forms of multiculturalism, see the collections *Multiculturalism: A Critical Reader*, ed. David Theo Goldberg, (Cambridge, Mass.: Blackwell, 1994) and *Mapping Multiculturalism*, ed. Avery F. Gordon and Christopher Newfield (Minneapolis: University of Minnesota Press, 1996).

14. Wahneema Lubiano, "Like Being Mugged by a Metaphor: Multiculturalism and State Narratives," *Mapping Multiculturalism*.

15. Ronald Takaki, *A Different Mirror: A History of Multicultural America* (Boston: Little, Brown and Company, 1993).

16. Homi K. Bhabha, "DissemiNation: Time, Narrative, and the Margins of the Modern Nation," *Nation and Narration*, ed. Homi K. Bhabha (New York: Routledge, 1990), 312.

17. Newfield and Avery, "Multiculturalism's Unfinished Business," *Mapping Multiculturalism*, 82.

18. Lora Romero, *Home Fronts: Domesticity and Its Critics in the Antebellum United States* (Durham, N.C.: Duke University Press, 1997), 4.

19. Although I do not discuss them at length, I would like to acknowledge several other works that have sharpened my understanding of "historical multiculturalism": José David Saldívar, *Border Matters: Remapping American Cultural Studies* (Berkeley: University of California Press, 1997); Amy Kaplan, " 'Left Alone with America': The Absence of Empire in the Study of American Culture," *Cultures of United States Imperialism* (Durham, N.C.: Duke University Press, 1993); Peter L. McLaren, "White Terror and Oppositional Agency: Toward a Critical Multiculturalism," *Multiculturalism: A Critical Reader* (Oxford: Basil Blackwell, 1994); Louis Owens, *Other Destinies* (Norman: University of Oklahoma Press, 1992); Rosaura Sánchez, *Telling Identities: The Californio Testimonios* (Minneapolis: University of Minnesota Press, 1995); Paul Gilroy, *The Black Atlantic: Modernity and Double Consciousness* (Cambridge, Mass.: Harvard University Press,

1993); Dana D. Nelson, *National Manhood: Capitalist Citizenship and the Imagined Fraternity of White Men* (Durham, N.C.: Duke University Press, 1998).

20. The term "historical multiculturalism" is meant to invoke two distinct traditions of literary criticism. On the one hand, my work has been informed by Cultural Studies scholars such as Houston A. Baker, Jr., Ronald Takaki, José David Saldívar, and Vine Deloria, Jr., without whom the field of "multiculturalism" would not be possible. The other major influence on my work is New Historicism. To my mind, the clearest definition of the term was given by Wai-Chee Dimock in *Empire for Liberty* (Princeton, N.J.: Princeton University Press, 1989): " 'text' and its 'context' are in every case inseparable, the latter being not so much external to the former as constitutive of it, encompassing it and permeating it as the condition of its textuality" (5). Although Dimock has recently distanced herself from New Historicism, her articulation of the interrelationship between history and literature remains fundamental to my understanding of the role of literary criticism. "Historical multiculturalism," like the work of the Cultural Studies scholars named above, is dedicated to recovering the "lost" voices of minorities and to deconstructing how the dominant white society enforces a monocultural conception of "America" (as in the opening paragraphs of "Roger Malvin's Burial," where Hawthorne self-consciously casts Native Americans "judicially into the shade"). *Ruthless Democracy* is also a study of how the historical context shapes the literary context and how literature provides a unique insight into the historical age in which it was written. For Dimock's discussion of the shortcomings of New Historicism, see Wai-Chee Dimock, *Residues of Justice: Literature, Law, Philosophy* (Berkeley: University of California Press, 1996), 77–79. I agree with Dimock's objection that New Historicism should not isolate the historical text in a given, and past, historical moment. As I attempt to demonstrate in chapter 4, Harriet Beecher Stowe's *Uncle Tom's Cabin* takes on very different meanings when read in 1850, 1985, or 1999, depending on whether it is read in a black nationalist, colonizationist, feminist, or multicultural context. I hope that "historical multiculturalism" lives up to Dimock's call to "engage the text not as the predictable part of a historical whole but as a perpetual witness to a history perpetually incomplete" (79).

21. My understanding of the relationship between history and literature is deeply indebted to the work of such new-historicist critics as Wai-Chee Dimock, *Empire for Liberty*; Philip Fisher, *Hard Facts: Setting and Form in the American Novel* (New York: Oxford University Press, 1985); Michael T. Gilmore, *American Romanticism and the Marketplace* (Chicago: University of Chicago Press, 1985); Priscilla Wald, *Constituting Americans* (Durham, N.C.: Duke University Press, 1995); Dana D. Nelson, *The Word in Black and White: Reading 'Race' in American Literature, 1638–1867* (New York: Oxford University Press, 1992).

22. For a virtual catalogue of the ways in which the forces of monoculturalism can manifest themselves as "logic," "aesthetics," or "sanity," see Herman Melville's "Benito Cereno," *Great Short Works of Herman Melville*, ed. Warner Berthoff (New York: Harper and Row, 1969). Melville explores with remarkable insight the differences between conscious and unconscious racism. For a fuller discussion of the knotty problem of authorial intent, see the beginning of chapter 1. For a fuller discussion of Stowe's claims not to be a colonizationist, see chapter 4.

23. The term "imagined community" comes from Benedict Anderson, *Imagined Communities: Reflections on the Origin and Spread of Nationalism* (New York: Verso, 1990). I am using it here in a more complicated sense of the term. Whereas Anderson speaks of "imagined community" in the singular, I intend to explore the theoretical implications of using it in the plural. At any given historical moment, I would argue, there always exist a multiplicity of "imagined communities." There is always, of course, the imagined community of "citizenship," the legal definition of national identity. But if one engages the notion of "ruthless democracy" in its fullest complexity and allows a multiplicity of groups (defined by race, class, gender, sexuality, region, religion, etc.) to define the nation on their own imaginative terms, a much more complicated theoretical notion of "American" identity begins to come into focus.

24. *Dictionary of Literary Terms and Literary Theory*, ed. J. A. Cuddon (Oxford: Basil Blackwell, 1979), 55.

25. Jacques Derrida, "*Ousia* and *Grammē*: Note on a Note from *Being and Time*," *Margins of Philosophy*, trans. Alan Bass (Chicago: University of Chicago Press, 1982), 43–44.

26. Herman Melville, *Moby-Dick; or, The Whale* (New York: Penguin Books, 1972), 685.

27. Reginald Horsman, *Race and Manifest Destiny* (Cambridge, Mass.: Harvard University Press, 1981), 235.

28. Quoted in Thomas R. Hietala, *Manifest Design: Anxious Aggrandizement in Late Jacksonian America* (Ithaca, N.Y.: Cornell University Press, 1985), 161.

29. The Treaty of Guadalupe Hidalgo, quoted in *Three Perspectives on Ethnicity: Blacks, Chicanos, and Native Americans*, ed. Carlos E. Cortés, Alrin I. Ginsberg, Alan W.F. Green, James A. Joseph (New York: G. P. Putnam's Sons, 1976), 113.

30. Rodolfo Acuña, *Occupied America: A History of the Chicanos* (New York: Harper and Row, 1981), 102.

31. The Senate Committee on Indian Affairs announced after Indian Removal had been completed, "They are on the outside of us, and in a place which will ever remain on the outside." Quoted in Michael Paul Rogin, *Fathers and Children: Andrew Jackson and the Subjugation of the American Indian* (New Brunswick, N.J.: Transaction Publishers, 1991), 244.

32. Horsman, *Race and Manifest Destiny*, 279.

33. Robert A. Trennert Jr., *Alternative to Extinction: Federal Indian Policy and the Beginnings of the Reservation System, 1846–51* (Philadelphia: Temple University Press, 1975), 57.

34. David Weber, *Foreigners in Their Native Land* (Albuquerque: University of New Mexico Press, 1973), 135.

35. Martin Delany, *The Condition, Elevation, Emigration, and Destiny of the Colored People of the United States* (New York: Arno Press, 1968), 203.

36. Acuña, *Occupied America*, 33–36.

37. Mary Gilbert Kelly, *Catholic Immigrant Colonization Projects in the United States, 1815–1860* (New York: U.S. Catholic Historical Society, 1939), 132–42.

38. Alexander Saxton, *The Indispensable Enemy: Labor and the Anti-Chinese Movement in California* (Berkeley: University of California Press, 1971), 19.

39. John W. Kuykendall, *Southern Enterprize: The Work of National Evangelical Societies in the Antebellum South* (Westport, Conn.: Greenwood Press, 1982), 150.

40. John McCardell, *The Idea of a Southern Nation: Southern Nationalists and Southern Nationalism, 1830–1860* (New York: W. W. Norton, 1979), 331.

41. *The Reader's Companion to American History*, ed. Eric Foner and John A. Garraty (Boston: Houghton Mifflin, 1991), 209.

42. Frederick Douglass, "The Meaning of July Fourth for the Negro, Speech at Rochester, New York, July 5, 1852," *The Life and Writings of Frederick Douglass*, vol. 2, ed. Philip S. Foner (New York: International Publishers, 1950), 189.

43. *Thoughts on African Colonization; or, An Impartial Exhibition of the Doctrines, Principles and Purposes of the American Colonization Society*, ed. William Lloyd Garrison (New York: Arno Press, 1968), 113.

44. Eugene Berwanger, *The Frontier against Slavery: Western Anti-Negro Prejudice and the Slavery Extension Controversy* (Urbana: University of Illinois Press, 1967), 45.

45. Hietala, *Manifest Design*, 74.

46. Paul Boyer, *Urban Masses and Moral Order in America, 1820–1920* (Cambridge, Mass.: Harvard University Press, 1978), 79.

47. Bruce Laurie, *Artisans into Workers: Labor in Nineteenth-Century America* (New York: Farrar, Straus and Giroux, 1989), 111.

48. Eleanor Flexner, *Century of Struggle: The Woman's Rights Movement in the United States* (Cambridge, Mass.: Belknap Press, 1975), 77.

49. Barbara Berg, *The Remembered Gate: Origins of American Feminism* (New York: Oxford University Press, 1978), 68.

50. Brian C. Mitchell, *The Paddy Camps: The Irish of Lowell, 1821–61* (Urbana: University of Illinois Press, 1988), 8.

51. David Roediger, *The Wages of Whiteness: Race and the Making of the American Working Class* (New York: Verso, 1991), 148.

52. Robert W. Fogel, *Without Consent or Contract* (New York: W. W. Norton, 1989), 354.

53. Henry David Thoreau, *Thoreau: Walden and Other Writings*, ed. Joseph Wood Krutch (New York: Bantam Books, 1979), 174.

54. Anne Norton, *Alternative Americas* (Chicago: University of Chicago Press, 1986), 78.

55. Laurie, *Artisans into Workers*, 104.

56. For a fuller discussion of how the Irish manipulated their whiteness to gain access to employment, see Roediger, *The Wages of Whiteness*.

57. Samuel F.B. Morse, *Imminent Dangers to the Free Institutions of the United States through Foreign Immigration, and the Present State of the Naturalization Laws . . . By an American* (New York: John F. Trow, 1854), 29.

58. Amy Bridges, *A City in the Republic: Antebellum New York and the Origins of Machine Politics* (New York: Cambridge University Press, 1984), 55.

59. Dimock, *Empire for Liberty*, 11.

60. Boyer, *Urban Masses*, 56.

61. Carroll Smith-Rosenberg, *Religion and the Rise of the American City: The New York City Mission Movement, 1812–1870* (Ithaca, N.Y.: Cornell University Press, 1971), 168, 170.

62. Boyer, *Urban Masses*, 98, 96.

63. Smith-Rosenberg, *Religion*, 217.

64. Anderson, *Imagined Communities*, 30.

65. M. M. Bakhtin, "Discourse in the Novel," *The Dialogic Imagination*, ed. Michael Holquist, trans. Caryl Emerson and Michael Holquist (Austin: University of Texas Press, 1981), 263, 291.

66. Bakhtin, "Discourse in the Novel," 367.

67. My conception of "transnational" identity has been influenced by theoretical works such as Donald E. Pease, "National Identities, Postmodern Artifacts, and Postnational Narratives," *National Identities and Post-Americanist Narratives*, ed. Donald E. Pease (Durham, N.C.: Duke University Press, 1994); Arjun Appadurai, "Sovereignty without Territoriality: Notes for a Postnational Geography," *The Geographies of Identity*, ed. Patricia Yaeger (Ann Arbor: Michigan University Press, 1996); and Saskia Sassen, "Identity in the Global City: Economic and Cultural Encasements,' *The Geographies of Identity.* Both Appadurai and Sassen are talking about late-twentieth-century social and geographical phenomena, such as multinational corporations, NAFTA, or Hindu organizations that cohere across national boundaries. Appadurai and Sassen's efforts to "think beyond the nation" by expanding identity beyond citizenship to include "guest workers, refugees, and illegal aliens" has, however, been helpful to me in trying to rethink "American" identity to include Indian Nations, African Americans living in exile because of the Fugitive Slave Act, Mexican Americans who found themselves living within the geographic borders of the United States after the Mexican-American War, the Irish and Chinese who came to build the railroads beginning in 1850, and the internationally diverse crews of the whale boats. See chapter 6 for a critique of Pease's notion of "postnational."

68. Bakhtin, "Discourse in the Novel," 412.

69. Ibid., 300.

70. Ernesto LaClau and Chantal Mouffe, *Hegemony and Socialist Strategy: Towards a Radical Democratic Politics* (London: Verso, 1992), 115, 103.

71. My conception of hybridity has been informed by Eric Lott's theorization of "the dialectical flickering of racial insult and racial envy" in *Love and Theft: Blackface Minstrelsy and the American Working Class* (New York: Oxford University Press, 1993), 18; Robert J. C. Young's explication of hybridity in *Colonial Desire: Hybridity in Theory, Culture and Race* (New York: Routledge, 1995); Paul Gilroy's conception of "fractal patterns of cultural and political exchange" in *The Black Atlantic*, 15; and Homi Bhabha's notion of "living perplexity" from "DissemiNation," 307.

HISTORICAL INTERLUDE
THE CIVIL POLITY DERANGED

1. Governor Troup to John C. Calhoun, February 28, 1824, U.S. Congress, *American State Papers: Indian Affairs* 2:735.

2. Michael Paul Rogin, *Fathers and Children: Andrew Jackson and the Subjugation of the American Indian* (New Brunswick, N.J.: Transaction Publishers, 1991), 83.

3. Troup, 735.

4. Ibid.
5. Ibid.
6. Ibid.

CHAPTER ONE
NATHANIEL HAWTHORNE: HISTORY IMAGINED
"FANTASTICALLY AWRY"

1. S. F. Cook, *The Indian Population of New England in the Seventeenth Century* (Berkeley: University of California Press, 1976), 26, 15.

2. Nathaniel Hawthorne, *The House of the Seven Gables* (New York: Collier Books, 1978), 20. Hereafter cited parenthetically in the text.

3. For a history of Hawthorne's place in the evolving canon of American literature, see Richard H. Brodhead, *The School of Hawthorne* (New York: Oxford University Press, 1986).

4. For more on representations of Indians in American "history" and literature, see Lucy Maddox, *Removals: Nineteenth-Century American Literature and the Politics of Indian Affairs* (New York: Oxford University Press, 1991); Dana D. Nelson, *The Word in Black and White: Reading "Race" in American Literature, 1638–1867* (New York: Oxford University Press, 1992), chapter 4; Richard Slotkin, *The Fatal Environment: The Myth of the Frontier in the Age of Industrialization, 1800–1890* (Middletown, Conn.: Wesleyan University Press, 1986), chapter 5; Eric Cheyfitz, "Savage Law: The Plot against American Indians in *Johnson and Graham's Lessee v. M'Intosh* and *The Pioneers,*" *Cultures of United States Imperialism*, ed. Amy Kaplan and Donald E. Pease (Durham, N.C.: Duke University Press, 1993); *The American Indian and the Problem of History*, ed. Calvin Martin (New York: Oxford University Press, 1987).

5. Susan L. Mizruchi, *The Power of Historical Knowledge: Narrating the Past in Hawthorne, James, and Dreisser* (Princeton, N.J.: Princeton University Press, 1988), 83.

6. John Marshall, *Worcester v. The State of Georgia, Reports of Decisions of the Supreme Court of the United States*, ed. B. R. Curtis, 5th ed., vol. 10 (Boston: Little, Brown & Co., 1870), 242.

7. Nathaniel Hawthorne, "Roger Malvin's Burial," *Selected Tales and Sketches* (New York: Holt, Rinehart and Winston, 1964), 34.

8. For an insightful account of Hawthorne's relationship to Indian removal, see Lucy Maddox, *Removals: Nineteenth-Century American Literature and the Politics of Indian Affairs* (New York: Oxford University Press, 1991). Hawthorne does not speak directly to the issue of Indian removal in either his literature or his personal correspondence. And yet, as Maddox points out, "whether the American writer in this period wanted to address the question of the place of the Indians in national culture or avoid it, there were few subjects that she or he could write about without in some way engaging it" (10–11).

9. The phrase "epistemology of unknowing" is adapted from Eve Kosofsky Sedgwick, *Epistemology of the Closet* (Berkeley: University of California Press, 1990), 11.

10. F. O. Matthiessen, *American Renaissance* (New York: Oxford University Press, 1985), ix.

11. Eric Lott, *Love and Theft: Blackface Minstrelsy and the American Working Class* (New York: Oxford University Press, 1993), 18, 52, 18.

12. Lauren Berlant writes, "To provide this analysis of national consciousness I will refer to the formation and operation of what I call the "National Symbolic"—the order of discursive practices whose reign within a national space produces, and also refers to, the 'law' in which the accident of birth within a geographic/political boundary transforms individuals into subjects of a collectively-held history." *The Anatomy of National Fantasy: Hawthorne, Utopia, and Everyday Life* (Chicago: University of Chicago Press, 1991), 20.

13. Robert Young, *Colonial Desire: Hybridity in Theory, Culture, and Race* (New York: Routledge, 1995), 22.

14. Frederic Jameson, *The Political Unconscious: Narrative as Socially Symbolic Act* (Ithaca, N.Y.: Cornell University Press, 1981), 82–83.

15. Eric Hobsbawm, "Introduction: Inventing Traditions," *The Invention of Tradition*, ed. Eric Hobsbawm and Terence Ranger (Cambridge: Cambridge University Press, 1983), 13.

16. The notion of a "crisis of indigenity" is indebted to Bill Ashcroft, Gareth Griffiths, and Helen Tiffin's *The Empire Writes Back* (New York: Routledge, 1989), 135.

17. Charles Warren, quoted in Robert A. Williams, *The American Indian in Western Legal Thought: The Discourse of Conquest* (New York: Oxford University Press, 1990), 306.

18. Williams, *The American Indian in Western Legal Thought*, 313, 315.

19. Ibid., 307.

20. Ibid., 315.

21. Ronald N. Satz, *American Indian Policy in the Jacksonian Era* (Lincoln: University of Nebraska Press, 1975), 45.

22. Marshall, *Worcester v. Georgia*, 228, 229, 242, 225.

23. Thurman Wilkins, *Cherokee Tragedy: The Story of the Ridge Family and of the Decimation of a People* (New York: Macmillan, 1970), 229, 242.

24. Wilcombe E. Washburn, *Red Man's Land / White Man's Law: A Study of the Past and Present Status of the American Indian* (New York: Charles Scribner's Sons, 1971), 69.

25. Wilkins, *Cherokee Tragedy*, 290, 314.

26. Four thousand deaths is a conservative estimate; Russell Thornton, for example, has estimated that as many as eight thousand Cherokee died on the Trail of Tears. Cf. Russell Thornton, "Cherokee Population Losses during the 'Trail of Tears': A New Perspective and a New Estimate," *Ethnohistory* 31 (November 1984): 289–300. For more on Cherokee removal, see Grant Foreman, *Indian Removal* (Norman: University of Oklahoma Press, 1989); Brian W. Dippie, *The Vanishing American: White Attitudes and U.S. Indian Policy* (Middletown, Conn.: Wesleyan University Press, 1982); Satz, *American Indian Policy*; Grace Steele Woodward, *The Cherokees* (Norman: University of Oklahoma Press, 1963); John R. Finger, *The Eastern Band of Cherokees, 1819–1900* (Knoxville: University of Tennessee Press, 1984).

27. Satz, *American Indian Policy*, 51.

28. Ralph Waldo Emerson, *The Complete Works of Ralph Waldo Emerson*, ed. Edward W. Emerson (Cambridge, Mass.: Riverside Press, 1904), 11:95.

29. Martin Van Buren, "Second Annual Message," *Messages and Papers of the Presidents*, ed. James D. Richardson, vol. 3 (Washington: Government Printing Office, 1896), 499.

30. Emerson, *Complete Works*, 11:95, my emphasis.

31. Philip Fisher, *Hard Facts: Setting and Form in the American Novel* (New York: Oxford University Press, 1985), 4. This is not to deny that Hawthorne's erasure of Native American presence is "racist" by late-twentieth-century standards. It is. My point is, however, that I am more interested in understanding the psychological, historical, and cultural *reasons* for Hawthorne's erasure of the Indians from his literary construction of early American history than I am in judging him as a "racist."

32. Hawthorne, "Roger Malvin's Burial," 34.

33. For details of Lovewell's Fight and the historical sources of "Roger Malvin's Burial," see James McIntosh's notes in *Nathaniel Hawthorne's Tales* (New York: W. W. Norton, 1987), 18; Michael Colacuricio, *The Province of Piety: Moral History in Hawthorne's Early Tales* (Cambridge, Mass.: Harvard University Press, 1977); G. H. Orians, "The Source of Hawthorne's 'Roger Malvin's Burial,'" *American Literature* 10 (1958).

34. Francis Jennings, *The Invasion of America: Indians, Colonialism and the Cant of Conquest* (Chapel Hill: University of North Carolina, 1975), 136.

35. Matthiessen, *American Renaissance*, xv.

36. Although I am critical of F. O. Matthiessen's construction of the American Renaissance, I do not want to be unfair. I think that we have to read Matthiessen as we do the literary authors in this study. That is to say, from a New Historicist perspective, his text is shaped by the historical context within which he was working. Writing at the outset of World War II, Matthiessen's critical conception of "America" is, not surprisingly, highly nationalistic. This is not to say, however, that *American Renaissance* is no longer an important work of literary criticism. It is a brilliant work, to be sure. Matthiessen effectively argues the merits of American literature according to the standards of Milton and Shakespeare. His criticism is also keenly sensitive to class conflict within nineteenth-century American society. It may seem unfair, to some, to criticize Matthiessen for not being more sensitive to issues of race and gender. My point is not that his analytical observations are wrong, but rather that the nature of literary criticism has changed in the last half-century such that we are now able to build on and to extend Matthiessen's insights. Having struggled with the same complex material, I am deeply respectful of his ability to articulate the meaning(s) of "American" identity. I am also aware, however, that the struggle needs to continue in new directions.

37. Maddox, *Removals*, 11.

38. Charles Brockden Brown, *Edgar Huntly* (New York: Macmillan, 1928), xxiii.

39. William Gilmore Simms, *The Yemassee* (New Haven, Conn.: College & University Press, 1964), 22.

40. Lydia Maria Child, *Hobomok and Other Writings on Indians*, ed. Carolyn L. Karcher (New Brunswick, N.J.: Rutgers University Press, 1986), 141, 150.

41. James Fenimore Cooper, *The Pioneers* (New York: Penguin, 1988), 452, 450.

42. Dippie, *The Vanishing American*, 21.

43. Jacques Derrida, *Of Grammatology*, trans. Gayatri Spivak (Baltimore: Johns Hopkins University Press, 1976), 18.

44. Satz, *American Indian Policy*, 112.

45. Horsman, *Race and Manifest Destiny*, 137, 136.

46. Patricia Limerick, *The Legacy of Conquest* (New York: W. W. Norton, 1985), 221.

47. Marshall, *Worcester v. Georgia*, 224.

48. Richard Drinnon, *Facing West: The Metaphysics of Indian Hating* (New York: Schocken Books, 1990), xii.

49. Williams, *The American Indian*, 315.

50. Washburn, *Red Man's Land / White Man's Law*, 109.

51. Drinnon, *Facing West*, 76.

52. Ernest Renan, "What is a Nation?" trans. Martin Thom, *Nation and Narration*, ed. Homi Bhabha (London: Routledge, 1990), 11.

53. House, *Indian Territory, West of the Mississippi*, 30th Cong., 1st sess., 1848, H. Rept. 736, serial 526, 1.

54. Ibid., 11.

55. Cornelius Vermeule, *Numismatic Art in America* (Cambridge, Mass.: Belknap Press of Harvard University Press, 1971), 55.

56. Vermeule, *Numismatic Art*, 55. Vermeule adds, "The first die-designer to represent the Indian with dignified accuracy, on the so-called Buffalo nickel" was James E. Fraser in 1912 (57).

HISTORICAL INTERLUDE
THE SHIFTING BORDERS OF CITIZENSHIP

1. J. Ross Browne, ed., *Report of the Debates in the Convention of California on the Formation of the State Constitution, 1849* (Washington: John T. Towers, 1850), appendix 3.

2. Ibid., 144.

3. Ibid., 62.

4. David J. Weber, *Foreigners in Their Native Land* (Albuquerque: University of New Mexico Press, 1973), 164.

5. Ibid., 148.

6. *Report of the Debates*, 63.

7. Weber, *Foreigners*, 152.

8. Priscilla Wald, *Constituting Americans: Cultural Anxiety and Narrative Forms* (Durham, N.C.: Duke University Press, 1995), 10.

CHAPTER TWO
JOHN ROLLIN RIDGE: EXTENDING THE BORDERS OF "AMERICA" FROM NEW ENGLAND TO ALTA CALIFORNIA

1. Thurman Wilkins, *Cherokee Tragedy: The Story of the Ridge Family and of the Decimation of a People* (New York: Macmillan, 1970), 215.

2. Ibid., 215.

3. John Rollin Ridge, *The Life and Adventures of Joaquín Murieta, the Celebrated California Bandit* (Norman: University of Oklahoma Press, 1955), 75. Hereafter cited parenthetically in the text.

4. For more on Ridge's novel, see Franklin Walker, *San Francisco's Literary Frontier* (New York: Alfred A. Knopf, 1939); Joseph Henry Jackson, introduction to Ridge, *The Life and Adventures of Joaquín Murieta*; Louis Owens, *Other Destinies: Understanding the American Indian Novel* (Norman: University of Oklahoma Press, 1992); John Lowe, "Space and Freedom in the Golden Republic: Yellow Bird's *The Life and Adventures of Joaquín Murieta, the Celebrated California Bandit*," *Studies in American Indian Literature* 4, nos. 2 and 3 (1992); Peter G. Christensen, "Minority Interaction in John Rollin Ridge's *The Life and Adventures of Joaquín Murieta*," *MELUS* 17, no. 2 (1991–92); Maria Mondragon, " 'The [Safe] White Side of the Line': History and Disguise in John Rollin Ridge's *The Life and Adventures of Joaquín Murieta, the Celebrated California Bandit*," *American Transcendental Quarterly* 8, no. 3 (1994); Timothy B. Powell, "Historical Multiculturalism: Cultural Complexity in the First Native American Novel," *Beyond the Binary: Reconstructing Cultural Identity in a Multicultural Context*, ed. Timothy B. Powell (New Brunswick, N.J.: Rutgers University Press, 1999).

5. Nathaniel Hawthorne, "Roger Malvin's Burial," *Selected Tales and Sketches* (New York: Holt, Rinehart, and Winston, 1964), 34.

6. J. S. Holliday, *The World Rushed In: The California Gold Rush Experience* (New York: Simon and Schuster, 1981), 297; George M. Frederickson, "Antislavery Racist: Hinton Howan Helper," *The Arrogance of Race: Historical Perspectives on Slavery, Racism, and Social Inequality* (Middletown, Conn.: Wesleyan University Press, 1988), 35.

7. F. O. Matthiessen, *The American Renaissance: Art and Expression in the Age of Emerson* (New York: Oxford University Press, 1985).

8. Sacvan Bercovitch discusses his theory of "consent" in *The American Jeremiad* (Madison: University of Wisconsin Press, 1978) and *The Rites of Assent: Transformations in the Symbolic Construction of America* (New York: Routledge, 1993).

9. Nathaniel Hawthorne, *The House of the Seven Gables* (New York: Collier Books, 1978), 282, 147.

10. Matthiessen, *American Renaissance*, 331, 324.

11. William G. McLouglin, *Cherokee Renascence in the New Republic* (Princeton, N.J.: Princeton University Press, 1986), 194–95.

12. James W. Parins, *John Rollin Ridge: His Life and Works* (Lincoln: University of Nebraska, 1991), 11.

13. Ibid., 13.

14. Wilkins, *Cherokee Tragedy*, 212, 268, 289.

15. Parins, *John Rollin Ridge*, 30.

16. Andrew Jackson, Second Annual Message, *The State of the Union Messages of the President, 1790–1960*, ed. Fred L. Israel (New York: Chelsea House Publishing, 1967), 333.

17. Parins, *John Rollin Ridge*, 36, 60.

18. Ibid., 99, 102, 106.

19. Rosaura Sánchez, *Telling Identities: The Californio Testimonios* (Minneapolis: University of Minnesota Press, 1995), 297, 291. Sánchez notes of the relationship between Ridge's novel and the *testimonios:* "Here Vallejo adopts the version of the bandit 'Joaquín' provided by 'Yellow Bird' [John Rollin] Ridge . . . in order to reconstruct the pervasive Californio rage against the invaders" (291). As Peter G. Christensen points out in "Minority Interaction in John Rollin Ridge's *The Life and Adventures of Joaquín Murieta*," Ridge's novel "begins two traditions in American literature. Not only is it the first novel written in English by a person of Native American ancestry, it is also the first novel by an American in English treating the Mexican community of post–Mexican War California" (61).

20. For more on the pitfalls of binary analysis and an overview of the way other critics have read Ridge's ideological stance in the novel, see Powell, "Historical Multiculturalism."

21. John Rollin Ridge, *A Trumpet of Our Own: Yellow Bird's Essay's on the North American Indians*, ed. David Farmer and Rennard Strickland (San Francisco: Book Club of San Francisco, 1981), 52.

22. Parins, *John Rollin Ridge*, 211.

23. Frederic Jameson, *The Political Unconscious: Narrative as Socially Symbolic Act* (Ithaca, N.Y.: Cornell University Press, 1981), 53, 10.

24. Bercovitch, *American Jeremiad*, 205; *Rites of Assent,* 20, 54, 47.

25. Bercovitch, *The Rites of Assent*, 43.

26. Jameson, *The Political Unconscious*, 10.

27. Bercovitch, *American Jeremiad*, 206.

28. As I noted earlier in regard to F. O. Matthiessen, it is with the utmost respect that I challenge Sacvan Bercovitch's conception of "America." Bercovitch's understanding of the way in which American society transforms dissent into consent constitutes, to my mind, one of the most insightful theoretical observations in the history of U.S. literary criticism. It has taken me many years to be able to articulate my conception of multiculturalism in relationship to his theories of consent. I would like to thank Professor Bercovitch for listening with great patience as I struggled to come to these conclusions.

29. José David Saldívar, *Border Matters: Remapping American Cultural Studies* (Berkeley: University of California Press, 1997), ix.

30. For an example of this line of argumentation, see Arthur M. Schlesinger, *The Disuniting of America: Reflections on a Multicultural Society* (New York: W. W. Norton, 1992).

31. Rodman Wilson Paul, *Mining Frontiers of the Far West, 1848–1880* (Albuquerque: University of New Mexico Press, 1963), 14.

32. Holliday, *The World Rushed In*, 402.

33. Ronald Takaki, *Strangers from a Different Shore: A History of Asian Americans* (New York: Penguin Books, 1989), 80.

34. Acuña, *Occupied America*, 99.

35. Holliday, *The World Rushed In*, 452, 455.

36. Richard Peterson, *Manifest Destiny in the Mines: A Cultural Interpretation of Anti-Mexican Nativism in California, 1848–1853* (San Francisco: R and E Research Associates, 1975), 49.

37. Weber, *Foreigners*, 146, 164.

38. Sánchez, *Telling Identities*, 276.

39. Acuña, *Occupied America*, 101.

40. Weber, *Foreigners*, 151.

41. Holliday, *The World Rushed In*, 401.

42. Weber, *Foreigners*, 151.

43. Berwanger, *The Frontier against Slavery*, 73.

44. *Racism, Dissent, and Asian Americans: A Documentary History*, ed. Philip S. Foner and Daniel Rosenberg (Westport, Conn.: Greenwood Press, 1993), 18.

45. Alexander Saxton, *The Indispensable Enemy: Labor and the Anti-Chinese Movement in California* (Berkeley: University of California Press, 1971), 4–7.

46. J. Ross Browne, ed., *Report of the Debates in the Convention of California on the Formation of the State Constitution, 1849* (Washington: John T. Towers, 1850), 48, 48, 335, 332.

47. Ibid., 150.

48. Berwanger, *The Frontier against Slavery*, 68.

49. Reginald Horsman, *Race and Manifest Destiny* (Cambridge, Mass.: Harvard University Press, 1981), 279.

50. Sánchez, *Telling Identities*, 290.

51. Horsman, *Race and Manifest Destiny*, 278.

52. Robert F. Heizer, *The Destruction of the California Indians* (Lincoln: University of Nebraska Press, 1974), 243–47.

53. *Report of the Debates*, 260, 265.

54. Holliday, *The World Rushed In*, 455.

55. Brian C. Mitchell, *The Paddy Camps: The Irish of Lowell, 1821–61* (Urbana: University of Illinois Press, 1988), 18.

56. R. A. Burchell, *The San Francisco Irish, 1848–1880* (Berkeley: University of California Press, 1980), 6–7.

57. David R. Roediger, *The Wages of Whiteness: Race and the Making of the American Working Class* (New York: Verso, 1991).

58. Remi A. Nadeau, *The Real Joaquín Murieta: Robin Hood or Gold Rush Gangster?* (Corona del Mar, Calif.: Trans-Anglo, 1974), 145.

59. Herman Melville, "Benito Cereno," *The Piazza Tales* (New York: Hendricks House, Farrar, Straus, 1948), 140.

60. For more on the theorization of "hybridity," see Robert Young, *Colonial Desire: Hybridity in Theory, Culture and Race* (New York: Routledge, 1995).

61. Americo Paredes, *"With His Pistol in His Hand": A Border Ballad and Its Hero* (Austin: University of Texas Press, 1958), 149.

62. William Gilmore Simms, *The Yemassee: A Romance of Carolina* (New Haven, Conn.: College & University Press, 1964), 301–2.

63. Ridge's own racist prejudices against the California tribes can be seen in both *Joaquín Murieta* (e.g., he describes the Tejon Indians as being "cautious"—"a quality that particularly distinguishes the California Indians amounting to so extreme a degree that it might safely be called cowardice"[37]) and in an essay entitled "A True Sketch of 'Si Bolla,' a Digger Indian," *A Trumpet of Our Own*.

64. James Mooney, "Ûñtsaiyĭ', The Gambler," *Myths of the Cherokee* (Nashville, Tenn.: Charles Elder Bookseller, 1972), 311. I would like to thank David Payne at the University of Georgia for pointing out this connection to me.

65. Simms, *The Yemassee*, 303.

66. Benedict Anderson, *Imagined Communities: Reflections on the Origin and Spread of Nationalism* (New York: Verso, 1990), 30.

HISTORICAL INTERLUDE
DEFINING "NATIVE AMERICAN"

1. Ray Allen Billington, *The Origins of Nativism in the United States, 1800–1844* (New York: Arno Press, 1974), 587.

2. Ibid., 591.

3. Carlton Beals, *Brass Knuckle Crusade* (New York: Hastings House Publishers, 1960), 26.

4. John Bach McMaster, *With the Fathers* (New York: D. Appleton and Co., 1896), 100.

CHAPTER THREE
HENRY DAVID THOREAU: "THE ONLY TRUE AMERICA"

1. Stanley Cavell, *The Senses of Walden* (New York: Viking Press, 1972), 8.

2. Samuel F.B. Morse, *Imminent Dangers to the Free Institutions of the United States through Foreign Immigration, and the Present State of the Naturalization Laws. . . . By an American* (New York: John F. Trow, 1854), 19.

3. Henry David Thoreau, *Walden, Thoreau: Walden and Other Writings*, ed. Joseph Wood Krutch (New York: Bantam Books, 1979), 220, 126. Hereafter cited parenthetically in the text.

4. Oscar Handlin, *Boston's Immigrants, 1790–1865: A Study in Acculturation* (Cambridge, Mass.: Harvard University Press, 1941), 57.

5. As I noted in the introduction, I am not particularly interested in the question of authorial intent; trying to discern the writer's intentionality can lead the critic far afield. Here, for example, I do not think that Thoreau consciously *meant* to erase Indians or African Americans from his text. On a conscious level, he would undoubtedly have seen himself as a scholar of Native American folklore and an abolitionist. This does not mean, however, that these erasures should be excused or overlooked. Whether Thoreau consciously excludes these minority groups or erases them as part of the transcendental reduction matters very little to me. I would, however, encourage other scholars interested in the inner workings of racism to continue this line of investigation. The relationship between racism and philosophy is poorly understood by cultural historians and philosophers alike. To uncover how racial exclusion is grounded in a philosophical quest for a transcendental truth might reveal, I suspect, why many white people have such a profoundly difficult time understanding racism.

6. This transcendental reduction is precisely the quality that Emerson admired when he praised Thoreau for his ability to infer the "universal law from the single

fact." Quoted in Lawrence Buell, *Literary Transcendentalism: Style and Vision in the American Renaissance* (Ithaca, N.Y.: Cornell University Press, 1973), 189.

7. This philosophical paradigm goes to the heart of "American" identity in the sense that the notion of *e pluribus unum* is founded on the premise that the cultural multiplicity of the nation can be reduced to a knowable, clearly defined unity.

8. William Lloyd Garrison, *Thoughts on African Colonization* (New York: Arno Press, 1968), 117.

9. Handlin, *Boston's Immigrants*, 192.

10. This passage is often cited as proof that Thoreau never *intended* to position himself as the "one man" who would become a philosophical model for "all men." I would argue, however, that Thoreau's statement that "each one [should] pursue *his own* way" does not necessarily contradict the logic of transcendental reduction. As he notes in the opening pages, "This is the only way, we say; but there are as many ways as there can be drawn radii from one centre" (113). Thus, even though there may be *many* ways to the truth, there is still only *one* truth. Transcendentalism constantly collapses multiplicity into Oneness and this, I would argue, is the philosophical source of the monocultural logic that Matthiessen implicitly draws on to argue that writers from one sex, one race, and one region of the country can be construed as "representative" of the nation at large. *Ruthless Democracy* is an extended attempt to think beyond such "centric" logic. That is to say, I am not calling for a "poly-centric" model but a dialogic paradigm with no centers and no margins, just positions.

11. My analysis has benefited from Toni Morrison's insights in "Unspeakable Things Unspoken: The Afro-American Presence in American Literature" (*Michigan Quarterly Review* 28, no. 1 [1989]), where she writes:

> The problem now is putting the question. Is the 19th century flight from blackness, for example, successful in mainstream American literature? Beautiful? Artistically problematic? Is the text sabotaged by its own proclamations of "universality"? Are there ghosts in the machine. . . . These kinds of questions have been consistently put by critics of Colonial Literature vis-à-vis Africa and India and other third world countries. American literature would benefit from similar critiques. (13)

12. Cavell, *The Senses of Walden*, 8.

13. Buell, *Literary Transcendentalism*, 189.

14. My point, then, is not to drum Thoreau out of the canon but rather to demonstrate that *Walden* is a multicultural literary text that provides an extremely important insight into the aporia that lies at the heart of "American" identity. In this sense, Thoreau's literary text will once again be situated at the heart of the canon, albeit for different reasons.

15. For more on Thoreau's Indian Notebooks, see Suzanne D. Rose, "Following the Trail of Footsteps: From the Indian Notebooks to *Walden*," *New England Quarterly* 67, no. 1 (1994).

16. Leonard Neufeldt, *The Economist: Henry David Thoreau and Enterprise* (New York: Oxford University Press, 1989), 54.

17. Brian W. Dippie, *The Vanishing American: White Attitudes and U.S. Indian Policy* (Middletown, Conn.: Wesleyan University Press, 1982), 41.

18. Quoted in Robert F. Sayre, *Thoreau and the American Indians* (Princeton, N.J.: Princeton University Press, 1977), 22–23.

19. Henry David Thoreau, *The Journal of Henry D. Thoreau*, ed. Bradford Torrey and Francis H. Allen (New York: Dover Publications, 1962), 2:42 (1850).

20. Josephine Latham Swayne, *The Story of Concord: Told by Concord Writers* (Boston: George H. Ellis Co., 1905), 29, 34.

21. Henry David Thoreau, *A Week on the Concord and Merrimack Rivers* (Boston: Houghton Mifflin, 1961), 53.

22. This interrogation of the role of aesthetics in perpetuating a monocultural conception of "American" identity needs to be pursued in much greater depth. I have chosen not to do so here but would encourage other scholars to continue thinking along these lines. The dissertation on which this book is based was originally entitled "The Beautiful Absurdity of American Identity" (after a line in the closing pages of Ralph Ellison's *Invisible Man*). The phrase invokes interesting questions about whether multiculturalism has a different aesthetic.

23. Michael Paul Rogin, *Fathers and Children: Andrew Jackson and the Subjugation of the American Indian* (New Brunswick, N.J.: Transaction Publishers, 1991), 247.

24. Homi K. Bhabha, "DissemiNation: Time, Narrative and the Margins of the Modern Nation," *Nation and Narration*, ed. Homi K. Bhabha (London: Routledge, 1990), 297.

25. Buell, *Literary Transcendentalism*, 304.

26. Philip J. Deloria, *Playing Indian* (New Haven, Conn.: Yale University Press, 1998), 5.

27. James Oliver Horton and Lois E. Horton, *Black Bostonians: Family Life and Community Struggle in the Antebellum North* (New York: Holmes & Meier Publishing, 1979), 104–5.

28. Horton, *Black Bostonians*, 108–11.

29. Henry David Thoreau, "Slavery in Massachusetts," *The Writings of Henry D. Thoreau*, ed. Wendell Glick (Princeton, N.J.: Princeton University Press, 1973), 96.

30. Henry David Thoreau, "Civil Disobedience," *Thoreau: Walden and Other Writings*, 88.

31. Sayre, *Thoreau and the American Indians*, 25.

32. Thoreau, *Journal*, 3:37–38.

33. Len Gougeon, *Virtue's Hero: Emerson, Antislavery, and Reform* (Athens, Ga.: University of Georgia Press, 1990), 103.

34. Thomas R. Hietala, *Manifest Design: Anxious Aggrandizement in Late Jacksonian America* (Ithaca, N.Y.: Cornell University Press, 1985), 123, 124.

35. Thoreau, *Journal*, 3:37–38.

36. Horton, *Black Bostonians*, 7.

37. Ibid., 71.

38. Richard Lebeaux, *Thoreau's Seasons* (Amherst: University of Massachusetts Press, 1984), 48.

39. Ibid., 48.

40. Ibid., 62.

41. Henry L. Golemba, *Thoreau's Wild Rhetoric* (New York: New York University Press, 1990), 177.

42. William Gleason, "Re-Creating *Walden*: Thoreau's Economy of Work and Play," *American Literature* 65, no. 4 (1993): 674.

43. See Lora Romero, *Home Fronts: Domesticity and Its Critics in the Antebellum United States* (Durham, N.C.: Duke University Press, 1997); "No More Separate Spheres!" *American Literature* 70, no. 3 (1998; special edition, ed. Cathy N. Davidson).

44. Philip Fisher, *Hard Facts: Setting and Form in the American Novel* (New York: Oxford University Press, 1985), 88.

45. For a fuller analysis of Thoreau's relationship to the economy, see Neufeldt, *The Economist*.

46. I am indebted to Philip J. Deloria for the idea of the Indian as "the other without." *Playing Indian*, 34–35.

47. Barbara Welter, "The Cult of True Womanhood: 1820–1860," *American Quarterly* 18 (September 1966): 163.

48. Harriet Beecher Stowe, *Uncle Tom's Cabin* (New York: Signet, 1966), 92.

49. Gillian Brown, "Getting in the Kitchen with Dinah: Domestic Politics in *Uncle Tom's Cabin*," *American Quarterly* 3, no. 4 (1984): 522.

50. For a more detailed discussion of men in antebellum America who became disassociated from the "masculine sphere," see Ann Douglas, *The Feminization of American Culture* (New York: Doubleday, 1988).

51. E. Anthony Rotundo, *American Manhood: Transformations in Masculinity from the Revolution to the Modern Era* (New York: Basic Books, 1993), 2, 3, 191, 175.

52. Thoreau, *Journal*, 5:365.

53. Stowe, *Uncle Tom's Cabin*, 21, 91.

54. Thomas H. O'Connor, *The Boston Irish: A Political History* (Boston: Northeastern University Press, 1995), 60.

55. Ibid., 60.

56. Tyler Anbinder, *Nativism and Slavery: The Northern Know Nothings and the Politics of the 1850s* (New York: Oxford University Press, 1992), 8.

57. O'Connor, *The Boston Irish*, 63.

58. Brian C. Mitchell, *The Paddy Camps: The Irish of Lowell, 1821–1861* (Urbana: University of Illinois Press, 1988), 92.

59. See David R. Roediger, *The Wages of Whiteness: Race and the Making of the American Working Class* (New York: Verso, 1991); Noel Ignatiev, *How the Irish Became White* (New York: Routledge, 1995); *Race Traitor*, ed. Noel Ignatiev and John Garvey (New York: Routledge, 1996).

60. O'Connor, *The Boston Irish*, 74.

61. Mitchell, *The Paddy Camps*, 134.

62. Anbinder, *Nativism and Slavery*, 121.

63. Gleason, "Re-Creating Walden," 676–77.

64. Lebeaux, *Thoreau's Seasons*, 63.

65. Ibid., 62.

HISTORICAL INTERLUDE
"A LITTLE BLACK AMERICA" IN AFRICA

1.　C. Abayomi Cassell, *Liberia: History of the First African Republic* (New York: Fountainhead Publishers, 1970), 143–53.

2.　J. Gus Liebenow, *Liberia: The Evolution of Privilege* (Ithaca, N.Y.:Cornell University Press), 13, 19.

3.　Charles Morrow Wilson, *Liberia: Black Africa in Microcosm* (New York: Harper and Row, 1971), xvii.

4.　Charles Henry Huberich, *The Political and Legislative History of Liberia* (New York: Central Book Company, 1947), 2:853.

5.　Liebenow, *Liberia*, 23.

6.　*Information about Going to Liberia: With Things Which Every Emigrant Ought to Know* (Washington: C. Alexander, 1852), 7.

7.　Liebenow, *Liberia*, 20, 21, 23.

8.　Thirty-Fifth Annual Report of the American Colonization Society, *African Repository* 28, no. 3 (1852; New York: Kraus Reprint Corporation, 1967), 68.

9.　P. J. Staudenraus, *The African Colonization Movement, 1816–1865* (New York: Columbia University Press, 1961), 199.

10.　Frederick Douglass, "Henry Clay and Colonization Cant, Sophistry, and Falsehood," address delivered in Rochester, New York, February 2, 1851, *The Frederick Douglass Papers*, ed. John Blassingame (New Haven, Conn.: Yale University Press, 1982), 2:322.

11.　Kwando M. Kinshasa, *Emigration vs. Assimilation: The Debate in the African American Press, 1827–1861* (Jefferson, N.C.: McFarland and Co., 1988), 95.

12.　John H. Bracey, August Meier, and Elliot Rudwick, eds., *Black Nationalism in America* (New York: Bobbs-Merrill, 1970), 86.

CHAPTER FOUR
HARRIET BEECHER STOWE: *UNCLE TOM'S CABIN* AND THE QUESTION OF
THE AMERICAN COLONIZATION SOCIETY

1.　William Lloyd Garrison, *Thoughts on African Colonization; or, An Impartial Exhibition of the Doctrines, Principles and Purposes of the American Colonization Society* (New York: Arno Press, 1968), 42.

2.　Harriet Beecher Stowe, *Uncle Tom's Cabin* (New York: Signet, 1981), 460.

3.　It is, admittedly, difficult to critically locate the "end" of Stowe's novel. In the penultimate chapter, "Results," Stowe sends Topsy and seven other black characters off to "her country" in Liberia (463). In the final chapter, "The Liberator," George Shelby returns to tell Aunt Chloe that Uncle Tom has died and "gone to a better country" (467). All of which is followed by Stowe's "Concluding Remarks," further complicating the idea that there is any singular "ending" to the novel. In this final chapter of the book, Stowe both argues in favor of African colonization (e.g., "Does not every American Christian owe to the African race some effort at reparation for the wrongs that the American nation has brought upon them?" [473]) and seems to suggest, somewhat after the fact, that there may indeed be a place for blacks in her imagined community of "America." In a brief "statement of facts . . . given to show the capability of the race," Stowe cites: "K———. Full black; dealer in real estate; worth thirty thousand dollars; about forty years old; free six years; paid eighteen hundred dollars for his family; member of the Baptist Church" (475). While acknowledging the multiplicity of endings (which I take to be yet another indication of Stowe's ambivalence and uncertainty about whether blacks should be included in a postabolition "America"), for the purposes of this analysis I will focus on the exodus of black characters that Stowe delineates in "Results."

4. For other interpretations of Stowe's colonizationist conclusion, see Gillian Brown, *Domestic Individualism: Imagining Self in Nineteenth-Century America* (Berkeley: University of California Press, 1990); Hortense J. Spillers, "Changing the Letter: The Yokes, the Jokes of Discourse, or, Mrs. Stowe, Mr. Reed," *Slavery and the Literary Imagination*, ed. Deborah E. McDowell and Arnold Rampersad (Baltimore: Johns Hopkins University Press, 1989); Robert B. Stepto, "Sharing the Thunder: The Literary Exchanges of Harriet Beecher Stowe, Henry Bibb, and Frederick Douglass," *New Essays on Uncle Tom's Cabin*, ed. Eric J. Sundquist (New York: Cambridge University Press, 1986); Richard Yarborough, "Strategies of Black Characterization in *Uncle Tom's Cabin* and the Early Afro-American Novel," *New Essays on Uncle Tom's Cabin*; Moira Davison Reynolds, *Uncle Tom's Cabin and Mid-Nineteenth Century United States: Pen and Conscience* (Jefferson, N.C.: McFarland and Co., 1985); Thomas F. Gossett, *Uncle Tom's Cabin and American Culture* (Dallas: Southern Methodist University, 1985); George M. Fredrickson, *The Black Image in the White Mind: The Debate on Afro-American Character and Destiny, 1817–1914* (New York: Harper and Row, 1971).

5. Joan Hedrick writes, "she was swayed by the forces nearest her . . . her father and Mr. Stowe," before the Fugitive Slave Act politicized her and "led her to write a book much more radical than its colonizationist valedictory," *Harriet Beecher Stowe: A Life* (New York: Oxford University Press, 1994), 235.

6. Jane Tompkins, *Sensational Designs: The Cultural Work of American Fiction, 1790–1860* (New York: Oxford University Press, 1985), 139.

7. Philip Fisher, *Hard Facts: Setting and Form in the American Novel* (New York: Oxford University Press, 1985), 4.

8. Martin Delany, "Mrs. Stowe's Position," *Frederick Douglass' Paper*, May 6, 1853.

9. Frederick Douglass, "Letter to Harriet Beecher Stowe," March 8, 1853, *The Life and Writings of Frederick Douglass*, ed. Philip S. Foner (New York: International Publishers, 1950), 2:233.

10. This subject has been treated at length by Robert Levine, *Martin Delany, Frederick Douglass, and the Politics of Representative Identity* (Chapel Hill: University of North Carolina Press, 1997).

11. More scholarly work needs to be done on African Americans who emigrated to Liberia. As Kwando M. Kinshasa argues in *Emigration vs. Assimilation*, one must be careful of relying too heavily on nineteenth-century African American newspapers, since, in most cases, they "articulated the goals and interests of an elite stratum among free blacks" (3). For an interesting, though controversial, attempt to recover what Liberia meant to black Americans who were still enslaved, see Miles Mark Fisher, *Negro Slave Songs in the United States* (New York: Russell

and Russell, 1968). Fisher argues that many spirituals contain messages encoding the desire of enslaved blacks to emigrate to Liberia. Fisher's book received mixed reviews among ethnomusicologists. To my mind, the argument that African Americans living in bondage would have felt very differently about African colonization than the free black communities who were so vocal in their discontent is compelling and has not been fully enough explored.

12. Martin Delany, introduction to William Nesbit, *Four Months in Liberia; or, African Colonization Exposed*, reprinted in *Two Black Views of Liberia*, ed. William Loren Katz (New York: Arno Press, 1969), 8.

13. Tom W. Shick, *Behold the Promised Land: A History of Afro-American Settler Society in Nineteenth-Century Liberia* (Baltimore: Johns Hopkins University Press, 1977), 27.

14. Samuel Williams, *Four Years in Liberia: A Sketch of the Life of Rev. Samuel Williams by Samuel Williams*, reprinted in *Two Black Views of Liberia*, ed. William Loren Katz (New York: Arno Press, 1969), 6.

15. I want to thank Dana Nelson for suggesting the term "miscege-nation" to me. By "sentimental imperialism," I do not mean to imply that it was the invention of women. It is the domestic quality—seeing Indians and "Africans" as children of the American family—that I wish to emphasize

16. My theory of "sentimental imperialism" has been informed by the essays collected in *Western Women and Imperialism: Complicity and Resistance*, ed. Nupur Chaudhuri and Margaret Strobel (Bloomington: Indiana University Press, 1992).

17. I will use the words "imperialism" and "colonization" as two manifestations of a single historical phenomenon. William Appleman Williams argues that the two terms are distinct in *Empire as a Way of Life: An Essay on the Causes and Character of America's Present Predicament along with a Few Thoughts about an Alternative* (New York: Oxford University Press, 1980). Neither Williams nor other scholars of United States imperialism, however, have adequately theorized how the "colony" of Liberia fits into European models of colonization.

18. Bernard DeVoto, *The Course of Empire* (Boston: Houghton Mifflin, 1952), 391.

19. Williams, *Empire as a Way of Life*, 37–38.

20. For an excellent analysis of the unique nature of U.S. imperialism in the Mexican-American War, see Thomas R. Hietala, *Manifest Design: Anxious Aggrandizement in Late Jacksonian America* (Ithaca, N.Y.: Cornell University Press, 1985).

21. Frank P. Blair, "Colonization and Commerce," address to the Young Men's Mercantile Library Association of Cincinnati, Ohio, November 29, 1859 (pamphlet, American Antiquarian Society, Worcester, Mass).

22. Even the founding fathers were not sure about America's right to imperial expansion. In *The Course of Empire*, DeVoto shows that Jefferson himself was unsure how to address the constitutional questions raised by the Louisiana Purchase and eventually decided it would be safer to avoid the problem altogether (396).

23. Staudenraus, *African Colonization*, 52.

24. *African Repository* 1, no. 4 (1825): 110.

25. For a fuller analysis of the use of the term "colony" in the nineteenth century see Timothy B. Powell, "Postcolonialism in an American Context: A Reading
of Martin Delany's *Blake*," *The Pre-Occupation of Post-Colonial Studies*, ed. Kalpana Seshadri-Crooks and Fawzia Azfal-Khan (Durham, N.C.: Duke University
Press, 2000).

26. House, *Indian Removal Bill, Index to Reports of Committee*, 21st Cong.,
1st sess., 1829–30, H. Rept. 227, 31.

27. Quoted in *Documents of United States Indian Policy*, ed. Francis Paul Prucha
(Lincoln: University of Nebraska Press, 1990), 71.

28. Staudenraus, *African Colonization*, 1.

29. Ibid., 20.

30. Ibid., 36, 50, 53.

31. Ibid., 22,19, 32.

32. August Meier and Elliot Rudwick, "The Role of Blacks in the Abolitionist
Movement," *Blacks in the Abolitionist Movement* (Belmont, Calif.: Wadsworth
Publishing, 1971), 108–9.

33. Staudenraus, *African Colonization*, 61.

34. Liebenow, *Liberia*, 25.

35. Staudenraus, *African Colonization*, 65.

36. Cassell, *Liberia*, 72–74. See also Warren L. D'Azevedo, "A Tribal Reaction
to Nationalism," *Liberian Studies Journal* 1, no. 2 (1969): 4; Svend E. Holsoe, "A
Study of Relations between Settlers and Indigenous Peoples in Western Liberia,
1821–1847," *African Historical Studies* 4, no. 1–3 (1971): 334–40.

37. "American Colonization and the Colony at Liberia" (Boston: Massachusetts Colonization Society, 1832), 4, in Garrison, *Thoughts*.

38. G. B. Stebbins, *Facts and Opinions Touching the Real Origin, Character,
and Influence of the American Colonization Society* (1853; New York: Negro Universities Press, 1969), 172.

39. "American Colonization Society," *African Repository* 1, no. 1 (1825): 5.

40. Staudenraus, *African Colonization*, 91–95.

41. Ibid., 153–57.

42. My notion of the historical complexity that lies beyond the colonized/colo-
nizer binary is indebted to Eve Troutt Powell, *Colonized Colonizers: Egyptian Nationalism and the Issue of the Sudan*, Ph.D. diss., Harvard University, 1995.

43. Tom W. Shick, *Behold the Promised Land: A History of Afro-American Settler Society in Nineteenth-Century Liberia* (Baltimore: Johns Hopkins University
Press, 1977), 67.

44. For a fuller analysis of the role of black Americans and Americo-Liberians
in the colonization of Africa, see V. Y. Mudimbe, *The Invention of Africa: Gnosis,
Philosophy, and the Order of Knowledge* (Bloomington: Indiana University Press,
1988).

45. The United States continued to provide military support to Liberia even
after independence in 1847. In President Joseph Jenkins Roberts's Fourth Annual
Message in 1851, for example, he states, "We are indebted to Captain Pearson of
the United States ship *Dale*, for his prompt response to my application to be con-
veyed in a ship to Grand Bassa." Quoted in Cassell, *Liberia*, 174.

46. Liebenow, *Liberia*, 5.

47. Staudenraus, *African Colonization*, 244.

48. Robert J. Breckinridge, "The Black Race," *African Repository* 27, no. 5 (1851): 143.

49. Garrison, *Thoughts*, 126.

50. Bruce E. Krikham, *The Building of Uncle Tom's Cabin* (Knoxville: University of Tennessee Press, 1977), 23.

51. Forrest Wilson, *Crusader in Crinoline* (New York: Lippincott, 1941), 137.

52. Wilson, *Crusader*, 137.

53. Hedrick, *Stowe*, 102–4.

54. Ibid., 105.

55. Staudenraus, *African Colonization*, 231.

56. Hedrick, *Stowe*, 236, 252.

57. *The Life and Letters of Harriet Beecher Stowe*, ed. Annie Fields (Boston: Houghton, Mifflin, and Co., 1897), 133–35.

58. Staudenraus, *African Colonization*, 244.

59. Eugene Berwanger, *The Frontier against Slavery: Western Anti-Negro Prejudice and the Slavery Extension Controversy* (Urbana: University of Illinois Press, 1967), 52, 47.

60. Fisher, *Hard Facts*, 4.

61. Garrison, *Thoughts*, 140.

62. Ibid., 117.

63. Stebbins, *Facts*, 96.

64. Garrison, *Thoughts*, 135.

65. Ibid., 114.

66. Ann Norton, *Alternative Americas: A Reading of Antebellum Political Culture* (Chicago: Chicago University Press, 1986), 65.

67. Rev. John Orcutt, "Annual Meeting of the Massachusetts Colonization Society," *African Repository* 28, no. 3 (1852): 248–49. It is ironic—and revealing of the complexity of "American" identity in the years preceding the Civil War—that in the 1850s the ACS was arguing that blacks were "native" to Africa (even though they had been born in the U.S.) while white nativists were laying claim to the title of "Native American" (even though the white race was not indigenous to the American continent).

68. Harriet Beecher Stowe, *The Key to Uncle Tom's Cabin* (New York: Arno Press, 1969), 41.

69. Ibid., 51, 52.

70. Garrison, *Thoughts*, 136.

71. Stowe, *Key*, 51.

72. Ibid., 55.

73. Ibid., 56.

74. Tompkins, *Sensational Designs*, 139.

75. Karen Sánchez-Eppler, "Bodily Bonds: The Intersecting Rhetorics of Feminism and Abolition," *Representations* 24 (Fall 1988): 28.

76. Catherine E. Beecher and Harriet Beecher Stowe, *The American Woman's Home; or, Principles of Domestic Science, Being a Guide to the Formation and Maintenance of Economical, Healthful, Beautiful and Christian Homes* (Watkins Glen, N.Y.: Library of Victorian Culture, American Life Foundation, 1979), 466.

77. Jacqueline Jones, *Labor of Love, Labor of Sorrow: Black Women, Work, and the Family from Slavery to the Present* (New York: Vintage Books, 1985), 128.

78. Gossett, *Uncle Tom's Cabin*, 294. Louis Tappan said in a letter to *Frederick Douglass' Paper*, that he "wrote to have it [the reference to emigration in *Uncle Tom's Cabin*] omitted; but it was too late; otherwise she would have done so." Quoted in Yarborough, "Strategies of Black Characterization," 69.

79. Gossett, *Uncle Tom's Cabin*, 170–71, 174, 172–73.

80. Harriet Beecher Stowe, *Dred; A Tale of the Great Dismal Swamp* (Boston: Sampson and Co., 1856), 240, 253, 257, 334.

81. Garrison, *Thoughts*, 29.

82. Frederick Douglass, "The Free Negro's Place Is in America" (1851), *The Frederick Douglass Papers*, 2:340.

83. Yarborough, "Strategies of Black Characterization," 57.

84. Ibid., 65.

85. Spillers, "Changing the Letter," 36.

86. James Baldwin, "Everybody's Protest Novel," *Notes from a Native Son* (Boston: Beacon Press, 1955), 14, 19.

87. Ibid., 22.

88. Eve Kosofsky Sedgwick, "Paranoid Reading and Reparative Reading," *Novel Gazing: Queer Readings in Fiction*, ed. Eve Kosofsky Sedgwick (Durham, N.C.: Duke University Press, 1997), 21.

89. Wilson Moses institutes a similar shift in *Black Messiahs and Uncle Toms* when he notes that "no less than Nat Turner, Uncle Tom represents the intrinsically Christian black nationalism of the nineteenth-century." Wilson Jeremiah Moses, *Black Messiahs and Uncle Toms: Social and Literary Manipulations of a Religious Myth* (University Park: Pennsylvania State University Press, 1982), 55.

90. Kinshasa, *Emigration vs. Assimilation*, 24.

91. Nesbit, *Four Months in Liberia*, 12.

92. Williams, *Four Years in Liberia*, 6, 52.

93. Peyton Skipwith, *"Dear Master": Letters of a Slave Family*, ed. Randall M. Miller (Ithaca, N.Y.: Cornell University Press, 1978), 43, 58, 59.

94. Shick, *Behold the Promised Land*, 28. For a more detailed analysis, see chapter 4 of Antonio McDaniel, *Swing Low, Sweet Chariot: The Mortality Cost of Colonizing Liberia in the Nineteenth Century* (Chicago: University of Chicago Press, 1995).

95. Skipwith, *"Dear Master,"* 82.

96. Ibid., 86, 82, 75.

97. Jane Tompkins, *Sensational Designs*, 139.

98. James Baldwin, "Everybody's Protest Novel," 19.

HISTORICAL INTERLUDE
DIS-FIGURING BLACK BODIES ON THE WHITE PAGE

1. William Stanton, *The Leopard's Spots: Scientific Attitudes toward Race in America, 1815–59* (Chicago: University of Chicago Press, 1960), 58–59.

2. Thomas R. Hietala, *Manifest Design: Anxious Aggrandizement in Late Jacksonian America* (Ithaca, N.Y.: Cornell University Press, 1985), 28–29, 39.

3. John C. Calhoun, Letter from the Secretary of State, Relative to the Alleged Errors of the Sixth Census, February 8, 1845, 28th Cong., 2d sess., 1845, S. Doc. 5.

4. Robert Walker, "Letter of Mr. Walker, of Mississippi, Relative to the Annexation of Texas" (1844), in Frederick Merk, *Fruits of Propaganda in the Tyler Administration* (Cambridge, Mass.: Harvard University Press, 1971), 234, 235.

CHAPTER FIVE
WILLIAM WELLS BROWN: MAPPING THE AMERICAN DIASPORA

1. The phrase "family of nations" comes from Chief Justice Roger Taney's decision in the *Dred Scott* case. The statement " 'all men are created equal,' " Taney wrote, "seems to embrace the whole human family. . . . But it is too clear for dispute, that the enslaved African race were not intended to be included . . . [in] the family of nations." Taney's *Dred Scott* decision (1857) was issued four years after the publication of *Clotel*, but the two documents have an interesting intertextual relationship, in that both seek to interpret the intentions of the "founding fathers," although in very different ways. See *The Black American: A Documentary History*, ed. Leslie H. Fishel, Jr. and Benjamin Quarles (New York: Morrow, 1970).

2. William Wells Brown, "Narrative of the Life and Escape of William Wells Brown," *Clotel; or, The President's Daughter* (New York: Carol Publishing, 1969), 52.

3. Harriet Beecher Stowe, *Uncle Tom's Cabin* (New York: Signet, 1966), 460.

4. My critique of Anderson here is indebted to Paul Gilroy, *"There Ain't No Black in the Union Jack": The Cultural Politics of Race and Nation* (Chicago: University of Chicago Press, 1991), 44–45.

5. William L. Andrews, *To Tell a Free Story: The First Century of Afro-American Autobiography, 1760–1865* (Urbana: University of Illinois Press, 1986), 26.

6. Reginald Horsman, *Race and Manifest Destiny* (Cambridge, Mass.: Harvard University Press, 1981), 274.

7. William Wells Brown, *Clotel; or, The President's Daughter*, ed. William Edward Farrison (New York: Carol Publishing, 1969), 59. Hereafter cited parenthetically in the text.

8. For more on the use of "authenticating documents," see James Olney, " 'I Was Born': Slave Narratives, Their Status as Autobiography and as Literature," *The Slave's Narrative*, ed. Charles T. Davis and Henry Louis Gates, Jr. (New York: Oxford University Press, 1985).

9. See William Edward Farrison's notes to *Clotel*, 249.

10. Nina Baym, *Woman's Fiction: A Guide to Novels by and about Women in America, 1820–1870* (Ithaca, N.Y.: Cornell University Press, 1978).

11. Werner Sollors, *Beyond Ethnicity: Consent and Descent in American Culture* (New York: Oxford University Press, 1986), 259.

12. Alexander Saxton, *The Rise and Fall of the White Republic: Class Politics and Mass Culture in Nineteenth-Century America* (London: Verso, 1990), 32. The debate about Jefferson's involvement with Sally Heming has recently been reopened with the findings of Eugene A. Foster, who traced DNA patterns from Jefferson to Sally Heming's descendants.

13. Cf. Frederick Douglass, *Narrative of the Life of Frederick Douglass* (Cambridge, Mass.: Belknap Press, 1960); Henry Bibb, *Narrative of the Life and Adventures of Henry Bibb*, Afro-American History Series (Wilmington, Del.: Scholarly Resources, 1972; William Wells Brown, "A Narrative of Slave Life in the United States," *Clotel*, 17–55.

14. Saxton, *White Republic*, 89.

15. Louis Ruchames, "Race, Marriage, and Abolition in Massachusetts, *Journal of Negro History* 40, no. 3 (1955): 253, 260.

16. Eugene Berwanger, *The Frontier against Slavery: Western Anti-Negro Prejudice and the Slavery Extension Controversy* (Urbana: University of Illinois Press, 1967), 36, 39.

17. *The Black Laws in the Old Northwest*, ed. Stephen Middleton (Westport, Conn.: Greenwood Press, 1993), 325.

18. Josiah C. Nott, "The Mulatto a Hybrid—Probable Extermination of the Two Races If the Whites and Blacks Are Allowed To Intermarry," *American Journal of the Medical Sciences* 6 (1843): 252–56.

19. Homi Bhabha, "Of Mimicry and Man: The Ambivalence of Colonial Discourse," *The Location of Culture* (New York: Routledge, 1994).

20. For a fuller discussion of the critical importance of Brown's fragmented chronology, see Russ Castronovo, introduction to *Fathering the Nation: American Genealogies of Slavery and Freedom* (Berkeley: University of California Press, 1995).

21. Castronovo, *Fathering the Nation*, 194–98.

22. By "discursive miscegenation" I do not mean to suggest that the black and white voices are seamlessly mixed into one singular body but rather that they coexist together wtihout losing their distinctive identities.

23. Middleton, *Black Laws*, 160.

24. Farrison, note to *Clotel*, 252.

25. Houston A. Baker, Jr., *Blues, Ideology, and Afro-American Literature: A Vernacular Theory* (Chicago: University of Chicago Press, 1984), 151.

26. V. Y. Mudimbe, *The Invention of Africa: Gnosis, Philosophy, and the Order of Knowledge* (Bloomington: Indiana University Press, 1988), 104.

27. William Wells Brown, *Clotelle: A Tale of the Southern States*, in *Violence and the Black Imagination*, ed. Ronald T. Takaki (New York: G. P. Putnam's Sons, 1972), 338.

28. Stowe, *Uncle Tom's Cabin*, v.

29. David M. Potter, *The Impending Crisis, 1848–1861* (New York: Harper and Row, 1976), 140.

30. William Wells Brown, Letter to the *Liberator*, June 3, 1853.

31. William Wells Brown, *The Anti-Slavery Harp: A Collection of Songs* (1848), Afro-American History Series (Wilmington, Del.: Scholarly Resources, 1972), 17.

32. William Wells Brown, *The Black Man, His Antecedents, His Genius, and His Achievements* (1865; Miami: Mnemosyne Publishing, 1969), 48.

33. Stowe, *Uncle Tom's Cabin*, 127, 462.

34. Houston A. Baker, Jr., *Workings of the Spirit: The Poetics of Afro-American Women's Writing* (Chicago: University of Chicago Press, 1991), 26.

35. William Edward Farrison, *William Wells Brown: Author and Reformer* (Chicago: University of Chicago Press, 1969), 14, 177, 240.

36. Daniel Webster, *Speech of Hon. Daniel Webster on Mr. Clay's Resolutions* (Washington: Gideon and Co., 1850), 5–6, 58, 62.

37. Potter, *The Impending Crisis*, 131.

38. Ibid., 134.

39. Stanley W. Campbell, *The Slave Catchers: Enforcement of the Fugitive Slave Law, 1850–1860* (Chapel Hill: University of North Carolina Press, 1970), 27.

40. Potter, *The Impending Crisis*, 128.

41. Frederick Douglass, "Do Not Send Back the Fugitive: An Address Delivered in Boston, Massachusetts, on 14 October 1850," *The Frederick Douglass Papers*, ed. John W. Blassingame (New Haven, Conn.: Yale University Press, 1982), 2:246.

42. Potter, *The Impending Crisis*, 133.

43. William Wells Brown, "Arrival of William and Ellen Craft in England," *Liberator*, January 24, 1851.

44. David Potter puts the number of fugitives slaves who migrated to Canada at less than eight thousand. *The Impending Crisis*, 136.

45. William Wells Brown, "Fugitive Slaves in England," *Liberator*, August 25, 1851.

46. William Wells Brown, "Emigration of Colored People to Jamaica," *Liberator*, October 24, 1851.

47. Brown, "Fugitive Slaves in England," my emphasis.

HISTORICAL INTERLUDE
"THE ANSWER IS NEVER EXPRESSED IN WORDS"

1. "Annual Meeting of the Massachusetts Colonization Society" (August 1852), *African Repository* 28, no. 3: 248 (my emphases).

2. For a fuller analysis of Jefferson's constitutional dilemma, see chapters 8 and 9 of Alexander DeConde, *This Affair of Louisiana* (New York: Scribner's Sons, 1976). For an enlightening analysis of the relationship between Jefferson's phrase and the works of Melville, see Wai-Chee Dimock, *Empire for Liberty: Melville and the Poetics of Individualism* (Princeton, N.J.: Princeton University Press, 1989).

3. See "Documents Relating to the Origins of the Monroe Doctrine," *Expansion and Reform, 1815–1850*, ed. Charles M. Wiltse (New York: Free Press, 1967).

4. Thomas R. Hietala, *Manifest Design: Anxious Aggrandizement in Late Jacksonian America* (Ithaca, N.Y.: Cornell University Press, 1985), 84.

5. Howard Zinn, *A People's History of the United States* (New York: Harper and Row, 1980) 166.

CHAPTER SIX
HERMAN MELVILLE: RUTHLESS DEMOCRACY

1. For a fuller explanation of how the nation's will to empire increased multicultural diversity, see the third section of the introduction.

2. Michael Paul Rogin, *Subversive Genealogy: The Politics and Art of Herman Melville* (New York: Alfred A. Knopf, 1983), 108, 144.

3. Herman Melville, *Moby-Dick; or, The Whale*, ed. Harold Beaver (New York: Penguin Books, 1986), 607. Hereafter cited parenthetically in the text.

4. Donald E. Pease, "Melville and Cultural Persuasion," *Ideology and Classic American Literature*, ed. Sacvan Bercovitch and Myra Jehlen (New York: Cambridge University Press, 1986), 415.

5. Herman Melville, *Correspondence* (Chicago: Northwestern University Press and Newberry Library, 1993), 190.

6. Harold Beaver supplies a map of the *Pequod*'s voyage Melville, *Moby-Dick*, 1014.

7. For a fuller analysis of the attempt to theorize the nation in a transnational context, see Arjun Appadurai, "Sovereignty without Territoriality: Notes for a Postnational Geography," *The Geographies of Identity*, ed. Patricia Yaeger (Ann Arbor: Michigan University Press, 1996).

8. For a detailed account of the history of the whaling industry, see Lance E. Davis, Robert E. Gallman, and Karin Gleiter, *In Pursuit of Leviathan: Technology, Institutions, Productivity, and Profits in American Whaling, 1816–1906* (Chicago: University of Chicago Press, 1997).

9. For a fuller analysis of the narrative structure of "Benito Cereno", see chapter 6 of Dana D. Nelson, *The Word in Black and White* (New York: Oxford University Press, 1992); Sterling Stuckey and Joshua Leslie, "The Death of Benito Cereno: A Reading of Herman Melville on Slavery," *Going through the Storm: The Influence of African-American Art in History* (New York: Oxford University Press, 1994); James H. Kavanagh, "That Hive of Subtlety: 'Benito Cereno' and the Liberal Hero," *Ideology and Classic American Literature*, ed. Sacvan Bercovitch and Myra Jehlen (New York: Cambridge University Press, 1986).

10. Eve Kosofsky Sedgwick, *Epistemology of the Closet* (Berkeley: University of California Press, 1990), 11.

11. Ibid., 5.

12. See F. O. Matthiessen, *The American Renaissance: Art and Expression in the Age of Emerson* (New York: Oxford University Press, 1985), 442–43; Nancy Fredericks, *Melville's Art of Democracy* (Athens, Ga.: University of Georgia Press, 1995), 11; for a darker reading of the passage see Dimock, *Empire for Liberty*, 122.

13. "Documents Relating to the Origins of the Monroe Doctrine," *Expansion and Reform, 1815–1850*, ed. Charles M. Wiltse (New York: Free Press, 1967), 61.

14. Herman Melville, *Typee: A Peep at Polynesian Life*, ed. Harrison Hayford, Hershel Parker, and G. Thomas Tanselle (Chicago: Northwestern University Press, 1968), 125.

15. Leon Howard, "Historical Note" to Melville, *Typee*, 3.

16. For more on Melville's relationship to Duyckinck, see chapter 4 of Rogin, *Subversive Genealogy*.

17. Melville, *Typee*, 195.

18. For a more detailed analysis of Melville's anti-imperialism, see John Carlos Rowe, "Melville's *Typee*: U.S. Imperialism at Home and Abroad," *National Identities and Post-Americanist Narratives*, ed. Donald E. Pease (Durham, N.C.: Duke University Press, 1994).

19. For an interesting overview of the critical history of "Benito Cereno," see Kavanagh, "That Hive of Subtlety," 353–55.

20. George Lipsitz, "The Possessive Investment in Whiteness: Racialized Social Democracy and the 'White' Problem in American Studies," *American Quarterly* 47, no. 3 (1995): 369.

21. Peter McLaren, "White Terror and Oppositional Agency: Towards a Critical Multiculturalism," *Multiculturalism: A Critical Reader*, ed. David Theo Goldberg (Cambridge, Mass.: Basil Blackwell, 1994), 61.

22. For an important critique of careless multiculturalism, see Wahneema Lubiano, "Like Being Mugged by a Metaphor: Multiculturalism and State Narratives," *Mapping Multiculturalism*, ed. Avery F. Gordon and Christopher Newfield, (Minneapolis: University of Minnesota Press, 1996), 67.

23. Herman Melville, "Benito Cereno," *Great Short Works of Herman Melville*, ed. Warner Berthoff (New York: Harper and Row, 1969), 270.

24. Barbara, Leitch, *A Concise Dictionary of Indian Tribes of North America* (Algonac, Mich.: Reference Publications, 1979), 502.

25. Russell Bourne, *The Red King's Rebellion: Racial Politics in New England, 1675–1678* (New York: Atheneum, 1990), 201.

26. Leitch, *Dictionary of Indian Tribes*, 502.

27. Frederick Douglass, "Emancipation, Racism and the Work before Us: An Address Delivered in Philadelphia, Pa. on 4 December 1863," *The Frederick Douglass Papers*, ed. John W. Blassingame (New Haven, Conn.: Yale University Press, 1982), 2:599.

28. W. Jeffrey Bolster, *Black Jacks: African American Seamen in the Age of the Sail* (Cambridge, Mass.: Harvard University Press, 1997), 194, 199, 202.

29. For a detailed account of Melville's time in the Marquesas Islands, see T. Walter Herbert Jr., *Marquesan Encounters: Melville and the Meaning of Civilization* (Cambridge, Mass.: Harvard University Press, 1980); Charles Roberts Anderson, *Melville in the South Seas* (New York: Columbia University Press, 1939).

30. Alfred Gell, *Wrapping in Images: Tattooing in Polynesia*, (New York: Oxford University Press, 1993), 163.

31. Herbert, *Marquesan Encounters*, 19, 79, 95, 97.

32. Toni Morrison, "Unspeakable Things Unspoken: The Afro-American Presence in American Literature," *Michigan Quarterly Review* 28 (1989): 17, 16. For earlier readings of the whiteness of the whale in racial terms, see D. H. Lawrence, *Studies in Classic American Literature* (New York: Doubleday and Co., 1951), and C.L.R. James, *Mariners, Renegades and Castaways* (New York: Allison and Busby, 1985).

33. My discussion of resistance to whiteness has been influenced here by John Garvey and Noel Ignatiev's work. See, for example, *Race Traitor*, ed. Noel Ignatiev and John Garvey (New York: Routledge, 1996).

34. Louis Ruchames, "Race, Marriage, and Abolition in Massachusetts," *Journal of Negro History* 40, no. 3 (1955): 253, 260.

35. William R. Lloyd Garrison to J. Miller McKim, October 4, 1851, *The Letters of William Lloyd Garrison*, ed. Louis Ruchames (Cambridge, Mass.: Belknap Press of Harvard University Press, 1975), 4:91–92.

36. Stephen B. Oates, *To Purge This Land with Blood: A Biography of John Brown* (New York: Harper and Row, 1970), 3.

37. David R. Roediger, *Towards the Abolition of Whiteness: Essays on Race, Politics, and Working Class History* (New York: Verso, 1994), 3.

38. The phrase "radical democracy" comes from Ernesto LaClau and Chantal Mouffe's *Hegemony and Socialist Strategy: Towards a Radical Democratic Politics* (London: Verso, 1992). "This proliferation of antagonisms and calling into question of relations of subordination should be considered as a moment of deepening of the democratic revolution" (163).

39. E. J. Hobsbawm, *Nations and Nationalism since 1780: Programme, Myth, and Reality* (Cambridge: Cambridge University Press, 1990), 11.

40. Edouard A. Stackpole, *The Sea-Hunters: The New England Whalemen during Two Centuries, 1635–1835* (New York: Bonanza Books, 1953), 15.

41. Edward Beyers, *The Nation of Nantucket: Society and Politics in an Early American Commercial Center, 1660–1820* (Boston: Northeastern University Press, 1987), 75.

42. Margaret Creighton, *Rites and Passages: The Experience of American Whaling, 1830–1870* (New York: Cambridge University Press, 1995), 22.

43. Stackpole, *The Sea-Hunters*, 23.

44. Beyers, *Nation of Nantucket*, 94.

45. Ibid., 97–98, 95, 99, 163.

46. James Farr, "A Slow Boat to Nowhere: The Multi-Racial Crews of the American Whaling Industry," *Journal of Negro History* 68, no. 2 (1983): 161.

47. Bolster, *Black Jacks*, 5, 177, 161, 162.

48. Creighton, *Rites and Passages*, 123.

49. Bolster, *Black Jacks*, 176, 172, 177.

50. Stackpole, *Sea-Hunters*, 165, 268.

51. Beyers, *Nation of Nantucket*, 249.

52. Marion Diamond, "Queequeg's Crewmates: Pacific Islanders in the European Shipping Industry," *International Journal of Maritime History* 1 (December 1989): 129.

53. Briton Cooper Busch, *"Whaling Will Never Do for Me": The American Whalemen in the Nineteenth Century* (Lexington: University Press of Kentucky, 1994), 46.

54. Busch, *"Whaling Will Never Do for Me,"* 46, 42, 48.

55. Beyers, *Nation of Nantucket*, 255, 298.

56. See *Iron Men, Wooden Women: Gender and Seafaring in the Atlantic World, 1700–1920*, ed. Margaret S. Creighton and Lisa Norling (Baltimore: Johns Hopkins University Press, 1996).

57. Lisa Norling, "Ahab's Wife: Women and the American Whaling Industry, 1820–1870," *Iron Men, Wooden Women*, ed. Creighton and Norling, 81.

58. Busch, *"Whaling Will Never Do for Me,"* 139.

59. Greg Dening, *Islands and Beaches: Discourse on a Silent Land, Marquesas, 1774–1880* (Honolulu: University Press of Hawaii, 1980), 270.

60. Donald Pease, "National Identities, Postmodern Artifacts, and Postnational Narratives," *National Identities and Post-Americanist Narratives*, 7. For another interpretation of "postnational," see Arjun Appadurai, "Sovereignty without Territoriality," 41–42.

61. Anne McClintock, "The Angel of Progress: Pitfalls of the Term 'Post-Colonialism,' " *Social Text* 10 (1992): 2–3, 31–32, 85.

62. For a detailed account of how the Trail of Tears was covered in the white press, see Thurman Wilkins, *Cherokee Tragedy: The Story of the Ridge Family and of the Decimation of a People* (New York: Macmillan, 1970), 304–20.

63. See Herbert, *Marquesan Encounters*, 79–111.

64. See chapter 4 of Rogin, *Subversive Genealogy*, and chapters 1 and 3 of Carolyn L. Karcher, *Shadow over the Promised Land: Slavery, Race, and Violence in Melville's America* (Baton Rouge: Louisiana State University Press, 1980).

BIBLIOGRAPHY

Acuña, Rodolfo. *Occupied America: A History of the Chicanos*. New York: Harper and Row, 1981.

Anbinder, Tyler. *Nativism and Slavery: The Northern Know Nothings and the Politics of the 1850s*. New York: Oxford University Press, 1992.

Anderson, Benedict. *Imagined Communities: Reflections on the Origin and Spread of Nationalism*. New York: Verso, 1990.

Anderson, Charles Roberts. *Melville in the South Seas*. New York: Columbia University Press, 1939.

Andrews, William L. *To Tell a Free Story: The First Century of Afro-American Autobiography, 1760–1865*. Urbana: University of Illinois Press, 1986.

Appaduri, Arjun. "Sovereignty without Territoriality: Notes for a Postnational Geography." *The Geographies of Identity*. Ed. Patricia Yaeger. Ann Arbor: Michigan University Press, 1996.

Ashcroft, Bill, Gareth Griffiths, and Helen Tiffin. *The Empire Writes Back*. New York: Routledge, 1989.

Baker, Houston A. Jr. *Blues, Ideology, and Afro-American Literature: A Vernacular Theory*. Chicago: University of Chicago Press, 1984.

———. *Workings of the Spirit: The Poetics of Afro-American Women's Writing*. Chicago: University of Chicago Press, 1991.

Bakhtin, M. M. "Discourse in the Novel." *The Dialogic Imagination*. Ed. Michael Holquist. Trans. Caryl Emerson and Michael Holquist. Austin: University of Texas Press, 1981.

Baldwin, James. "Everybody's Protest Novel." *Notes from a Native Son*. Boston: Beacon Press, 1955.

Baym, Nina. *Woman's Fiction: A Guide to Novels by and about Women in America, 1820–1870*. Ithaca, N.Y.: Cornell University Press, 1978.

Beals, Carlton. *Brass Knuckle Crusade*. New York: Hastings House Publishers, 1960.

Beecher, Catherine E., and Harriet Beecher Stowe. *The American Woman's Home; or, Principles of Domestic Science, Being a Guide to the Formation and Maintenance of Economical, Healthful, Beautiful and Christian Homes*. Watkins Glen, N.Y.: Library of Victorian Culture, American Life Foundation, 1979.

Bercovitch, Sacvan. *The American Jeremiad*. Madison: University of Wisconsin Press, 1978.

———. *The Rites of Assent: Transformations in the Symbolic Construction of America*. New York: Routledge, 1993.

Berg, Barbara. *The Remembered Gate: Origins of American Feminism*. New York: Oxford University Press, 1978.

Berlant, Lauren. *The Anatomy of National Fantasy: Hawthorne, Utopia, and Everyday Life*. Chicago: University of Chicago Press, 1991.

Berwanger, Eugene. *The Frontier against Slavery: Western Anti-Negro Prejudice and the Slavery Extension Controversy*. Urbana: University of Illinois Press, 1967.

Beyers, Edward. *The Nation of Nantucket: Society and Politics in an Early American Commercial Center, 1660–1820*. Boston: Northeastern University Press, 1987.

Bhabha, Homi K. "DissemiNation: Time, Narrative, and the Margins of the Modern Nation." *Nation and Narration*. Ed. Homi K. Bhabha. New York: Routledge, 1990.

———. "Of Mimicry and Man: The Ambivalence of Colonial Discourse." *The Location of Culture*. New York: Routledge, 1994.

Bibb, Henry. *Narrative of the Life and Adventures of Henry Bibb, Afro-American History Series*. Wilmington, Del.: Scholarly Resources, 1972.

Billington, Ray Allen. *The Origins of Nativism in the United States, 1800–1844*. New York: Arno Press, 1974.

Blair, Frank P. "Colonization and Commerce." Address to the Young Men's Mercantile Library Association of Cincinnati, Ohio, November 29, 1859. Pamphlet, American Antiquarian Society, Worcester, Mass.

Bolster, W. Jeffrey. *Black Jacks: African American Seamen in the Age of the Sail*. Cambridge, Mass.: Harvard University Press, 1997.

Bourne, Russell. *The Red King's Rebellion: Racial Politics in New England, 1675–1678*. New York: Atheneum, 1990.

Boyer, Paul. *Urban Masses and Moral Order in America, 1820-1920*. Cambridge, Mass.: Harvard University Press, 1978.

Bracey, John H., August Meier, and Elliot Rudwick. *Black Nationalism in America*. New York: Bobbs-Merrill, 1970.

Breckinridge, Robert J. "The Black Race." *African Repository* 27, no. 5 (1851).

Bridges, Amy. *A City in the Republic: Antebellum New York and the Origins of Machine Politics*. New York: Cambridge University Press, 1984.

Brodhead, Richard H. *The School of Hawthorne*. New York: Oxford University Press, 1986.

Brown, Charles Brockden. *Edgar Huntly*. New York: Macmillan, 1928.

Brown, Gillian. *Domestic Individualism: Imagining Self in Nineteenth-Century America*. Berkeley: University of California Press, 1990.

———. "Getting in the Kitchen with Dinah: Domestic Politics in *Uncle Tom's Cabin*." *American Quarterly* 3, no. 4 (1984).

Brown, William Wells. "The Anti-Slavery Harp: A Collection of Songs." *Afro-American History Series*. Wilmington, Del.: Scholarly Resources, 1972.

———. *The Black Man, His Antecedents, His Genius, and His Achievements*. Miami: Mnemosyne Publishing, 1969.

———. *Clotel; or, The President's Daughter*. Ed. William Edward Farrison. New York: Carol Publishing, 1969.

———. *Clotelle: A Tale of the Southern States. Violence and the Black Imagination*. Ed. Ronald T. Takaki. New York: G. P. Putnam's Sons, 1972.

———. "Narrative of the Life and Escape of William Wells Brown." *Clotel; or, The President's Daughter*. Ed. William Edward Farrison. New York: Carol Publishing, 1969.

Browne, J. Ross. *Report of the Debates in the Convention of California on the Formation of the State Constitution, 1849*. Washington: John T. Towers, 1850.

Buell, Lawrence. *Literary Transcendentalism: Style and Vision in the American Renaissance*. Ithaca, N.Y.: Cornell University Press, 1973.

Burchell, R. A. *The San Francisco Irish, 1848–1880*. Berkeley: University of California Press, 1980.

Busch, Briton Cooper. *"Whaling Will Never Do for Me": The American Whalemen in the Nineteenth Century*. Lexington: University Press of Kentucky, 1994.

Cain, William E. *F. O. Matthiessen and the Politics of Criticism*. Madison: University of Wisconsin, 1988.

Calhoun, John C. "Letter from the Secretary of State, Relative to the Alleged Errors of the Sixth Census." February 8, 1845. 28th Cong., 2d sess., 1845. S. Doc 5.

Campbell, Stanley W. *The Slave Catchers: Enforcement of the Fugitive Slave Law, 1850–1860*. Chapel Hill: University of North Carolina Press, 1970.

Cassell, C. Abayomi. *Liberia: History of the First African Republic*. New York: Fountainhead Publishers, 1970.

Castronovo, Russ. *Fathering the Nation: American Genealogies of Slavery and Freedom*. Berkeley: University of California Press, 1995.

Cavell, Stanley. *The Senses of Walden*. New York: Viking Press, 1972.

Chaudhuri, Nupur, and Margaret Strobel. *Western Women and Imperialism: Complicity and Resistance*. Bloomington: Indiana University Press, 1992.

Cheyfitz, Eric. "Savage Law: The Plot against American Indians in *Johnson and Graham's Lessee v. M'Intosh* and *The Pioneers*." *Cultures of United States Imperialism*. Ed. Amy Kaplan and Donald E. Pease. Durham, N.C.: Duke University Press, 1993).

Child, Lydia Maria. *Hobomok and Other Writings on Indians*. Ed. Carolyn L. Karcher. New Brunswick, N.J.: Rutgers University Press, 1986.

Christensen, Peter G. "Minority Interaction in John Rollin Ridge's *The Life and Adventures of Joaquín Murieta*." *MELUS* 17, no. 2 (1991–92).

Colacuricio, Michael. *The Province of Piety: Moral History in Hawthorne's Early Tales*. Cambridge, Mass.: Harvard University Press, 1977.

Cook, S. F. *The Indian Population of New England in the Seventeenth Century*. Berkeley: University of California Press, 1976.

Cooper, James Fenimore. *The Pioneers*. New York: Penguin, 1988.

Cortés, Carlos E., Alrin I. Ginsberg, Alan W.F. Green, and James A. Joseph, eds. *Three Perspectives on Ethnicity: Blacks, Chicanos, and Native Americans*. New York: G. P. Putnam's Sons, 1976.

Creighton, Margaret S. *Rites and Passages: The Experience of American Whaling, 1830–1870*. New York: Cambridge University Press, 1995.

Creighton, Margaret S., and Lisa Norling. *Iron Men, Wooden Women: Gender and Seafaring in the Atlantic World, 1700–1920*. Baltimore: Johns Hopkins University Press, 1996.

Cuddon, J. A., ed. *Dictionary of Literary Terms and Literary Theory*. Cambridge, Mass.: Basil Blackwell, 1979.

Davis, Lance E., Robert E. Gallman, and Karin Gleiter. *In Pursuit of Leviathan: Technology, Institutions, Productivity, and Profits in American Whaling, 1816–1906*. Chicago: University of Chicago Press, 1997.

D'Azevedo, Warren L. "A Tribal Reaction to Nationalism." *Liberian Studies Journal* 1, no. 2 (1969): 4.

DeConde, Alexander. *This Affair of Louisiana*. New York: Scribner's Sons, 1976.

Delany, Martin. *The Condition, Elevation, Emigration, and Destiny of the Colored People of the United States.* New York: Arno Press, 1968.

———. Introduction to William Nesbit, *Four Months in Liberia: Or, African Colonization Exposed. Two Black Views of Liberia.* Ed. William Loren Katz. New York: Arno Press, 1969.

Deloria, Philip J. *Playing Indian.* New Haven, Conn.: Yale University Press, 1998.

Dening, Greg. *Islands and Beaches: Discourse on a Silent Land Marquesas, 1774–1880.* Honolulu: University Press of Hawaii, 1980.

Derrida, Jacques. *Of Grammatology.* Trans. Gayatri Spivak. Baltimore: Johns Hopkins University Press, 1976.

———. "*Ouisa* and *Grammē*: Note on a Note from *Being and Time.*" *Margins of Philosophy.* Trans. Alan Bass. Chicago: University of Chicago Press, 1982.

DeVoto, Bernard. *The Course of Empire.* Boston: Houghton Mifflin, 1952.

Diamond, Marion. "Queequeg's Crewmates: Pacific Islanders in the European Shipping Industry." *International Journal of Maritime History* 1 (December 1989).

Dimock, Wai-Chee. *Empire for Liberty: Melville and the Poetics of Individualism.* Princeton, N.J.: Princeton University Press, 1989.

———. *Residues of Justice: Literature, Law, Philosophy.* Berkeley: University of California Press, 1996.

Dippie, Brian W. *The Vanishing American: White Attitudes and U.S. Indian Policy.* Middletown, Conn.: Wesleyan University Press, 1982.

Douglas, Ann. *The Feminization of American Culture.* New York: Doubleday, 1988.

Douglass, Frederick. "Do Not Send Back the Fugitive: An Address Delivered in Boston, Massachusetts, on 14 October 1850." *The Frederick Douglass Papers.* Ed. John W. Blassingame. Vol. 2. New Haven, Conn.: Yale University Press, 1982.

———. "Emancipation, Racism and the Work before Us: An Address Delivered in Philadelphia, Pa. on 4 December 1863." *The Frederick Douglass Papers.* Ed. John W. Blassingame. Vol. 2. New Haven, Conn.: Yale University Press, 1982.

———. "The Free Negro's Place Is in America." *The Frederick Douglass Papers.* Ed. John Blassingame. Vol. 2. New Haven, Conn.: Yale University Press, 1982.

———. "Henry Clay and Colonization Cant, Sophistry, and Falsehood." *The Frederick Douglass Papers.* Vol. 2. Ed. John Blassingame. New Haven, Conn.: Yale University Press, 1982.

———. Letter to Harriet Beecher Stowe, March 8, 1853. *The Life and Writings of Frederick Douglass.* Vol. 2. Ed. Philip S. Foner. New York: International Publishers, 1950.

———. "The Meaning of July Fourth for the Negro." Speech delivered at Rochester, N.Y., July 5, 1852. *The Life and Writings of Frederick Douglass.* Vol. 2. Ed. Philip S. Foner. New York: International Publishers, 1950.

———. *Narrative of the Life of Frederick Douglass.* Cambridge, Mass.: Belknap Press, 1960.

Drinnon, Richard. *Facing West: The Metaphysics of Indian Hating.* New York: Schocken Books, 1990.

Emerson, Ralph Waldo. *The Complete Works of Ralph Waldo Emerson*. Ed. Edward W. Emerson. Cambridge, Mass.: Riverside Press, 1904.

Farr, James. "A Slow Boat to Nowhere: The Multi-Racial Crews of the American Whaling Industry." *Journal of Negro History* 68, no. 2 (1983).

Fields, Annie. *The Life and Letters of Harriet Beecher Stowe*. Boston: Houghton, Mifflin, and Co., 1897.

Finger, John R. *The Eastern Band of Cherokees, 1819–1900*. Knoxville: University of Tennessee Press, 1984.

Fishel, Leslie H. Jr., and Benjamin Quarles, *The Black American: A Documentary History*. New York: Morrow, 1970.

Fisher, Miles Mark. *Negro Slave Songs in the United States*. New York: Russell and Russell, 1968.

Fisher, Philip. *Hard Facts: Setting and Form in the American Novel*. New York: Oxford University Press, 1985.

Flexner, Eleanor. *Century of Struggle: The Woman's Rights Movement in the United States*. Cambridge, Mass.: Belknap Press, 1975.

Flores, William V., and Rina Benmayor. "Constructing Cultural Citizenship." *Latino Cultural Citizenship: Claiming Identity, Space, and Rights*. Ed. William V. Flores and Rina Benmayor. Boston: Beacon Press, 1997.

Fogel, Robert W. *Without Consent or Contract*. New York: W. W. Norton, 1989.

Foner, Eric, and John A. Garraty, eds. *The Reader's Companion to American History*. Boston: Houghton Mifflin, 1991.

Foner, Philip S., and Daniel Rosenberg, eds. *Racism, Dissent, and Asian Americans: A Documentary History*. Westport, Conn.: Greenwood Press, 1993.

Foreman, Grant. *Indian Removal*. Norman: University of Oklahoma Press, 1989.

Fredericks, Nancy. *Melville's Art of Democracy*. Athens, Ga.: University of Georgia Press, 1995.

Fredrickson, George M. "Antislavery Racist: Hinton Howan Helper." *The Arrogance of Race: Historical Perspectives on Slavery, Racism, and Social Inequality*. Middletown, Conn.: Wesleyan University Press, 1988.

———. *The Black Image in the White Mind: The Debate on Afro-American Character and Destiny, 1817–1914*. New York: Harper and Row, 1971.

Garrison, William Lloyd, ed. *Thoughts on African Colonization; or, An Impartial Exhibition of the Doctrines, Principles and Purposes of the American Colonization Society*. New York: Arno Press, 1968.

Gell, Alfred. *Wrapping in Images: Tattooing in Polynesia*. New York: Oxford University Press, 1993.

Gilmore, Michael T. *American Romanticism and the Marketplace*. Chicago: University of Chicago Press, 1985.

Gilroy, Paul. *The Black Atlantic: Modernity and Double Consciousness*. Cambridge, Mass,: Harvard University Press, 1993.

———. *"There Ain't No Black in the Union Jack": The Cultural Politics of Race and Nation*. Chicago: University of Chicago Press, 1991.

Gleason, William. "Re-Creating *Walden*: Thoreau's Economy of Work and Play." *American Literature* 65, no. 4 (1993).

Goldberg, David Theo, ed. *Multiculturalism: A Critical Reader*. Oxford: Basil Blackwell, 1994.

Golemba, Henry L. *Thoreau's Wild Rhetoric*. New York: New York University Press, 1990.

Gordon, Avery F., and Christopher Newfield, eds. *Mapping Multiculturalism*. Minneapolis: University of Minnesota Press, 1996.

Gossett, Thomas F. *Uncle Tom's Cabin and American Culture*. Dallas: Southern Methodist University, 1985.

Gougeon, Len. *Virtue's Hero: Emerson, Antislavery, and Reform*. Athens, Ga.: University of Georgia Press, 1990.

Handlin, Oscar. *Boston's Immigrants, 1790–1865: A Study in Acculturation*. Cambridge, Mass.: Harvard University Press, 1941.

Hawthorne, Nathaniel. *The House of the Seven Gables*. New York: Collier Books, 1978.

———. "Roger Malvin's Burial." *Selected Tales and Sketches*. New York: Holt, Rinehart and Winston, 1964.

Hedrick, Joan. *Harriet Beecher Stowe: A Life*. New York: Oxford University Press, 1994.

Heizer, Robert F. *The Destruction of the California Indians*. Lincoln: University of Nebraska Press, 1974.

Herbert, T. Walter Jr. *Marquesan Encounters: Melville and the Meaning of Civilization*. Cambridge, Mass.: Harvard University Press, 1980.

Hietala, Thomas R. *Manifest Design: Anxious Aggrandizement in Late Jacksonian America*. Ithaca, N.Y.: Cornell University Press, 1985.

Hobsbawm, E. J. "Introduction: Inventing Traditions." *The Invention of Tradition*. Ed. Eric Hobsbawm and Terence Ranger. Cambridge: Cambridge University Press, 1983.

———. *Nations and Nationalism since 1780: Programme, Myth, and Reality*. Cambridge: Cambridge University Press, 1990.

Holliday, J. S. *The World Rushed In: The California Gold Rush Experience*. New York: Simon and Schuster, 1981.

Holsoe, Svend E. "A Study of Relations between Settlers and Indigenous Peoples in Western Liberia, 1821–1847." *African Historical Studies* 4, nos. 1–3 (1971).

Horsman, Reginald. *Race and Manifest Destiny*. Cambridge, Mass.: Harvard University Press, 1981.

Horton, James Oliver, and Lois E. Horton. *Black Bostonians: Family Life and Community Struggle in the Antebellum North*. New York: Holmes and Meier Publishing, 1979.

Howard, Leon. "Historical Note." Herman Melville, *Typee: A Peep at Polynesian Life*. Ed. Harrison Hayford, Hershel Parker, and G. Thomas Tanselle. Chicago: Northwestern University Press, 1968.

Huberich, Charles Henry. *The Political and Legislative History of Liberia*. Vol. 2. New York: Central Book, 1947.

Ignatiev, Noel. *How the Irish Became White*. New York: Routledge, 1995.

Ignatiev, Noel, and John Garvey, eds. *Race Traitor*. New York: Routledge, 1996.

Jackson, Joseph Henry. Introduction to *The Life and Adventures of Joaquín Murieta*. Norman: University of Oklahoma Press, 1955.

James, C.L.R. *Mariners, Renegades and Castaways*. New York: Allison and Busby, 1985.

Jameson, Frederic. *The Political Unconscious: Narrative as Socially Symbolic Act.* Ithaca, N.Y.: Cornell University Press, 1981.

Jennings, Francis. *The Invasion of America: Indians, Colonialism and the Cant of Conquest.* Chapel Hill: University of North Carolina Press, 1975.

Jones, Jacqueline. *Labor of Love, Labor of Sorrow: Black Women, Work, and the Family from Slavery to the Present.* New York: Vintage Books, 1985.

Kaplan, Amy. " 'Left Alone with America': The Absence of Empire in the Study of American Culture." *Cultures of United States Imperialism.* Ed. Amy Kaplan and Donald E. Pease. Durham, N.C.: Duke University Press, 1993.

Karcher, Carolyn L. *Shadow over the Promised Land: Slavery, Race, and Violence in Melville's America.* Baton Rouge: Louisiana State University Press, 1980.

Kavanagh, James H. "That Hive of Subtlety: 'Benito Cereno' and the Liberal Hero." *Ideology and Classic American Literature.* Ed. Sacvan Bercovitch and Myra Jehlen. New York: Cambridge University Press, 1986.

Kelly, Mary Gilbert. *Catholic Immigrant Colonization Projects in the United States, 1815–1860.* New York: U.S. Catholic Historical Society, 1939.

Kinshasa, Kwando M. *Emigration vs. Assimilation: The Debate in the African American Press, 1827–1861.* Jefferson, N.C.: McFarland and Co., 1988.

Krikham, Bruce E. *The Building of Uncle Tom's Cabin.* Knoxville: University of Tennessee Press, 1977.

Kuykendall, John W. *Southern Enterprize: The Work of National Evangelical Societies in the Antebellum South.* Westport, Conn.: Greenwood Press, 1982.

LaClau, Ernesto, and Chantal Mouffe. *Hegemony and Socialist Strategy: Towards A Radical Democratic Politics.* London: Verso, 1992.

Laurie, Bruce. *Artisans into Workers: Labor in Nineteenth-Century America.* New York: Farrar, Straus and Giroux, 1989.

Lawrence, D. H. *Studies in Classic American Literature.* New York: Doubleday and Co., 1951.

Lebeaux, Richard. *Thoreau's Seasons.* Amherst: University of Massachusetts Press, 1984.

Leitch, Barbara. *A Concise Dictionary of Indian Tribes of North America.* Algonac, Mich.: Reference Publications, 1979.

Levine, Robert. *Martin Delany, Frederick Douglass, and the Politics of Representative Identity.* Chapel Hill: University of North Carolina Press, 1997.

Liebenow, J. Gus. *Liberia: The Evolution of Privilege.* Ithaca, N.Y.: Cornell University Press.

Limerick, Patricia Nelson. *The Legacy of Conquest.* New York: W. W. Norton, 1985.

Lipsitz, George. "The Possessive Investment in Whiteness: Racialized Social Democracy and the 'White' Problem in American Studies." *American Quarterly* 47, no. 3 (1995).

Lott, Eric. *Love and Theft: Blackface Minstrelsy and the American Working Class.* New York: Oxford University Press, 1993.

Lowe, John. "Space and Freedom in the Golden Republic: Yellow Bird's *The Life and Adventures of Joaquín Murieta, the Celebrated California Bandit.*" *Studies in American Indian Literature* 4, nos. 2–3 (1992).

Lubiano, Wahneema. "Like Being Mugged by a Metaphor: Multiculturalism and State Narratives." *Mapping Multiculturalism*. Ed. Avery F. Gordon and Christopher Newfield. Minneapolis: University of Minnesota Press, 1996.

Maddox, Lucy. *Removals: Nineteenth-Century American Literature and the Politics of Indian Affairs*. New York: Oxford University Press, 1991.

Marshall, John. *Worcester v. The State of Georgia. Reports of Decisions of the Supreme Court of the United States*. Ed. B. R. Curtis. 5th ed. Boston: Little, Brown and Co., 1870.

Martin, Calvin, ed. *The American Indian and the Problem of History*, New York: Oxford University Press, 1987.

Matthiessen, F. O. *American Renaissance*. New York: Oxford University Press, 1985.

McCardell, John. *The Idea of a Southern Nation: Southern Nationalists and Southern Nationalism, 1830–1860*. New York: W. W. Norton, 1979.

McClintock, Anne. "The Angel of Progress: Pitfalls of the Term 'Post-Colonialism.' " *Social Text* 10, nos. 2–3 (1992): 85.

McDaniel, Antonio. *Swing Low, Sweet Chariot: The Mortality Cost of Colonizing Liberia in the Nineteenth Century*. Chicago: University of Chicago Press, 1995.

McLaren, Peter L. "White Terror and Oppositional Agency: Toward a Critical Multiculturalism." *Multiculturalism: A Critical Reader*. Ed. David Theo Goldberg. Oxford: Basil Blackwell, 1994.

McLoughlin, William G. *Cherokee Renascence in the New Republic*. Princeton, N.J.: Princeton University Press, 1986.

McMaster, John Bach. *With the Fathers*. New York: D. Appleton and Co., 1896.

Meier, August, and Elliot Rudwick. "The Role of Blacks in the Abolitionist Movement." *Blacks in the Abolitionist Movement*. Belmont, Calif.: Wadsworth Publishing, 1971.

Melville, Herman. "Benito Cereno." *Great Short Works of Herman Melville*. Ed. Warner Berthoff. New York: Harper and Row, 1969.

———. *Correspondence*. Chicago: Northwestern University Press and Newberry Library, 1993.

———. *Moby-Dick; or, The Whale*. New York: Penguin, 1972.

———. *Typee: A Peep at Polynesian Life*. Ed. Harrison Hayford, Hershel Parker, and G. Thomas Tanselle. Chicago: Northwestern University Press, 1968.

Middleton, Stephen. *The Black Laws in the Old Northwest*. Westport, Conn.: Greenwood Press, 1993.

Mitchell, Brian C. *The Paddy Camps: The Irish of Lowell, 1821–1861*. Urbana: University of Illinois Press, 1988.

Mizruchi, Susan L. *The Power of Historical Knowledge: Narrating the Past in Hawthorne, James, and Dreisser*. Princeton, N.J.: Princeton University Press, 1988.

Mondragon, Maria. " 'The [Safe] White Side of the Line': History and Disguise in John Rollin Ridge's *The Life and Adventures of Joaquín Murieta, the Celebrated California Bandit*." *American Transcendental Quarterly* 8, no. 3 (1994).

Mooney, James. "Ûñtsaiyï̱', The Gambler." *Myths of the Cherokee*. Nashville, Tenn.: Charles Elder, Bookseller, 1972.

Morrison, Toni. "Unspeakable Things Unspoken: The Afro-American Presence in American Literature." *Michigan Quarterly Review* 28, no. 1 (1989).

Morse, Samuel F.B. *Imminent Dangers to the Free Institutions of the United States through Foreign Immigration, and the Present State of the Naturalization Laws. . . . By an American.* New York: John F. Trow, 1854.

Moses, Wilson Jeremiah. *Black Messiahs and Uncle Toms: Social and Literary Manipulations of a Religious Myth.* University Park: Pennsylvania State University Press, 1982.

Mudimbe, V. Y. *The Invention of Africa: Gnosis, Philosophy, and the Order of Knowledge.* Bloomington: Indiana University Press, 1988.

Nadeau, Remi A. *The Real Joaquín Murieta: Robin Hood or Gold Rush Gangster?* Corona del Mar, Calif.: Trans-Anglo, 1974.

Nelson, Dana. *National Manhood: Capitalist Citizenship and the Imagined Fraternity of White Men.* Durham, N.C.: Duke University Press, 1998.

————. *The Word in Black and White: Reading "Race" in American Literature, 1638–1867.* New York: Oxford University Press, 1992.

Neufeldt, Leonard. *The Economist: Henry David Thoreau and Enterprise.* New York: Oxford University Press, 1989.

Norling, Lisa. "Ahab's Wife: Women and the American Whaling Industry, 1820–1870." *Iron Men, Wooden Women: Gender and Seafaring in the Atlantic World, 1700–1920.* Ed. Margaret Creighton and Lisa Norling. Baltimore: Johns Hopkins University Press, 1996.

Norton, Anne. *Alternative Americas.* Chicago: University of Chicago Press, 1986.

Nott, Josiah C. "The Mulatto a Hybrid—Probable Extermination of the Two Races if the Whites and Blacks are Allowed to Intermarry." *American Journal of the Medical Sciences* 6 (1843): 252–56.

Oates, Stephen B. *To Purge This Land with Blood: A Biography of John Brown.* New York: Harper and Row, 1970.

O'Connor, Thomas H. *The Boston Irish: A Political History.* Boston: Northeastern University Press, 1995.

Olney, James. " 'I Was Born': Slave Narratives, Their Status as Autobiography and as Literature." *The Slave's Narrative.* Ed. Charles T. Davis and Henry Louis Gates Jr. New York: Oxford University Press, 1985.

Orians, G. H. "The Source of Hawthorne's 'Roger Malvin's Burial.' " *American Literature* 10 (1958).

Owens, Louis. *Other Destinies.* Norman: University of Oklahoma Press, 1992.

Paredes, Americo. *"With His Pistol in His Hand": A Border Ballad and Its Hero.* Austin: University of Texas Press, 1958.

Parins, James W. *John Rollin Ridge: His Life and Works.* Lincoln: University of Nebraska, 1991.

Paul, Rodman Wilson. *Mining Frontiers of the Far West, 1848–1880.* Albuquerque: University of New Mexico Press, 1963.

Pease, Donald E. "Melville and Cultural Persuasion." *Ideology and Classic American Literature.* Ed. Sacvan Bercovitch and Myra Jehlen. New York: Cambridge University Press, 1986.

————. "National Identities, Postmodern Artifacts, and Postnational Narratives." *National Identities and Post-Americanist Narratives.* Ed. Donald E. Pease. Durham, N.C.: Duke University Press, 1994.

Pease, Donald E. "New Americanists: Revisionist Interventions into the Canon." *Revisionary Interventions into the Americanist Canon*. Ed. Donald E. Pease. Durham, N.C.: Duke University Press, 1994.

Peterson, Richard. *Manifest Destiny in the Mines: A Cultural Interpretation of Anti-Mexican Nativism in California, 1848–1853*. San Francisco: R and E Research Associates, 1975.

Potter, David M. *The Impending Crisis, 1848–1861*. New York: Harper and Row, 1976.

Powell, Eve Troutt. "Colonized Colonizers: Egyptian Nationalism and the Issue of the Sudan." Ph.D. diss., Harvard University, 1995.

Powell, Timothy B. "Historical Multiculturalism: Cultural Complexity in the First Native American Novel." *Beyond the Binary: Reconstructing Cultural Identity in a Multicultural Context*. Ed. Timothy B. Powell. New Brunswick, N.J.: Rutgers University Press, 1999.

———. "Postcolonialism in an American Context: A Reading of Martin Delany's *Blake*." *The Pre-Occupation of Post-Colonial Studies*. Ed. Kalpana Seshadri-Crooks and Fawzia Azfal-Khan. Durham, N.C.: Duke University Press, 2000.

Prucha, Francis Paul. *Documents of United States Indian Policy*. Lincoln: University of Nebraska Press, 1990.

Renan, Ernest. "What Is a Nation?" Trans. Martin Thom. *Nation and Narration*. Ed. Homi Bhabha. London: Routledge, 1990.

Reynolds, David S. *Beneath the American Renaissance: The Subversive Imagination in the Age of Emerson and Melville*. Cambridge, Mass.: Harvard University Press, 1988.

Reynolds, Moira Davison. *Uncle Tom's Cabin and Mid-Nineteenth Century United States: Pen and Conscience*. Jefferson, N.C.: McFarland and Co., 1985.

Ridge, John Rollin. *The Life and Adventures of Joaquín Murieta, the Celebrated California Bandit*. Norman: University of Oklahoma Press, 1955.

———. *A Trumpet of Our Own: Yellow Bird's Essays on the North American Indians*. Ed. David Farmer and Rennard Strickland. San Francisco: Book Club of San Francisco, 1981.

Roediger, David R. *Towards the Abolition of Whiteness: Essays on Race, Politics, and Working Class History*. New York: Verso, 1994.

———. *The Wages of Whiteness: Race and the Making of the American Working Class*. New York: Verso, 1991.

Rogin, Michael Paul. *Fathers and Children: Andrew Jackson and the Subjugation of the American Indian*. New Brunswick, N.J.: Transaction Publishers, 1991.

———. *Subversive Genealogy: The Politics and Art of Herman Melville*. New York: Alfred A. Knopf, 1983.

Romero, Lora. *Home Fronts: Domesticity and Its Critics in the Antebellum United States*. Durham, N.C.: Duke University Press, 1997.

Rose, Suzanne D. "Following the Trail of Footsteps: From the Indian Notebooks to *Walden*." *New England Quarterly* 67, no. 1 (1994).

Rotundo, E. Anthony. *American Manhood: Transformations in Masculinity from the Revolution to the Modern Era*. New York: Basic Books, 1993.

Rowe, John Carlos. "Melville's *Typee*: U.S. Imperialism at Home and Abroad." *National Identities and Post-Americanist Narratives*. Ed. Donald E. Pease. Durham, N.C.: Duke University Press, 1994.

Ruchames, Louis. "Race, Marriage, and Abolition in Massachusetts." *Journal of Negro History* 40, no. 3 (1955).

Saldívar, José David. *Border Matters: Remapping American Cultural Studies.* Berkeley: University of California Press, 1997.

Sánchez, Rosaura. *Telling Identities: The Californio Testimonios.* Minneapolis: University of Minnesota Press, 1995.

Sánchez-Eppler, Karen. "Bodily Bonds: The Intersecting Rhetorics of Feminism and Abolition." *Representations* 28 (Fall 1988).

Sassen, Saskia. "Identity in the Global City: Economic and Cultural Encasements." *The Geographies of Identity.* Ed. Patricia Yaeger. Ann Arbor: Michigan University Press, 1996.

Satz, Ronald N. *American Indian Policy in the Jacksonian Era.* Lincoln: University of Nebraska Press, 1975.

Saxton, Alexander. *The Indispensable Enemy: Labor and the Anti-Chinese Movement in California.* Berkeley: University of California Press, 1971.

———. *The Rise and Fall of the White Republic: Class Politics and Mass Culture in Nineteenth-Century America.* London: Verso, 1990.

Sayre, Robert F. *Thoreau and the American Indians.* Princeton, N.J.: Princeton University Press, 1977.

Schlesinger, Arthur M. *The Disuniting of America: Reflections on a Multicultural Society.* New York: W. W. Norton, 1992.

Sedgwick, Eve Kosofsky. *Epistemology of the Closet.* Berkeley: University of California Press, 1990.

———. "Paranoid Reading and Reparative Reading." *Novel Gazing: Queer Readings in Fiction.* Ed. Eve Kosofsky Sedgwick. Durham, N.C.: Duke University Press, 1997.

Shick, Tom W. *Behold the Promised Land: A History of Afro-American Settler Society in Nineteenth-Century Liberia.* Baltimore: Johns Hopkins University Press, 1977.

Simms, William Gilmore. *The Yemassee.* New Haven, Conn.: College and University Press, 1964.

Skipwith, Peyton. *"Dear Master": Letters of a Slave Family.* Ed. Randall M. Miller. Ithaca, N.Y.: Cornell University Press, 1978.

Slotkin, Richard. *The Fatal Environment: The Myth of the Frontier in the Age of Industrialization, 1800–1890.* Middletown, Conn.: Wesleyan University Press, 1986.

Smith-Rosenberg, Carroll. *Religion and the Rise of the American City: The New York City Mission Movement, 1812–1870.* Ithaca, N.Y.: Cornell University Press, 1971.

Sollors, Werner. *Beyond Ethnicity: Consent and Descent in American Culture.* New York: Oxford University Press, 1986.

Spillers, Hortense J. "Changing the Letter: The Yokes, the Jokes of Discourse, or, Mrs. Stowe, Mr. Reed." *Slavery and the Literary Imagination.* Ed. Deborah E. McDowell and Arnold Rampersad. Baltimore: Johns Hopkins University Press, 1989.

Stackpole, Edouard A. *The Sea-Hunters: The New England Whalemen during Two Centuries, 1635–1835.* New York: Bonanza Books, 1953.

Stanton, William. *The Leopard's Spots: Scientific Attitudes Toward Race in America, 1815–59.* Chicago: University of Chicago Press, 1960.

Staudenraus, P. J. *The African Colonization Movement, 1816–1865.* New York: Columbia University Press, 1961.

Stebbins, G. B. *Facts and Opinions Touching the Real Origin, Character, and Influence of the American Colonization Society.* New York: Negro Universities Press, 1969.

Stepto, Robert B. "Sharing the Thunder: The Literary Exchanges of Harriet Beecher Stowe, Henry Bibb, and Frederick Douglass." *New Essays on Uncle Tom's Cabin.* Ed. Eric J. Sundquist. New York: Cambridge University Press, 1986.

Stowe, Harriet Beecher. *Dred; A Tale of the Great Dismal Swamp.* Boston: Sampson and Co., 1856.

———. *The Key to Uncle Tom's Cabin.* New York: Arno Press, 1969.

———. *Uncle Tom's Cabin.* New York: Signet, 1966.

Stuckey, Sterling, and Joshua Leslie. "The Death of Benito Cereno: A Reading of Herman Melville on Slavery." *Going through the Storm: The Influence of African-American Art in History.* New York: Oxford University Press, 1994.

Swayne, Josephine Latham. *The Story of Concord Told by Concord Writers.* Boston: George H. Ellis, 1905.

Takaki, Ronald. *A Different Mirror: A History of Multicultural America.* Boston: Little, Brown and Co., 1993.

———. *Strangers from a Different Shore: A History of Asian Americans.* New York: Penguin Books, 1989.

Talbert, Charles Gano. *Benjamin Logan: Kentucky Frontiersman.* Louisville: University of Kentucky Press, 1962.

Thoreau, Henry David. "Civil Disobedience." *Thoreau: Walden and Other Writings.* Ed. Joseph Wood Krutch. New York: Bantam Books, 1979.

———. *The Journal of Henry D. Thoreau.* Ed. Bradford Torrey and Francis H. Allen. New York: Dover Publications, 1962.

———. "Slavery in Massachusetts." *The Writings of Henry D. Thoreau.* Ed. Wendell Glick. Princeton, N.J.: Princeton University Press, 1973.

———. *Walden. Thoreau: Walden and Other Writings.* Ed. Joseph Wood Krutch. New York: Bantam Books, 1979.

———. *A Week on the Concord and Merrimack Rivers.* Boston: Houghton Mifflin, 1961.

Thornton, Russell. "Cherokee Population Losses during the 'Trail of Tears': A New Perspective and a New Estimate." *Ethnohistory* 31 (November 1984): 289–300.

Tompkins, Jane. *Sensational Designs.* New York: Oxford University Press, 1985.

Trennert, Robert A. Jr. *Alternative to Extinction: Federal Indian Policy and the Beginnings of the Reservation System, 1846–51.* Philadelphia: Temple University Press, 1975.

Vermeule, Cornelius. *Numismatic Art in America.* Cambridge, Mass.: Belknap Press of Harvard University Press, 1971.

Wald, Priscilla. *Constituting Americans.* Durham, N.C.: Duke University Press, 1995.

Walker, Franklin. *San Francisco's Literary Frontier*. New York: Alfred A. Knopf, 1939.

Walker, Robert. "Letter of Mr. Walker, of Mississippi, Relative to the Annexation of Texas." 1844. Frederick Merk, *Fruits of Propaganda in the Tyler Administration*. Cambridge, Mass.: Harvard University Press, 1971.

Washburn, Wilcombe E. *Red Man's Land / White Man's Law: A Study of the Past and Present Status of the American Indian*. New York: Charles Scribner's Sons, 1971.

Weber, David. *Foreigners in Their Native Land*. Albuquerque: University of New Mexico Press, 1973.

Webster, Daniel. *Speech of Hon. Daniel Webster on Mr. Clay's Resolutions*. March 7, 1850. Washington: Gideon and Co., 1850.

Welter, Barbara. "The Cult of True Womanhood: 1820–1860." *American Quarterly* 18 (September 1966).

Wilkins, Thurman. *Cherokee Tragedy: The Story of the Ridge Family and of the Decimation of a People*. New York: Macmillan, 1970.

Williams, Robert A. *The American Indian in Western Legal Thought: The Discourse of Conquest*. New York: Oxford University Press, 1990.

Williams, Samuel. *Four Years in Liberia: A Sketch of the Life of Rev. Samuel Williams, by Samuel Williams. Two Black Views of Liberia*. Ed. William Loren Katz. New York: Arno Press, 1969.

Williams, William Appleman. *Empire as a Way of Life: An Essay on the Causes and Character of America's Present Predicament, along with a Few Thoughts about an Alternative*. New York: Oxford University Press, 1980.

Wilson, Charles Morrow. *Liberia: Black Africa in Microcosm*. New York: Harper and Row, 1971.

Wilson, Forrest. *Crusader in Crinoline*. New York: Lippincott, 1941.

Wiltse, Charles M. *Expansion and Reform, 1815–1850*. New York: Free Press, 1967.

Woodward, Grace Steele. *The Cherokees*. Norman: University of Oklahoma Press, 1963.

Yarborough, Richard. "Strategies of Black Characterization in *Uncle Tom's Cabin* and the Early Afro-American Novel." *New Essays on Uncle Tom's Cabin*. Ed. Eric J. Sundquist. New York: Cambridge University Press, 1986.

Young, Robert J. C. *Colonial Desire: Hybridity in Theory, Culture and Race*. New York: Routledge, 1995.

Zinn, Howard. *A People's History of the United States*. New York: Harper and Row, 1980.

INDEX